The IRQ Book

The IRQ Book

Kate Chase

McGraw-Hill

New York   San Francisco   Washington, D.C.   Auckland   Bogotá
Caracas   Lisbon   London   Madrid   Mexico City   Milan
Montreal   New Delhi   San Juan   Singapore
Sydney   Tokyo   Toronto

Library of Congress Cataloging-in-Publication Data

Chase, Kate.
   The IRQ book / Kate Chase
       p. cm.
   ISBN 0-07-134698-8
   1. Microcomputers.   2. Software configuration management.
  I. Title.
   QA76.5.C434   1999
   004.165—dc21   98-14544
                                               CIP

McGraw-Hill

A Division of The McGraw·Hill Companies

1 2 3 4 5 6 7 8 9 0   DOC/DOC   9 0 4 3 2 1 0 9

P/N 0-07-134693-7

PART OF

ISBN 0-07-134698-8

*The sponsoring editor for this book was Michael Sprague, the editing supervisor
was Penny Linskey, and the production supervisor was Clare Stanley. It was set
in Sabon by North Market Street Graphics.*

Printed and bound by R. R. Donnelley & Sons Company.

 This book is printed on recycled, acid-free paper containing a minimum
of 50% recycled, de-inked fiber.

Contents

Preface

Solid research and planning maximize the chance for optimal results. It's true in career advancement, true in shopping for a house, true in investments, and it's true with PC performance as well. As users, regardless of our experience level, we will all come face-to-face with hardware incompatibility or resource conflicts, or convoluted configurations. We will also come up against the need to accommodate just one more add-on card or peripheral long after we have exhausted our PC's sometimes draconian upgrade limitations. New hardware types and models are introduced each week, but we really don't have a lot more ways to connect them to our PCs than we did several years ago.

Only two major factors differentiate a seasoned technician (titled or someone trying to achieve maximum capability out of his or her home/office system) from someone very hesitant to change his or her configuration. The first factor is the knowledge of what the hardware is, what it needs, and how it works together. The second is solid, logical troubleshooting skills. A talented tech is able to do more than resolve a conflict when it arises; he or she takes the steps necessary to try to prevent any from occurring in the first place. This, again, is achieved through careful configuration and planning.

Hardware conflicts are one of *the* most common problems with a PC. Industry groups report that hardware product return rates are at an all-time high, accounting for an average 15 to 30% of all such products purchased. They estimate that a substantial percentage of these returns are not because of defective merchandise, but instead because they were too difficult for a person to install and configure properly. Even the advent of Plug and Play (PnP) technology, discussed later, has not changed that, although PnP was specifically designed to help overcome this issue for less technically proficient users.

I have worked with PCs since the first XT was introduced by IBM. Yet I have been known to disable the so-called easy-to-install PnP capability (by jumpering, also discussed in the book) just to get a problematic modem installed where I want it to go, instead of where Plug and Play tries to insist it should go. And this is what mastery is all about: knowing what you have to work with, the potential possibilities for it, and the logical steps to take it where you want it to go.

This book is an attempt to provide you with the information you need to begin moving from casual ability to true skill. My goal is to have you read this and then apply what you learn to your PC. The result should be a PC packed with the hardware you need, tuned for maximum performance, and free from the conflicts and lockups that cost us precious time and productivity.

However, this book's greatest challenge is also the same one facing most of us as end users: This is a time of considerable chaos and change in PC hardware. The mainstreaming of PCs and the Internet, combined with various factors driving down PC pricing, are giving us incredible choices for hardware in the marketplace. In fact, one of the most severe limitations imposed on the majority of users right now is not price or availability of the add-on hardware for our computers. It is instead how the hardware must connect given the design of the PC itself.

The products—and the PCs we use—span several years' worth of technology. Even the newest PCs still have to accommodate some of our older hardware to ensure compatibility. We're still stuck, to a large degree, with the same number of physical ways to connect hardware to our PCs, while being offered an abundance of products we increasingly need to add. Sure, we have a few more choices, but not a lot more.

A PC just 5 years ago usually boasted a sound card in addition to a video card, often with a printer as its single external peripheral. Today it's not uncommon to have a second video card just to produce 3D gaming enhancements, a multifunction sound card, and a scanner, along with perhaps a digital camera, a removable mass storage backup unit, and a digitizing tablet.

Just how you accommodate these heavier demands with the physical connections you have to work with—and how to resolve the hardware conflicts likely to result as we pack our PCs with more—is the focus of this book. Whether you are using a Pentium III-500 MHz screaming machine or a souped-up 486 you continue to keep alive, there are three central resources available on a PC to alert the processor to the presence and immediate demands of hardware you have attached to it. These three system resources are known as IRQ, DMA, and I/O (with memory addressing). I'll tell you about these in a moment.

If there is one piece of information you need to remember in configuring hardware to work with your PC, it's that you should only have one device per system resource. Putting two devices together on the same resource is an invitation to conflicts, crashes, and headaches. Yes, there are exceptions and workarounds, as I will detail later in this book (Peripheral Component Interconnect, or PCI, for example, allows resource sharing for IRQs). But you need to know the rules in order to break them with any intelligence or success.

System resources are integral to a PC's performance because they are responsible for communication and information handling. If you think of the central processing unit (CPU) as the brain of the PC, then the system resources make up the network of nerves known as the central nervous system. On a PC, data moves through your system along metal conductors, which we collectively refer to as the *bus*.

A PC has three basic types of bus, which include address (bus), control (bus), and data (bus). Besides these, there are several different types of bus architecture, depending on your type of PC, including PCI, EISA, ISA, and VL, or VESA local. With some exceptions, most of today's Pentium-class machines (original, or "classic," Pentium Pros, Pentium MMX, and Pentium IIs) and ilk are equipped with motherboards supporting a combination of PCI/ISA bus slots for adding expansion cards such as internal modems, sound cards, video cards, SCSI adapters, or ISA-based scanner cards. PCI and ISA slots are reasonably easy to distinguish from one another. For one thing, PCI slots are usually white, short, and have just one section. (You might see brown slots as well—sometimes in PCI, sometimes for VESA local—but these are very long.) ISA slots, on the other hand, are often black and are always divided into two sections.

It is important that you understand there are three basic ways to get data into your PC:

◀ Through the keyboard

◀ Through the data bus, also known as the expansion bus, which provides a set of slots on the motherboard through which expansion cards are added and connected

◀ Through the serial (COM or communications) and parallel (LPT or printer) ports that you find originally connected to the motherboard or available as part of a separate expansion card

Now realize that using any of these methods to get data into your PC requires resources to handle them. There has to be a reliable way for the keyboard or the ISA bus or the printer port to get the attention of the CPU to transfer data and get back the information it needs. And this is where IRQ, DMA, and I/O come in.

You also need to know that, traditionally, there are two ways for add-on hardware to be recognized by the CPU to perform the task at hand: polling or interrupts. Polling means that the processor polls or checks with each device constantly to see if a device needs to perform a task. This works, but it's wasteful of the CPU's time. Instead of performing more critical functions, part of the CPU's time is lost asking each device again and again "Do you need me?" when the answer the majority of the time will be "No!"

Plus, there is an added problem in that different devices or types of hardware need the CPU's attention at differing rates of demand. Moving your mouse or typing away at your keyboard is less demanding of the CPU than a major file transfer to your hard drive. This is where hardware interrupts come in, because they take the responsibility off the CPU to check for requests and place it on the hardware to have the interrupt demand the CPU's attention. This brings us back to interrupts or IRQs, DMA, and I/O, which I'll describe briefly here:

◀ *IRQ (Interrupt Request)*. Also simply called an interrupt, this acts as a signal to the CPU or processor to indicate that a device attached requires its attention; there are 16 IRQs in today's PCs, numbered 0 to 15.

◀ *DMA (Direct Memory Address channels)*. A method of transferring data between two locations—a hard drive and memory, for example—without requiring the CPU's constant attention, which can save time and resources; today's PCs have eight DMA channels, numbered 0 to 7.

◄ *I/O (Input/Output addresses).* The actual physical address at which a piece of hardware can be reached; usually referenced as a three-digit hexadecimal number, such as 378h (the *h* indicating "hexadecimal").

What makes the issue of system resources even more critical is their very limited availability, and how they must work in having many different types of hardware and components communicate with each other in a logical fashion. As touched upon briefly, we continue to function on a PC design foundation created way back in the early 1980s with the original PC/XTs. Only some modifications have been made in this to help keep PCs a steady evolution instead of a radical reengineering each time a new generation of PC processors is introduced. The limitations are a direct price we pay for that compatibility.

Slowly, we're moving into faster hardware and more and more peripherals needed for a basic PC setup. With this come changes like the introduction of universal serial buses (USBs), discussed later in the book, which enable us to connect a large number of slower-speed devices like modems, keyboards, cameras, and printers to one port that utilizes only a single system resource. But for the most part, we continue to straddle the old world with the brave new one we may see PCs enter in the next millennium.

The good news is that, although you have to scrupulously monitor what you add via each resource—IRQs, DMA, and I/O—you do not have to worry about one set of resources conflicting with another. For instance, a DMA address you set should not then conflict with an IRQ you set elsewhere. Assigning two devices to IRQ9 would present a problem, assigning two devices to DMA channel 5 is a problem, but assigning one to IRQ9 and one to DMA channel 5 won't cause a problem.

Something else limits you, too, in the upgrade/expansion process: the physical number of available slots in your PC. If you buy a typical preconfigured PC, some of those slots are already occupied by expansion cards such as sound cards and internal modems. Also, you can only install an ISA card in an ISA slot; the same being true with PCI (unless you have a shared slot, meaning it will accommodate either). Once you exhaust your available slots of that type, you have to stop and consider your configuration.

One option, if you're using a Pentium-class machine with a motherboard based on the Intel LX, BX, or even GX chipset, is to move your video card from ISA or PCI to AGP (Accelerated Graphics Port), which plugs directly into its own socket on the motherboard. This frees up a slot. In most cases, however, it will not necessarily free up an IRQ, because some video cards do not use them. Another solution is to shift connection types from an ISA or PCI modem to a USB modem, for example. USB does require an IRQ, but just one for any and all USB devices connected. This requires both a PC and an operating system that is USB-capable, of which not all are. Some older machines can be made USB-capable easily; some cannot. I'll cover this more later in the book.

There are other worries, too, along this bridge between the old hardware and what we want to do in the future. Our current demands stating our need for speed are valid ones. Yet we may only be able to go so far, so fast, and still support all of the older equipment. ISA is slated to begin disappearing, but serial and parallel ports—not exactly two speed-demon connections—continue to be supported in specifications for the PC of 1998, as put forth by Microsoft and Intel. In one effort to widen the bridge, some computer manufacturers have recommended Intel expand the PCI bus in a new design called PCIx.

But if you are left with the impression from this that times are messy, your assessment may be right on the money. It's our world, however, and we have to do our best to survive and compute in it around the logjams, the imperfect innovations, and the wait for a better design implementation.

By now, you almost certainly have to be asking yourself—particularly if you are running a recently minted PC and know of the hardware install wizards packed into all 32-bit versions of Windows (including Windows 95/98 and NT)—*why must I consider all this fine detail?* There are, after all, Plug and Play devices, as mentioned, that are supposed to be load-set-and-use easy, and software/utilities out there that offer to help you diagnose, resolve, and monitor various aspects of your operating system, including hardware specifics. Additionally, there are always recovery disks and reinstalls and reformats to fall back on.

You need to learn and understand the finer details because you will, as a PC user, encounter situations that do not offer easy or obvious solutions. You may, for instance, need to install a specific piece of hardware for a work project or personal use that requires true tweaking to get recognized, configured, and working. You may run out of IRQs when you desperately need to add something that requires one. You could experience unusual conflicts between a sound card and a SCSI adapter. Or you could encounter frequent lockups and crashes in Windows that are not permanently resolved with a refreshing or a reformatting and reinstallation of your operating system. To use your PC the way you want and need to use it, you have to understand the rules and follow certain designated steps to be able to overcome such conflicts and crises.

No utility in existence—and only very good, specialized outside technical support—can offer you the troubleshooting capability possible once you are armed with the information you need to sort through conflicts combined with your own intimate knowledge of your PC's unique configuration and what you need it to do. Sure, utilities like Cybermedia's First Aid and Symantec's Norton CrashGuard, along with the various uninstaller/ cleaner programs available, can help those less knowledgeable about PC workings. But let me add why I would not recommend them personally. One reason is that while such utilities try to optimize and work for a vast range of possible setups and configurations, they will never know your system as well as you can.

Another is that they tend to add a layer of "management" between you and your PC/operating system. When things are going along well and your PC performs for you as it needs to do, you are content enough. But that extra layer separating you from the nuts and bolts won't always take kindly to your attempts to work around it, and in my experience as an online technical support manager, these utilities can add problems of their own. They may delete files you need and cause lockups when you run software the utilities do not work well with, and they often appear to fight with Windows for control of your environment. This is one power struggle to avoid at all costs.

Another issue for me is that they seem to give the user a false sense of security, as in "I can do this because the utility will protect me." While this is great when it happens to work, those using such products are often the least technically proficient to resolve a real crisis when it erupts.

The final reason I will offer is that these programs can be a nightmare at upgrade time, because they may, under the guise of helping protect you from yourself, interfere when you are performing maintenance updates. Last year's Microsoft Internet Explorer 4.0 upgrade is a prime example of this because the frequency of problems experienced with those trying to upgrade with protective utilities in place, including various antivirus utilities that run in the background, were serious. Part of the problem encountered involves the fact that Internet Explorer 4.0 supplies many hooks into the operating system, and it wants a very clean environment in which to do this. Another is that users did not always upgrade these "protector" utilities first to versions compatible with IE 4.0. But most of these complications would have been avoided had the utilities been turned off or at least disabled during the upgrade—something too few did.

Nor do these utilities always disable easily; they may leave footprints throughout the integrated Windows environment, resulting in some of the same problems you might see if not disabled at all. Far too often, the only solution for those who ended up with a mess was to reformat their hard disk, reload their operating system, and start over.

Let me add too that while there are many utilities out there to report what hardware you have connected and where—including the shareware program, Snoop, and even Microsoft's older MSD (Microsoft Diagnostic) DOS-based utility, plus ones that pack in popular management packages like Symantec's Norton Utilities—you can't depend on them 100 percent. Why? Almost all of them, from time -to time, misreport resources in use. As one example, some Cyrix processors, which are Pentium class-compatible, are seen as 486s instead. Over the years, I have seen them erroneously report the amount of RAM on a system, the type of video card implemented, the size or nature of a hard disk, and less frequently, the proper operating system version. Sometimes running three different hardware information utilities can produce three differing hardware summaries.

Thus, my advice is to use them for help, but do not depend on them to supply all of the information you may need with perfect accuracy. Too many variations—as well as less than "standard" standards—exist in today's hardware to allow these utilities such perfection in recognizing and reporting them.

So while you have tools at your disposal, the ultimate solution lies with you and your own skills as your own PC mechanic and configuration specialist. The failure to master certain basic PC design principles and limitations, coupled with a subpar understanding of what you need to do when you perform an upgrade (software or hardware), will dump you into a reactive rather than a proactive stance when you encounter the inevitable incompatibility or error. It will leave you at the mercy of others to help—and these others may know even less than you. Certainly, they are less likely to appreciate your particular PC needs and are more inclined to offer general solutions applicable to the masses. You will get their solution, and not necessarily the one you want. It will impede your ability to make your PC evolve as your work and needs do. Often, it can impede your very ability to work at all.

The PC is, after all, your tool. But a malfunctioning tool is of far less use to you. Also, if you don't have the knowledge you need to understand what problems are the fault of which offender, it will be tougher to find them and fix them appropriately. For example, let's say you don't know that in 32-bit Windows, DOS operates in real address mode, also known as real mode, with its own set of drivers, while Windows operates in protected mode using its own protected-mode drivers. Not understanding this means several big errors in Windows could leave you completely in the dark. But it also means you won't understand that Windows uses its own drivers (protected mode, as indicated) in Windows 95 and 98, and that to have the same hardware function in DOS or real mode as it does in Windows protected mode, you need to load real-mode drivers or DOS drivers in the DOS configuration files—CONFIG.SYS and AUTOEXEC.BAT.

Failing to know the above means you may assume a CD-ROM drive that only operates some of the time (like only in Windows) may be defective and need replacement. But unless you load DOS or real-mode drivers for the replacement, it won't work in DOS either.

Join me as we explore the issues related to proper configuration and hardware installation, see how the integrated nature of Windows helps you work easily on the desktop but requires a systematic and complete approach to conflict resolution, and discuss common conflicts and their solutions. This book will also help you identify and implement the steps necessary for successful troubleshooting, which includes trickier concepts, such as dealing with the Windows Registry (in Windows 95/98 and NT), as well as assisting you in devising a logical, workable game plan for future upgrades.

Near the end of the book, we will also tackle PC cooling and power concerns, because problems with either can masquerade as more traditional conflicts and can lead to full-blown hardware failures if left unchecked. If you have questions about what the normal operating temperature of your internal PC should be or how you determine whether the cooling system is adequate, look at Chapter 12. Also, do you know how "dirty" the power is in our homes and offices? So-called "noise" in the wiring can hurt a PC's rather delicate electronics, and you need to know how to minimize the risk potential.

For additional help with any of the terms discussed here, please refer to Appendix A, which offers a glossary of terminology. Appendix B provides you with online resources for getting needed support and information in working through problems and researching planned upgrades and configuration tweaks. Appendix C offers a checklist to use to keep track of your PC's configuration. If hexadecimal notation confuses you when you read something like 3F8h, jump to Appendix D.

One final note: This book spans several operating system platforms, all based on Microsoft Windows. These include DOS/Windows 3.1x; Windows 95, first released in August 1995; Windows 98, which came out in June 1998; and Windows NT 4.0, which released in 1996 (its major overhaul, NT 5.0, remains in a prolonged beta as of this writing but is referenced in this book where appropriate). Concepts like Plug and Play are not supported natively by either Windows 3.1x or NT 4.0, though I detail how you can work PnP devices into a non-PnP operating system.

Other complicating factors arise beyond this. Windows 95 had several interim releases between its debut and mid 1998, when Windows 98 came on the market. The list of releases for Windows 95 with their version numbers as reported by the system include:

Full retail release _____V.950

OEM* Service release 1 _____V.950a

OEM Service release 2 (OSR 2.0) _____V.950b

OEM Service release 2.1 _____V.950b
     With USB supplement (OSR 2.1)

OEM Service release 2.5 (OSR 2.5) _____V.950c

For quick reference, let's look at a chart of what kinds of features and services span these different Windows' versions, as illustrated in the table below.

	Supports PnP	Supports FAT 32	Max. Drive Size	Supports USB	Supports FireWire	Supports AGP
DOS/Win 3.1x	No	No		No	No	No
Win v. 950	Yes	No	2 GB	No	No	No
Win v. 950a	Yes	No	2 GB	No	No	No
Win v. 950b	Yes	Yes	8 GB	Yes	No	No
Win v. 950c	Yes	Yes	8 GB	Yes	No	No
Windows 98	Yes	Yes	2 TB	Yes	Minimal	Yes
Windows NT 4.0	No	No		No	No	No

◀ "Supports PnP" means that it embraces the Plug and Play specification throughout; while you can get PnP devices to operate under DOS/Windows 3.1x and Windows NT 4.0, it's not the more complete support of Windows 95 and 98.

◀ "Supports FAT32" means it supports drives converted to FAT32, which reduces the size of clusters used in storing files to a hard disk and can save an appreciable amount of wasted drive space. DOS, early Windows versions, and Windows NT 4.0 when using FAT (NT has the choice of using NTFS format, too) use FAT 16 (FAT12 is sometimes used on floppy drives, for example).

◀ "Maximum drive supported" refers to the maximum-size drive or drive partition the operating system will support without requiring multiple partitions (dividing one large physical drive into sequential logical drives).

◀ "Supports USB" means that support for universal serial bus connectivity is implemented in the operating system itself.

◀ "Supports FireWire" means that support for FireWire/IEEE 1394 high-speed interconnect technology is implemented in the operating system itself.

◀ "Supports AGP" means that support for an Accelerated Graphics Port is implemented in the operating system itself.

Also, though USB support was added to Windows 95 starting with OSR v. 2.5, full support didn't arrive until Windows 98. This means that some keyboards and other devices might not work under later revisions of Windows 95 but should under Windows 98. FireWire, while discussed more and more, still isn't a player in terms of full operating system support for it—even though a few FireWire devices are already on the market and some motherboards incorporate FireWire connections into their design.

Beyond that, more and more of us are choosing to have a dual-boot situation between a consumer-focused operating system like Windows 95/98 and the professional power of Windows NT 4.0. How do you accommodate a Plug and Play operating system with a non-Plug and Play one? How do you deal with the disparities in drivers, hardware compatibility, and other issues that arise? There's a steady rise in home-based PC networks, as well: As more of us have more than one PC in our homes and home offices, we want to network them to share services and files. But network cards have a reputation for being fussy around other resources. And even if you don't have a network, you may soon (if you don't already) have access to a cable modem that requires (if you don't have a USB cable modem) a network card to work with.

These things need resources; you can't escape it. Just like you can't escape the fact that whenever you add hardware, you run the risk of creating a conflict in those resource assignments.

All of these factor into the complications you will experience supporting and maintaining your PC as an important tool in your work, so these are things covered here under the broad subject of hardware conflict resolution.

Kate Chase
Wired to the Net from rural Connecticut

Acknowledgements

This book would not have been possible without the efforts and vision of certain key people and the richness of the online technical community where I work and learn each day.

Thanks go to Senior Editor Michael Sprague of McGraw-Hill for making it work, editing supervisor Penny Linskey, and my agent, Neil J Salkind and his colleagues, David and Sherry Rogelberg of the Studio-B Literary Agency for their generous assistance.

Many others deserve credit as well, including the Hardware Forum community of Microsoft/MSN ComputingCentral and my colleagues there, Jeff Marchi, Robert Proffitt, William Ball, and Deepak Midha. They have taught me the joy of hardware comes with its mastery and application—to control it and make it work for you.

Additional thanks go to Rick McMillion, also of ComputingCentral, Tracy Martin and Robin Bush, formerly of America Online (my colleagues there a few years back) and my partner, Chris Bedell, who has helped hone my technical expertise.

Also, more personal gratitude is extended to those others who supported my efforts and calmed my hair-tearing, and who reminded me that a reference like this could indeed be accomplished in so short a time.

Finally, let me add my heartfelt thanks to CK Phalon, a member of the online tech community, a master at demanding more from hardware and getting it, too, as well as a dear friend. He never failed to offer me the courage and strength to proceed.

Kate Chase

CHAPTER 1

Configuration Primer: What You Need to Know and Do

Included in this chapter are the following topics:

◀ Understanding configuration

◀ Essential elements of configuration

◀ Configuration maintenance

◀ What you need to save copies of for later reference or restoration

Let me introduce you to one of the most fundamental principles of computing: The best equipment will not achieve its best performance unless all components of the system are configured properly to reduce conflicts and maximize results.

In other words, you won't have a reliable, well-performing PC without both understanding its configuration and taking an active role in making sure your configuration is tuned to work best for your system. A brand-new PII-450 MHz screamer shipped from the factory should perform well right out of the box, but it won't continue performing well for long without your vigilance.

Why? Because each time you may have to reboot without shutting down properly, each time an application crashes, each time you install an application or try to remove one, and each time you try finessing hardware to do something it's not necessarily designed to do—and these are just a very few examples—changes are made to your system that can begin to deteriorate its overall performance.

The changes are likely to start out small (a lost file here, a corrupted file there, a removal of an application that doesn't remove its Windows Registry entry), when you may barely notice small warning messages, if they pop up at all. Over time, however, you notice that the hard disk and the system overall just seems slower. Windows takes longer to load, for instance. Defragmenting—which means a reorganization of the physical hard disk data to try to clump used space with used space and free space with free space—may not seem to do the trick anymore for restoring some speed. Soon thereafter, you may start getting error messages layered one on top of another, or so severe they halt further work on your PC until they are remedied.

By then, if you haven't learned your system and exerted some due diligence in maintaining it in peak form, you may be facing not just one problem (a missing driver, for example), but a slew of unrelated problems that have aggregated together to form one large mess. This is a real dilemma. Realize that an isolated, single PC problem can be tough enough to identify (many are easier to correct than find initially, by the way). When you have a layering of problem upon problem, you have a snarl far worse than trying to detangle many snarled sets of holiday lights just an hour before party guests are due to arrive. It's very tough to know where to start, or how to separate out one conflict from another in trying to get all of them resolved.

Don't believe that configuration relates to a specific issue or set of resources, because it truly does not. A symphony of components—the operating system, the peripheral devices totally and in terms of their parts, the Windows initialization files, how that hardware is read and influenced by the BIOS (the intelligent "settings" part of a motherboard), the adequacy of PC memory and the virtual swap file, and so much more—all come together to compose what we think of as total configuration and performance. If any component presents a real decline in optimization, or a full failure in performance, everything else will (eventually) feel it.

Part of this is because Windows—particularly the 32-bit Windows found in Windows 95 and 98, as well as in NT 4.0—is both intelligent and integrated. It is designed to work with most of the hardware we toss at it, with the smarter BIOSes that control more of our hardware settings, to make notations in its central Registry related to particular needs and custom settings, and to let its applications freely work with peripherals such as scanners, printers, and digitizing devices. In fact, the more you begin to understand how all these different pieces must come together and work in asymptomatic unison, the more you will appreciate the actual wonder of your PC, both in its design and function, and how the operating system works with it.

To exemplify this, let's look at Windows 95, the first regular consumer 32-bit Windows released by Microsoft in August 1995. Prior to its release, running Windows was simpler (and yet sometimes harder), because Windows wasn't an operating system of its own. It was what is referred to as a graphical operating environment—sort of like a colorful, icon-driven graphical shell—sitting above DOS. Only once the system was fully booted and DOS was loaded as an operating system could you run WIN.EXE to launch Windows itself. Likewise, when you quit Windows, you didn't drop out of your operating system, you just exited Windows and returned to good old basic DOS.

Windows isn't quite as smart in Windows 3.1x and earlier, not in the same way Windows 95 and 98 are. This is particularly true where hardware is concerned. With 16-bit Windows 3.1 and before, Windows only knew about installed hardware if you told it that a device existed.

This changed in Windows 95 with the arrival of Plug and Play technology, which we examine in some detail in Chapter 7. For now, understand that Plug and Play is a standard by which a PC's motherboard BIOS (which allows you to store settings to be remembered on each PC boot) can work in conjunction with the PC's operating system to identify and properly assign devices that are Plug and Play-compatible. These devices are identified by a bit of encoding done on the device itself to report information to the connection on the motherboard (either directly through a port or by plugging it into an expansion slot on the motherboard itself) stating, "This is what type of device I am and these are my standard settings."

As a companion to Plug and Play's introduction came a feature in Windows 95 known as Configuration Manager. This is actually loaded as part of Virtual Memory Manager (VMM32.EXE) and is specifically charged with coordinating the configuration process between your PC and your Windows operating system. If you are using Windows 95 or 98, one of your jobs will be to clean up around the configuration work Configuration Manager does (sometimes, you'll need to try to circumvent it even), though it usually does a pretty decent job of identifying hardware and assigning resources appropriately.

Configuration Manager has a tough job. It not only has to work with a number of different PC buses such as PCI and ISA and SCSI, it has to be able to distinguish from different types of hardware connected to each, and sort through each one's particular configuration requirements. Once Configuration Manager has identified and assessed, it needs to juggle system resources like hardware interrupt requests (IRQs) and DMA channels to meet the needs of these hardware devices. And it needs to do this without creating a conflict, if it can avoid one, even though some hardware seems almost designed to require the same set of system resources needed by totally different types of hardware. Sound cards and network interface cards (NICs) are a prime example of this, often opting for the same IRQ and the same I/O address.

You'll appreciate more the job Configuration Manager does when you read Chapter 3 on system resources, because you come to see how little room Configuration Manager has to work in. There aren't a slew of system resources available. Though there are 16 interrupt requests on most PCs, several are already assumed by the system itself, and some of these don't even have a physical connection (a wire) present to allow you to use them to work with a hardware device in being recognized and working with the PC and Windows.

Beyond that, Configuration Manager is also charged with spotting changes made to your system that affect other things. For instance, it needs to know when you have inserted a PC card (formerly PCMCIA) modem in your notebook PC's PCMCIA slot and when you've removed it. This way, you don't sit for an hour trying to fax a document to the central office using your PC card modem wondering why it's not doing anything; Windows will tell you there is no modem available when you try to run the fax application. Or take the case of my parallel/printer port, which sometimes has a printer attached to it and, sometimes, a digital camera. Configuration Manager helps the process by which Windows has some idea which is attached—though there is probably little danger that my Word documents will try to print to my Connectix camera instead of my Hewlett-Packard Inkjet printer.

Much of how Configuration Manager keeps all this straight is by looking to something called *bus enumerators* (enumeration versus hardware detection is discussed in detail in Chapter 7) to see what hardware is connected to each bus and what specific system resource needs each device on each bus requires to operate properly. More rarely, Configuration Manager will consult the bus or device itself for this information.

What the bus enumerators do here is create a sort of physical mapping of the hardware connected to the PC by way of the various buses. This is also called a hardware tree, which is the term for a hierarchical delineation of all the buses and devices on those buses that make up a PC. See Figure 1.1.

Along with enumerators, there are things built into your operating system known as *resource arbitrators*. As their name should imply, it's their job to try to resolve conflicts that come up between the devices attached to your PC and the system resources each wants to use. Most of the time, your system will attempt to correct a problem before it becomes an issue you can see or need to worry about.

The majority of the time, when we make changes to our PCs—to add hardware, to upgrade the operating system or major integrated software packages, to make it part of a network—those changes cascade throughout the system. They *have* to do this for all parts of the PC—including its operating system and all the applications installed within it—to recognize the changes and work properly with them.

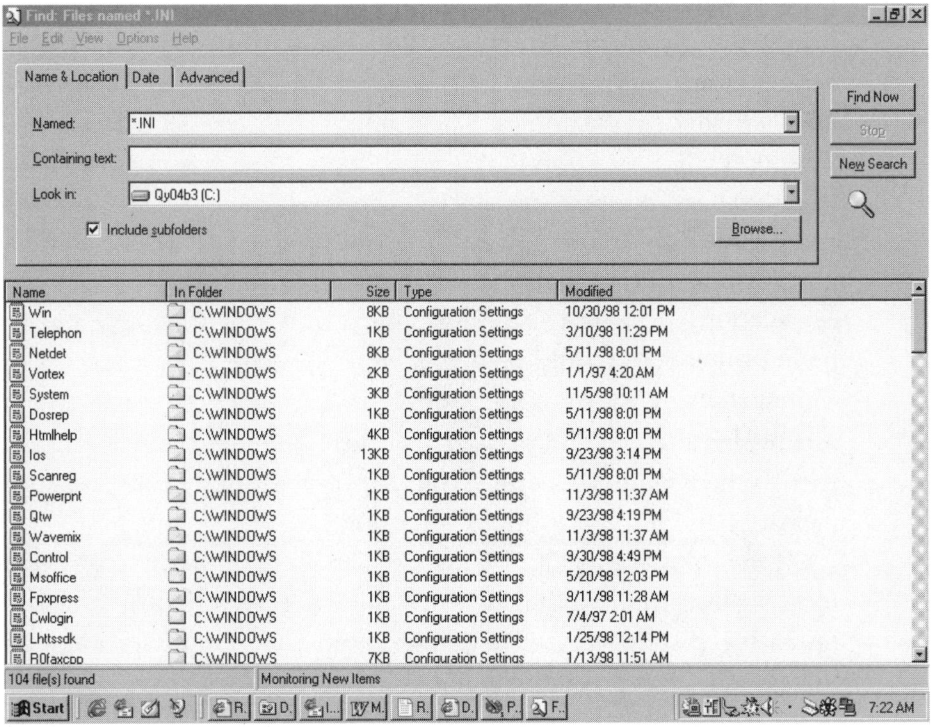

Figure 1.1 Finding all *.INI files.

But as far as we have come since IBM introduced the first PC/XT in the early 1980s, we have not found a way to make a PC work at its most capable without human intervention. The arrival of hardware ease-of-interface concepts like Plug and Play (PnP) has aided us, for example, but it remains up to the user to troubleshoot conflicts and try to configure his or her system for optimal performance, taking into account the specific components of the specific PC in question.

Too many types of equipment and even too many close-but-not-the-same standards, too many types of computer bus types and processors and motherboards, and hardware interfaces and operating systems, too, make it impossible for us to devise more than very general rules about "what works best," given the range of equipment types available. So it becomes the user's responsibility to understand the PC in question and make the right configuration choices based around that understanding of what it has and what it needs to do. No software or no other third-party agent can achieve what users cognizant of their PCs can.

A big part of what I want you to have when you're finished with this book is a much better understanding of all the ways hardware (and software) gets documented to your system, via CMOS/BIOS, through .INI and other system information files, through the Windows Registry, through data supplied in Windows 95/98 and Windows NT's Device Manager. These are all places you will need to look when trying to make a recalcitrant problem disappear.

I start off this book talking about configuration, because that's how key it is to the success of your PC productivity. Almost all versions of Windows can plod along half-broken and poorly configured for an amazingly long time before they finally may not boot. But the PC's rather amazing resources get squandered here as surely as buying a very expensive racing car just to drive to the end of your driveway to fetch the morning mail. The user's time gets wasted too, trying to work around pesky, repetitive error messages and hardware and/or program failures.

If the PC is your tool, you need to keep it in optimum shape. One of the most significant factors in great PC tuning is to configure the PC and your operating system correctly, and to keep that configuration maintained throughout changes that you make.

Windows adds a whole level of complexity to the configuration issue because many configuration files are pulled together—and must work in harmony—in its operation. These include WIN.INI and SYSTEM.INI. A flaw in these files can reverberate throughout the operating systems and your work. Those needing DOS abilities under Windows 95 or Windows 98 also must prepare and keep tweaked the DOS configuration files. Likewise, a problem in the Registry can result in anything from an annoying error to a hardcore failure.

Also important to realize: You need to know what your total configuration looks like *before* a problem occurs, so that you can better objectively see the difference. Knowing what an optimal configuration should look like—and how the settings read—can guide you in repairing a situation and restoring your configuration to proper operation.

Though we will tackle this more in Chapter 3, "The Work Before You Begin Work or Buy New Hardware," our discussion of configuration makes it appropriate now to talk about creating an overall picture of your PC. Consider it something of a personal computer inventory, noting specific facts about your PC as it is currently configured—and facts you can take with you to the next PC.

The difference between the inventory we take here and the one we take in Chapter 3 is detail. Here, we're mapping your overall physical PC, then we discuss what the system resources are on a PC in this context, taking you to the System Resource Inventory we do later, which will map each device to the system resources like IRQs that they use. You should come away with a much better idea of your total PC than you had before you started, and the work you do in gathering the information should save you time and frustration.

To start, locate any documentation that accompanied your PC if you bought it as a complete unit. This includes not just the user's manual but any supplemental literature about your video adapter, motherboard, CD-ROM drive, and so on that was packed as part of your PC. Most include these, even if they are not terribly well detailed (and may not be written in the most understandable language). If you have tossed these out, duplicates may be available at a small charge from your dealer or PC manufacturer. Also, much of the information may be available via the manufacturer's Web site as long as you can identify the make and model number of your PC (you may find this on a metal label on the back of the PC if located nowhere else). If instead you built your PC or had it custom-built for you, you likely retained the documentation relating to the various components of your system.

Now using the form listing in Table 1.1 below, try to fill in all the information you can for each of the blanks related to the PC you are looking at right now.

You may not be able to fill in all the information immediately, and you may want to amend the format for your own use. For instance, you may want to incorporate the inventory here with a more in-depth one that includes the resources used for devices like the sound card, the network card, and the video adapter, all into one sheet you can keep for the life of that PC. You will want to familiarize yourself with CMOS settings for your motherboard's BIOS, where many specifications and assignments are made. We'll talk more about this later.

Identifying the Key Configuration Files

Believe it or not considering the size of Windows (even Windows 3.1x), the majority of the primary configuration settings you will assign in your Windows (and DOS) environment are contained within just a small set of files. What is contained in them largely designates and customizes your entire working operation. These files, which are discussed in detail in subsequent chapters, are as follows:

◀ *CONFIG.SYS.* DOS-based file (optional in Windows 95 and 98) that loads memory management and device drivers.

◀ *AUTOEXEC.BAT* DOS-based file (also optional) that loads a DOS mouse driver (if ending in .EXE or .COM), the MSCDEX file (which may be more properly run in a file called DOSSTART.BAT) needed for CD-ROM drive operation, as well as any terminate-and-stay-resident (TSR) programs such as virus scanners.

◀ *PROGMAN.INI* This file is more important to Windows 3.1x but remains in Windows 95 and 98 for compatibility and may contain settings required for 16-bit programs.

◀ *WIN.INI* Defines many user-defined settings for Windows, including desktop settings such as wallpaper, programs to load or run on Windows' launch, and programs associated with types of files (as you might find under My Computer in Windows)

TABLE 1.1 PC Inventory

PC Make: Qualantex Operating System Version: Windows 98	Model #: xx450 Total RAM: 64 MB PC 100	Purchased: 9/1/98 OS Updates Applied: None
Device Type	Make	Notes
Monitor	Sceptre	15" VLMF Model 123AB
CPU	Intel	PII-450
Hard disk	IBM Deskstar 123AB Maxtor 789XX	8.1 GB master, assigned as drive C 5.4 GB slave assigned as Drive F
CD-ROM	Toshiba	32x; new driver applied 10/2/98; assigned as Drive E
Floppy drive	Toshiba	1.44 MB
Video adapter- Regular	Matrox Millenium II	8 MB, 250 MHZ RAMDAC; driver applied 10/2/98
3D	N/A	
Sound card	SB AWE64	Will change for SB Live in 11/98
COM Ports		Mouse on COM 1; modem on COM 2
Parallel Ports	LPT1	Shared between printer and Connectix camera, which also shares connection through keyboard port
Mouse	Microsoft IntelliMouse	Purchased 6/98—works on laptop, too
Keyboard	generic	
Modem	3Com/US Robotics voice/ data/fax	V.90 applied; driver updated 7/98
Printer	HP Deskjet 660 Cse	Purchased 11/93
Network Card	N/A	
Additional Storage	Iomega	ZIP drive 100 MB capacity allocated as Drive D
SCSI	N/A	
Universal Serial Bus		2, both unused (have powered hub for future use)

* Old ISA scanner and WACOM tablet available but not added at this time

◄ *SYSTEM.INI* Defines many of the system settings for Windows—including key core components like GDI.EXE and USER.EXE, basic drivers to load, and VCACHE information—and points you at your password list(s), if any.

◄ *SYSTEM.DAT* One of the key Windows Registry data files; see the Registry chapter for more information on this file.

◄ *USER.DAT* User settings for the Windows Registry; see above.

For those using Windows NT 4.0, these files are also important in operation and should be backed up regularly :

◄ NTUSER.DAT

◄ USER.DMP

You should make a copy of these whenever you have occasion to install Windows fresh, or when you have a new PC. You should also make a copy of them prior to beginning any modifications to your system, including installing service packs or updates, new drivers, or upgrading your operating system. After making changes, check the new versions of these files against the now-older saved copies. This should give you an indication of what got altered and may give you better insight into some of the cause-and-effect that goes on with your PC and even small modifications you may make. Everything you learn can help build your experience base for analyzing and troubleshooting difficulties down the road.

Except for the Registry .DAT files, which are handled through manipulation of the Registry itself through something like the REGEDIT.EXE utility that packs with Windows, all of these files are text-based and easy to edit using any text editor. SYSEDIT is included in Windows specifically to allow you to edit these basic system files.

Remember, serious changes, for example ones to your CONFIG.SYS or your SYSTEM.INI, require you to save the changes, then shut down and reboot your PC for the changes to take effect. As you gain mastery in using your PC, you'll become aware of what you can edit in these files to achieve the best results. But so long as you have a copy of the previous working versions of these files, combined with a system boot disk (which we cover in Chapter 3), you can test and tweak a bit to start without being in any grave danger. Registry editing is a bit more advanced. Wait until you read Chapter 5 on Registry manipulation before you play in there.

Other Things You Want to Copy

Other files you may want to back up include your .PWL or password files (logon for Windows or logon for services passwords, such as for mail in Outlook Express), your .GRP files (which are Group Manager files left over from Windows 3.1x), as well as other .INI files you may feel are important to keep. If you're using a mail client, such as Microsoft Outlook or Outlook Express, you will want to backup your .PST and other mail index files.

Are you running a network? Then you want to locate and copy any network configuration files, too, to save you time down the line. Do you have questions about what should be backed up for data in an application? Consult the online Help file for it or its documentation.

If you're not using a full-fledged regular backup routine (also discussed later in the book), you may want to just copy these files to a floppy drive, to a removable storage medium like a writable CD-ROM, a ZIP drive, and so on, but be sure to keep versions of these files separate. This means that if you want to keep a copy of the default versions of these files, you want to file them separately from copies you make after installing a new operating system or performing some other modification. This way, you have a sort of historical reference to check back into to see what the default values were, how they changed when you did something, and how that may vary from the settings you may have now (which may be causing you difficulties). This method, by the way, is an excellent tool in learning the cause-and-effect we've already discussed.

More than just the major .INI files discussed above can be found on your system, as indicated by this Find on all (*.INI) INI files on my system (Figure 1.1). You may choose to back all of these up or just the primary ones noted.

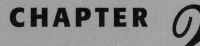

How PC Hardware Spans the Years: How It Jams Us; How It Helps Us

In this chapter, the following topics are covered:

◀ History of PC architecture as it relates to how hardware is added, configured, and used

◀ Current state and standards for PC hardware

◀ What PC99 specs are and what they tell us about the PC we will use in the next century

History of PC Bus Architecture

If you know anything about PCs, you know how far and fast they have developed. Ten years ago, 386 machines were big news. We were just beginning to see PCs that embodied the kind of computing power formerly reserved for much more expensive mini-computers, the type only big business owned.

But now we've left 80386 and even 80486 technology in the dust and traveled on past Pentium classics, Pentium Pros (an update to the Pentium specifically designed for Windows NT 4.0, then all but abandoned until Intel announced an overdrive chip for it in late summer 1998), and Pentium MMXs, which added multimedia extensions, to today's Pentium IIs and IIIs and the Xeons meant for the multiprocessor heavy processing already available now. Merced (IA=64 architecture), Intel's 64-bit CPU, should be out before another year passes.

Compared to the motherboards and central processing units (CPUs) we ran 5 and 10 years ago, we now have ones that run at clock speeds of 100 MHz and 450 plus MHz, respectively, with a 1000-MHz CPU in our not-too-distant future. Many take these rated clock speeds up a notch through a process known as *overclocking*.

Yet although our PCs can operate much faster overall—applications are loaded with amazing speed; our telecommunications have jumped from 1200 bps to 56 KB and beyond to cable-modem speed and ISDN; our video pace races along, comparatively speaking; and our hard drives are much improved in terms of both transfer rate and physical size—we're still tied to the relative dark days of PCs, back when lots of folks continued to own and use XTs.

As you will read in Chapter 7, which discusses recent innovations like Peripheral Component Interconnect (PCI), Accelerated Graphics Ports (AGP), universal serial bus (USB), and IEEE 1394/FireWire, technology has begun moving us away from some of the old restrictions, such as one set of system resources (e.g., interrupt requests) per device and more speed. Still, ISA remains. Most PCs today continue to pack at least one ISA slot, if just one it can share with PCI adapters (some, a few ISA slots).

Though ISA has been both accommodated for despite its slowness and accommodates us because it allows us to continue using older hardware, it is past ready to die. Keeping it in our PC architecture for backward compatibility has impeded our ability to move forward. As we clamor ever onward for faster and faster equipment, we need to leave some of the old connections behind, and these include the ISA bus (as later buses like MCA and VLB came and went, as discussed shortly).

ISA won't disappear instantly though. Sure, new equipment will not be manufactured in ISA format and new PCs wanting to carry the Microsoft Windows logo won't feature an ISA bus anymore. Yet many of us—perhaps even the majority of us—will likely retain at least one or two favored ISA devices. We may not let them go until they are wrenched away from us, in fact. We're still reticent to give up those old ISA-based scanners, for example, that we paid an arm-and-a-leg for a few years ago, before scanner prices really bottomed out. ISA-based video and sound adapters continue to be commonly seen.

So what is ISA and the buses that developed in response to it? But, first, what is a PC bus?

Understanding PC Buses

Since we will be talking a fair amount about PC bus architecture and the limitations of each, you need to realize that there is more than one type of bus in a PC. They may all operate at different speeds, depending on how close to the processor or central processing unit (CPU) they are located (the closer, the faster).

Think of a bus as a data channel. The width of the bus has a direct effect on the speed of the bus, because a wider bus means more data can be moved at once. Original PCs had 8-bit buses; today's often use a mix between 16 and 64 bits wide. Bus bandwidth, or throughput, refers to how much data can move across the bus simultaneously during a set amount of time (a table of these is included in Chapter 8). Buses are connected to one another by means of bus bridges, including today's common PCI-ISA bridge.

Other bridges connect these buses to the processor, which means the bus acts as a subset of the PC system to the whole system. Buses may allow the addition of hardware that is connected to the individual bus, and thus in turn connected to the whole PC. It's a design that allows the PC to work more effectively, because rather than have every peripheral feeding directly into the main highway of traffic on a PC at the same place and pace, they come in along access points, some designed to work faster than others. Hardware needing faster response time is installed to faster buses; hardware with slower needs go to slower buses.

Most PCs today include at least four types of buses, and sometimes more. These are as follows:

- ◀ *Processor bus*. Highest level of PC bus, used for moving data back and forth between the chipset and processor; some systems—for all practical purposes—combine the processor and memory bus (see below).
- ◀ *Memory bus*. Connects the PC's memory subsystem to the CPU and chipset; if it doesn't reside with the processor bus, it's a second-level bus below the cache bus.
- ◀ *Cache bus*. Dedicated bus found in Pentium Pro and Pentium II PCs to access system cache.

◁ *Local I/O bus.* "Local" means local to the processor, which should mean faster performance, as these devices interact more directly with the CPU, chipset, and memory. You can see this with PCI devices over standard ISA. Peripheral Component Interconnect (PCI) and VESA Local Bus (VLB) are examples of a local I/O bus.

◁ *Standard I/O bus.* Older bus architecture still included on today's machines for compatibility with older-format hardware devices and for more modern ones with slower demands than PCI devices. For example, Industry Standard Architecture (ISA) is still included in machines being sold right now (and it's from that original ISA bus architecture design that we get IRQs, DMA, and I/O).

Additionally, PCs using the LX- and BX-chipset motherboards (and beyond) have an additional means of connecting hardware to the system: the Accelerated Graphics Port, or AGP (discussed more in Chapter 7). While it's not an exclusive bus of its own, its unique role in connecting a higher-speed video adapter to the motherboard means some refer to it as a bus. It is, however, a port, because of the limitations of what you can plug into it (only video).

Types of PC Expansion Buses

ISA (INDUSTRY STANDARD ARCHITECTURE)

ISA dates back to the original IBM PCs in the early 1980s. If you think we're limited in terms of system resources for our hardware now, you should have seen those early days when we had half the number of interrupts (IRQs), DMA channels, and data lines that we do on today's ISA bus. But there was an excuse for it then: We had so little we needed to attach. There weren't specially featured sound and video adapters for them, nor ISA scanner cards to power and control a scanner. We didn't even generally use pointing devices like mice, because we were using a command-line operating system with little need for point-and-shoot capability. PCs in those days were a big case with a floppy and perhaps a hard drive, and the peripherals were usually limited to a keyboard, monitor, and if you were most fortunate, a printer.

ISA was for a long time the only way to connect peripherals other than internal hard drives and such into the PC internally. COM or serial ports and LPT or printer ports, both fairly slow technologies too, were the primary way to get external devices like printers, scanners, pointing devices, tape or disk backup units, and such connected to a PC (and each of these needed an individual IRQ in which to work). These will continue on after ISA is scheduled to be eliminated on January 1, 2000.

The advent of the AT-style (80286) PC a few years later brought some needed changes to the ISA bus when it expanded it from an 8-bit to a 16-bit data path, doubling the total number of IRQs to 16 and DMA channels to 8, and added four more address lines. When you hear people refer to the AT bus, it is this, what we have reverted back to calling ISA today.

By today's standards, ISA is really too slow and prissy in its work inside the higher-end Pentiums and Pentium IIs, and Pentium IIIs but it's been kept viable, partnered with other, faster buses. It has remained to support our older hardware, but its time is coming to an end, as put forth by the PC99 hardware specifications discussed later in this chapter. This will put an end to some of the strangleholds we have experienced in trying to refit the PC to be a much more capable tool, to accommodate our lifestyle as well as our work needs.

MCA (MICRO CHANNEL ARCHITECTURE)

If you know your computing history, you know that IBM created the original line of personal computers (PC/XT) that still serves as the basis for the PC architecture we use today. But IBM lost control over its creation quickly, as various hardware manufacturers and PC clone firms sprang up to offer wider developments and better pricing. The result was that PC clones became more popular than the brand name itself. Tiny hardware companies sprang up into PC clone giants almost overnight to take on the Evil Empire in Armonk, NY (if you are a history buff, you remember that IBM was the so-called Evil Empire of computing long before Microsoft). IBM found itself being eased out of a market it had effectively invented.

In 1987, IBM announced its counterattack: Micro Channel Architecture and the IBM PS/2 line of personal computers. Having learned its business lesson from the original PC, IBM decided to forge its own PC design that would be hard to copy. But it was also meant to offer alternatives to what IBM came to view as flaws with its original PC, including the very limited ISA bus.

MCA improved speed, but not by much: It rose to a modest 10 MHz from a low of 8 MHz, and it widened the data path to allow either 16- or 32-bit. In fact, in streaming mode, it was possible to open it up to 64 bits moved at a time.

What it offered up was so distinctly proprietary as to be completely incompatible with anything else that had come before it. You couldn't plug your original ISA hardware into your MCA slots. There were different connectors to consider too. While most PC software ran fine on either a PS/2 or standard PC, operating systems (DOS predominantly then) sometimes needed special accommodations made for PS/2's uniqueness. This left those buying PCs in those days to choose between the cheaper PC clones and the streamlined, proprietary, and often more expensive PS/2. Most of MCA's market appeared to be corporate users, while consumers and smaller business operations continued along the more traditional PC route.

That MCA didn't catch as a long-term player may or may not seem like a surprise. IBM didn't want to repeat bad history by making it too easy to clone, so it became very close-mouthed about certain specifics and demanded royalties of any company that wanted to create third-party-compatible hardware on the MCA design.

That it held on in the industry as long as it did is in part a function of what distinguished MCA. Besides hardware changes discussed, MCA introduced the configuration of hardware through software menus through a single main configuration program, hardware that could share IRQs, and hardware that could bus master its operations (discussed more in the PCI section) to relieve the CPU of some of the workload. Software configuration of hardware was particularly unique, especially if you recall that original IBM PCs didn't offer CMOS setup options. Of course, I remember the dark days when installing a hard disk meant using something as complex and prone to errors as DEBUG, and having to predetermine a host of settings related to the hard disk type that were pulled from dense technical specifications from the manufacturer.

EISA (EXTENDED ISA)

EISA, or Extended Industry Standard Architecture (because it is indeed an extension of ISA), was developed largely in response to IBM's MCA design and came about 2 years after MCA's announcement. Its backers were IBM competitors, including Compaq, Epson, Hewlett-Packard, NEC, and Tandy.

As the name suggests, this group didn't want to reinvent PC design; it wanted to extend the capability of what was already in place with the ISA bus. Forget MCA's whole new direction when you can upgrade performance and potential along a steady path was the message.

EISA brought some changes, but not all some desired. The system clock rate remained the same as ISA, a puttering 8 MHz. The number of interrupts (IRQs) and DMA channels didn't increase (continuing at 16 and 8, respectively), but I/O addresses hopped up to 64 KB, and the speed at which DMA will run is higher. The data path also increased to 32-bit, and address lines were expanded to provide for up to 4 GB of memory.

Some well-liked additions in MCA—namely, bus-mastering ability and the ability to set up hardware configurations from software—were built in, which would reduce some of the reasons PC buyers might choose the MCA model over an EISA-based PC.

But a nice side benefit was that EISA design finally allowed for physically larger expansion cards/adapters. While we think of smaller as better in microelectronic design, it's also usually more expensive. Larger expansion cards were cheaper to produce overall than the smaller original ISA cards. If you want a parallel, look at how much more expensive a portable PC is than a desktop PC—part of that additional cost is borne by the fact that everything has to be designed to work in a much smaller case weighing far less. While notebooks and laptops have dropped in price significantly over the last 12 to 18 months, you still pay a premium. And repair costs on a portable versus a desktop can be dramatic, to say the least.

But EISA's slow clock rate made the industry itch for more. Move the bus closer to the processor and watch the speed rise, they thought. Thus, the seeds of the next generation of bus were sown.

VESA LOCAL BUS (VLB)

VESA Local Bus, or VLB, is notable because it represented the very first local bus, meaning that the system bus is positioned on or near (local to) the much zippier memory bus of the PC's CPU. Repositioning it in this way helps the local bus run at or near the actual external speed of the CPU itself. But it also keeps higher-speed operations from having to wade through the noise and sluggishness of the very slow ISA bus, which remained on the PC for backward compatibility for older equipment (as it continues to do as of this writing).

VLB has been largely abandoned now and tends to be present only on older 486 systems (newer 486s use the PCIset). VLB devices are notable because they are much longer than ISA and PCI adapters, with the VLB also (of course) offering a much longer slot to accommodate the adapters.

PERIPHERAL COMPONENT INTERCONNECT

Peripheral Component Interconnect, or PCI, is the latest and most commonly used non-ISA bus in today's PCs, and offers a nice performance boost above all other older competitors. We'll talk a lot more about PCI in Chapter 7, but understand that its speed and ability to share system resources like IRQ assignments with other PCI devices and the ability to help with the bus mastering of drives helped win its place on today's PC motherboards.

USB, FIREWIRE, AND BEYOND

Universal serial bus (USB), IEEE 1394 specification or FireWire technology, and Device Bay are part of the expansion of the interconnect concept— meaning, plug it in and use. Again, these will all be covered in more depth in Chapter 7. USB is already here, of course, found on notebook computers more often before their wider implementation on the desktop PC with the advent of an operating system and BIOS to support it.

OK, at this point we can start putting together some of the facts learned earlier with some deeper-detailed reality of the state of hardware today. With different chipsets and PC bus types, there has been an evolution over time to increase the performance possibilities. Different markers measure this evolution, including:

◄ *Bus width*. How wide (measured in bits) the channel is through which data must move back and forth

◄ *Bus speed*. Rate at which data bits move across each wire along the bus each second (measured in MHz)

TABLE 2.1   Bus Type Specifications

Bus Type	Bus Width (bits)	Bus Speed (MHz)	Bus Bandwidth (MB/second)
ISA (8-bit)	8	8.33	8.3
ISA (16-bit)	16	8.33	16.6
EISA	32	8.33	33.3
VLB (VESA Local)	32	33	133.3
PCI	32	33	133.3
PCI 2.1 (64-bit)	64	66	533.3
AGP	32	66	266.6
AGP x 2 mode	32	66x2	533.3
AGP x 4 mode	32	66x4	1066.6

◀ *Bus bandwidth*. Maximum potential of the bus as viewed through data that can move along the bus against a set time frame (standardly measured in MB per second; also known as *throughput*).

Table 2.1 shows the specifications for various bus types.
The method by which different types of system buses (often PCI and ISA today) communicate with each other and the devices attached to each different bus is called a *bus bridge*. In the case of PCI and ISA, there is what is known as a PCI-ISA bridge, first introduced with the Pentium classic line.

NOTE The PCI bus has another bridge that connects it to the CPU bus. You can see this in Windows 95/98 and Windows NT 4.0 Device Manager by looking under the System Devices listing.

PC99 Specifications—What They Are, What They Mean

When Microsoft and Intel (or "Wintel")—in association with other PC manufacturers—release their PC system design guidelines for the coming year, the industry listens, and it affects your hardware purchases. Basically, what PC99 (and its predecessors) offers are guidelines for what should be considered the standard of equipment for home and office machines in the year ahead. Only PC manufacturers offering equipment that meets the guidelines set forth within PC99 are eligible to carry the much-coveted

"Designed for Windows" Microsoft logo. This is the PC world equivalent of the "Good Housekeeping Seal of Approval." More importantly, many consumers look for the label and may not buy a PC without it.

According to PC99 guidelines released on July 20, 1998, the average system of the immediate tomorrow will include:

◀ 300 MHz CPU (processor)

◀ 128 KB integrated Level 2 (L2) cache

◀ 64 megabytes of RAM for office/32 for homes

◀ Support for Instantly Available PC standard (which defines power management issues for things like power supplies, the PCI bus, and add-in cards)

◀ DVD to replace the traditional CD-ROM (recommended, not required)

Other changes required or recommended include:

◀ The presence of two USB ports (1 for mobile PCs)

◀ Improved ACPI and BIOS support

◀ Required 56 Kbps V.90 modem

◀ AGP video recommended as the primary adapter

◀ Clarifications provided for graphic adapter support for 3-D video hardware acceleration, as well as incremental enhancements to audio performance standards

What has been allowed in past PC guidelines but is being eliminated in this new round is support for older ISA cards. ISA is a notoriously fussy platform (now relegated to "legacy" status) that is not only harder to configure but also much slower than later model PCI- and USB-based hardware. Another big negative with ISA: older ISA cards don't support Plug and Play (PnP), a so-called ease-of-installation technology that Microsoft widely introduced with its support in Windows 95 in August 1995. Newer PnP-ISA devices tend to present their own problems on installation.

PC99 effectively calls for the elimination of all ISA slots by January 1, 2000, although most motherboards today include at least one ISA-usable slot. While ISA is less and less popular, the equipment is still in wide use today, even in Pentium II PCs, which may offer as many as three or four ISA slots.

TABLE 2.2   Color Codes for Connectors

Connector Type	Color	Pantone*
PS/2-compatible mouse	Green	3395C
PS/2-compatible keyboard	Purple	2715C
Universal serial bus (USB)	Black	426C
FireWire/IEEE 1394	Grey	424C
VGA (analog)	Blue	661C
Monitor (digital)	White	
MIDI/Gameport	Gold	131C
Serial (com)	Teal or Turquoise	322C
Parallel (printer)	Burgundy	235C
Microphone	Pink	701C
Audio Line-in	Light Blue	284C
Audio Line-out	Lime Green	577C
Speaker out (subwoofer)	Orange	157C
SCSI	None	
Modem in	None	
Modem out	None	
Network adapters	None	
Video out	Yellow	123C
Speaker (right to left)	Brown	4645C

* Pantone is a standard set of colors; each color is specified by a specific number.

Industry pundits expected PC99 would call for an end to the older serial and parallel ports as well. Instead of elimination, PC99 seems to recommend a phase-out. Since it continues to allow support for the older hardware types, some analysts are saying PC99 doesn't go far enough to push support for USB and FireWire IEE1394, two faster and more flexible means of connecting hardware to the PC. While two USB ports are required under PC99 specs, failure to remove serial and parallel connections may slow down its adoption by consumers (like us) who retain all those older printers and such. It also may mean the implementation of Device Bay, a sort of universal hardware expansion scheme concept that supports both USB and FireWire, gets put on a back burner. USB, FireWire or 1394, and Device Bay are discussed in more detail in Chapter 7.

PC99 also recommends requiring the color coding of connectors used for hardware, to help ensure proper installation in low-light or low-visibility situations (behind or under a desk, for example) and to help those with visual problems. It's also intended to help reduce "connection confusion" for PC newcomers performing some of their first PC hardware work.

For example, a microphone would be coded "pink," a USB connection "black," and a PS/2-compatible keyboard "purple," as indicated in the proposed color coding standards offered in Table 2.2.

To get a copy of the PC99 specs for yourself, you can visit *http://www.microsoft.com/hwdev/pc99.htm* on the World Wide Web.

CHAPTER 3

The Work Before You Begin Work or Buy New Hardware

The following topics are included in this chapter:

◀ Doing your homework on what you want to add

◀ Assessing your system and how your resources are currently used

◀ Identifying resources for information

◀ Acquainting yourself with information and diagnostic utilities before you have to troubleshoot

◀ Boot disks—how to create them; how you need to augment them

Let me advise you of *the* single best tip for curing a hardware conflict: Don't let yourself have one in the first place.

It may sound simple, but the best time- and frustration-saver of all is to analyze your PC and determine what you have and how you can make it work with what you wish to add. When this is all done thoughtfully and with a view toward full compatibility, you achieve better results and less downtime troubleshooting through a tricky setup.

With Windows NT 4.0, this preinstallation homework is even more necessary. NT has very specific products it supports, and it doesn't always play kindly when you try to "fool" it into thinking it's using one device when it is really using another. It wants the right hardware and the right configuration from the start. Just setting up an unsupported modem to work with NT's Remote Access Service (RAS) and Dial-Up Networking (DUN) can be an exercise in humility. Translation: If you value your time, you will use some of the recommendations offered here.

Remember: Many difficulties can start to crop up long before you begin experiencing failures and crashes. You can reduce the minor problems from occurring at all, or impede their development into larger issues that can halt your work, if you take a proactive approach to managing your system. As you plan your new equipment purchases and installations, this approach can help you prepare for the best configuration and assess problems ahead of time.

Assessing Your System to Understand Current Resource Use

To know what you can add and how, you need to determine what you have already. Then you can use this base of information to build upon as you analyze the particular needs of proposed new equipment. You know your system and the basics of system resources well enough that you can consider adding a network card, for example, and immediately realize the network card may present a problem. You know this because you have come to know that the only IRQ you have free is IRQ5, for example, while network cards really, truly prefer being installed on an available interrupt above IRQ9.

This base of information lets you make adjustments before you start installing to increase the odds that the new hardware—along with the rest of the devices already installed—works well from the first boot and recognition. You have wrested the situation from the realm of hit or miss and delivered yourself and your PC into the world of strategic resource planning.

Using Windows 95/98 and Windows NT's Device Manager in Documenting Your Resources

Windows Device Manager, available in Windows 95/98 and Windows NT, is really the first place to start when assessing what you currently have and identifying what you may need to change to add what you need (as well as to overcome conflicts; you can read more about this in Chapter 5 on troubleshooting).

If you're using Windows 98, however, do check out MSINFO/System

Information utility, because it presents much of the same information (and often more) in an easier to read format (more about this in a little bit). We will also look at other system information utilities later in this chapter.

What Device Manager provides is an easy graphical interface that lists device properties and allows you to modify these as needed. Let's take a closer look at this application. To access Device Manager, choose Start|Settings|Control Panel, then double-click on the System icon and then choose the Device Manager tab.

TIP The deeper you get into Device Manager's nested menus, the more useful the information tends to be, particularly when you are trying to identify current resources and potential conflicts.

You have two options:

1. *View devices by type.* Gives a listing of connected devices by their category or class (all printers are displayed under the Printer category, all display adapters grouped under Display adapters, for example). See Figure 3.1.

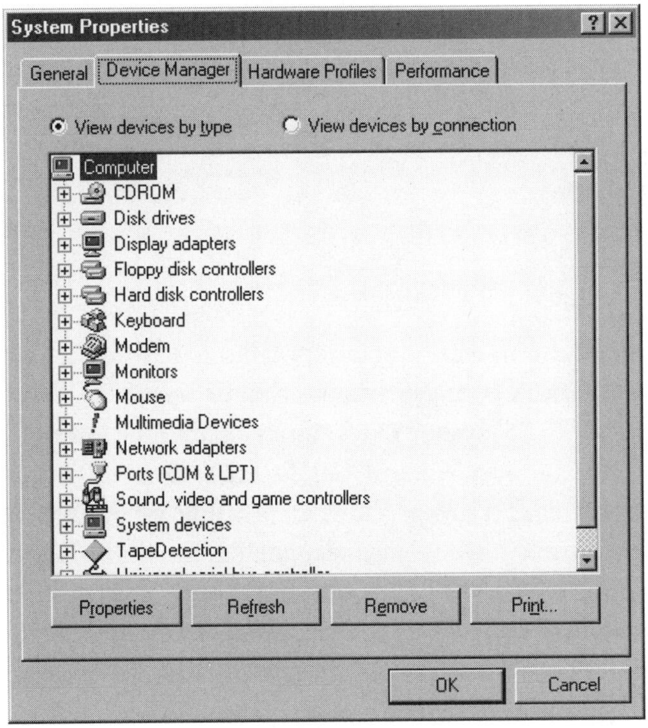

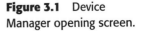

Figure 3.1 Device Manager opening screen.

2. *View devices by connection.* Gives a listing of connected devices by hardware they are connected by.

The first option is best for giving you an overview. Let's say you have just taken one sound card out to exchange for a new and better one. If you're having trouble getting the new sound card recognized, it's wise to check here first to see if the old sound card driver is still listed. If you found it there, you can remove it to resolve the problem, but more about this in Chapter 5. Right now, use this option for determining your hardware inventory.

On the listing shown in the Figure 3.1, the following device categories are given, representing major hardware components of a P200 MMX computer:

◀ CD-ROM
◀ Disk drives
◀ Display adapters
◀ Floppy disk controllers
◀ Hard disk controllers
◀ Keyboard
◀ Modem
◀ Monitor
◀ Mouse
◀ Network adapters
◀ Ports (COM & LPT)
◀ Sound, video, and game controllers

System devices (these include but are not limited to advanced system power management, DMA controller, motherboard resources, PCI bus and bridges, Plug and Play BIOS, system clock, and system timer); see Figure 3.2.

Use the plus (+) signs to expand out listings. One or more devices should be shown for each type or class, depending on how many such devices of each you have connected and recognized. In Figure 3.3, you'll see the listing if you click on View by Connection.

Enumeration, in case you are wondering, refers to the process by which Plug and Play devices are identified by the PC (discussed in depth in the "Plug and Play" section in Chapter 7).

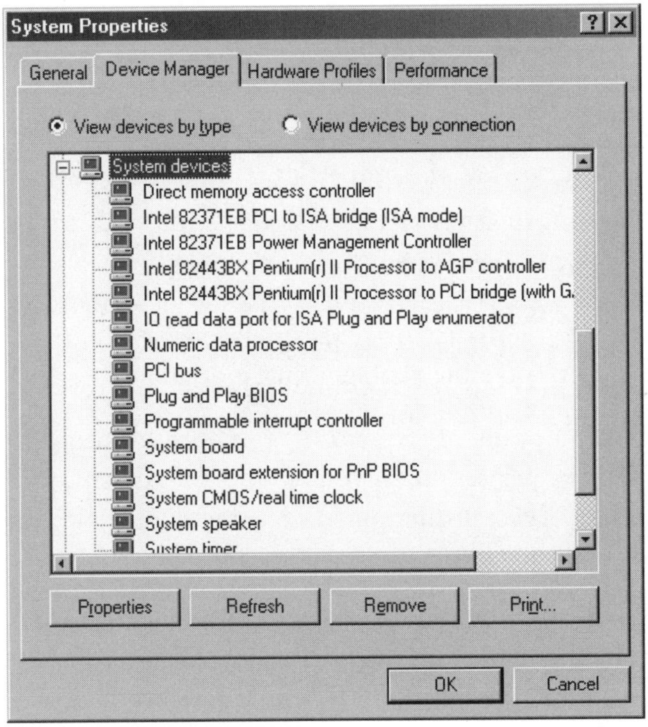

System Properties

General | Device Manager | Hardware Profiles | Performance

○ View devices by type   ○ View devices by connection

System devices
  Direct memory access controller
  Intel 82371EB PCI to ISA bridge (ISA mode)
  Intel 82371EB Power Management Controller
  Intel 82443BX Pentium(r) II Processor to AGP controller
  Intel 82443BX Pentium(r) II Processor to PCI bridge (with G.
  IO read data port for ISA Plug and Play enumerator
  Numeric data processor
  PCI bus
  Plug and Play BIOS
  Programmable interrupt controller
  System board
  System board extension for PnP BIOS
  System CMOS/real time clock
  System speaker
  System timer

Properties | Refresh | Remove | Print...

OK | Cancel

Figure 3.2 Device Manager/view by type/System Devices.

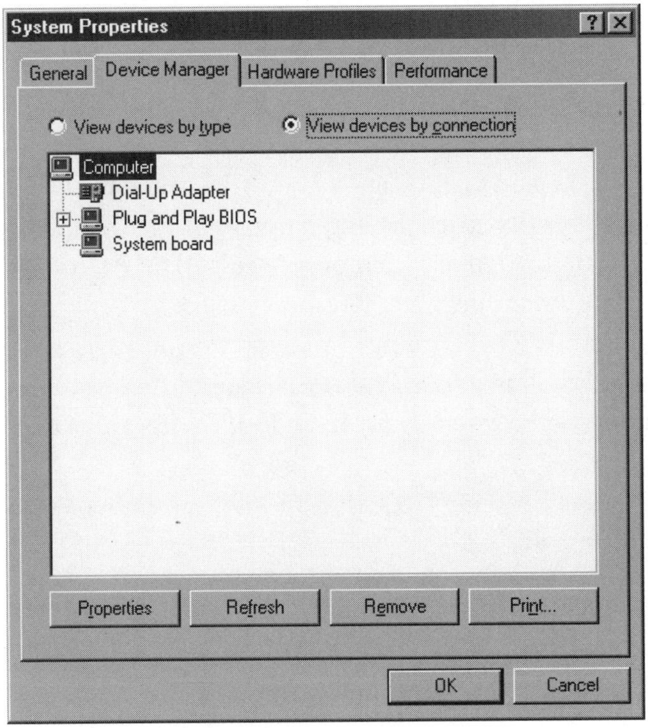

System Properties

General | Device Manager | Hardware Profiles | Performance

○ View devices by type   ● View devices by connection

Computer
  Dial-Up Adapter
  Plug and Play BIOS
  System board

Properties | Refresh | Remove | Print...

OK | Cancel

Figure 3.3 Device Manager/view devices by connection.

Your four options are:

◄ *Properties*. Allows you to view the properties for a specific device

◄ *Refresh*. Refreshes information about the devices listed to be updated because it forces your system to reenumerate

◄ *Remove*. Allows you to remove a device from the listing, which also removes it from memory as well as the Registry (that is, hopefully it does—more on this in Chapter 8 on the Windows Registry)

◄ *Print*. Gives you the option of generating a report (printing to screen, rather than your printer unless you redirect it to do so), providing a summary of this information that contains a listing of devices, as well as their properties and resources.

The presence of yellow circles containing exclamation points or red x's indicate warnings or problems, which we will discuss in Chapter 5. Just briefly, it is important to note all the information you can about these as a tool in helping you overcome them.

Let's take a look at your PC properties, according to Device Manager. To do so, find Computer at the top of your Device Manager listing, click on it, and select Properties. This breaks out the information into two windows:

◄ View Resources

◄ Reserve Resources

Under View Resources, as shown in Figure 3.4, you can tell Device Manager to show you the devices listed by Interrupt Request (IRQ), by Input/Output Address (I/O), by Direct Memory Access (DMA), or by Memory. Do this to inventory your devices by resource used.

Use the View Resources tab when you need to assign resources manually. Windows will then assign Plug and Play devices around the resources you reserve here. Resources can be reserved for IRQ, I/O, DMA, and Memory, depending on your needs.

For example, if you need to reserve IRQ5 for an internal modem, you would:

1. Open Device Manager (Start|Settings|Control Panel|System|Device Manager).

2. Click on the line in the list labeled simply Computer.

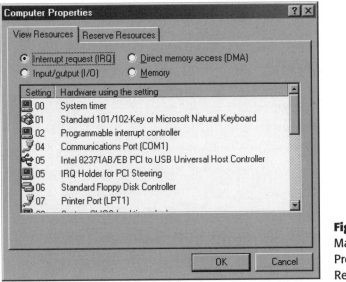

Figure 3.4 Device Manager/Computer/ Properties/View Resources/IRQs.

3. In the Computer Properties window, select the Reserve Resources tab.

4. Click on the type of resource you wish to reserve; in this case, Interrupt Request (IRQ).

5. Click on the Add button, then type in the value for the resource you are reserving; in this case, "5". See Figure 3.5.

6. Click OK.

IRQ5 should now be reserved for your assignment. When your system boots, the Plug and Play BIOS (supported in Windows 95 and beyond, and on most machines of 486 generation and beyond) will configure its devices around the resource you reserve (or that the system needs).

NOTE You can modify a setting now or later by highlighting it and clicking the Modify button. You can remove a resource the same way.

The second option (View Devices by Connection) permits you to view devices prefaced by their overall means of connection (COM port hardware connections show an RS-232 connector picturegram; add-on cards and adapters show a PC add-on card picturegram, etc.). See Figure 3.6. Click on the COM1 to see what is using it; click on PCI Bus category, for instance.

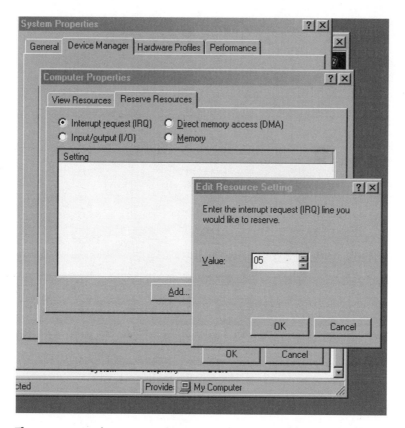

Figure 3.5 Device Manager/Computer/Reserve Resources/Add IRQ5.

Now, what other useful information can we glean from Device Manager without jumping too far ahead?

Go back to the main window of Device Manager, with View Devices by Type checked. On my P200MMX test system, I want to check what is listed under Hard Drive Controllers, because I'm not sure I'm using bus mastering (explained in greater detail in Chapter 4). So I click on the plus (+) sign or the Hard Disk Controllers menu item to expand the entry. As illustrated in Figure 3.7, Device Manager tells me I not only have primary and secondary bus master IDE controller, I have the VX-pro II PC82371 IDE controller to round out the process.

Now I want to take a closer look at how my primary bus master IDE controller is configured. I know what IRQ it should be occupying, but I want to double-check. By double-clicking on the primary bus master IDE controller entry, a window with three tabs pops into view, labeled as follows:

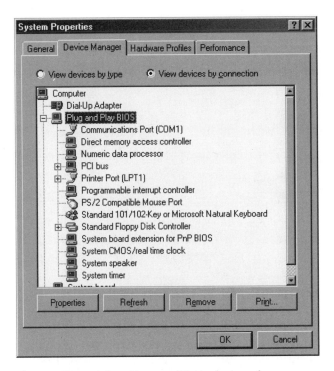

Figure 3.6 Device Manager/View devices by connection—another view.

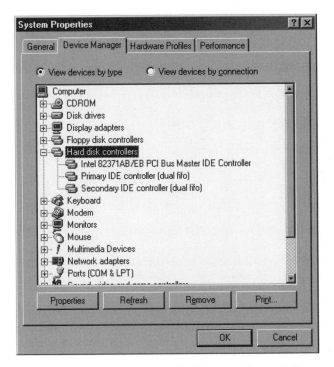

Figure 3.7 Device Manager/view by type/HD controller.

◄ *General.* Reports device type, manufacturer, hardware version, device status (you want to see "This device is working properly."), and checkbox options to disable this device in the hardware profile or make sure it exists in all hardware profiles

◄ *Driver.* Reports device driver information and gives you the option of changing/updating the driver for the particular device

◄ *Resource.* Reports vital information about resource addressing, including the input/output (I/O address) and the interrupt request (IRQ). As shown in Figure 3.8, this bus master IDE controller is taking I/O address 01F0-01F7, 03F6-03F6, with an IRQ of 14, with no conflicts reported.

If you need to modify a resource listed here, to clear a conflict, for instance, follow these steps:

1. Click the Use Automatic Settings checkbox to clear this.

2. When presented with the Settings Based On entry, choose an appropriate setting.

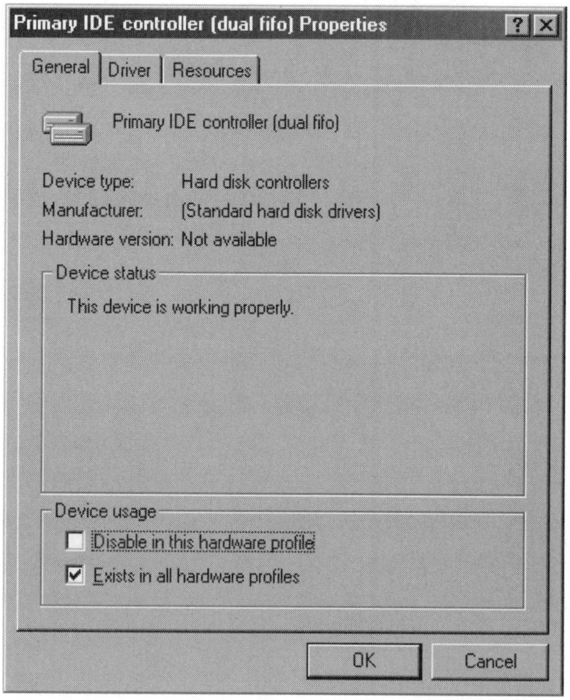

Figure 3.8 Device Manager/ view by type expanded/ HD controller/primary IDE controller.

3. Click on the resource type you need to modify, then click Change Setting.

4. Choose the value required from the Value options. Before you close, check the Conflict Information window to see if it is reporting any problems.

Please remember if your hardware required specific physical jumper or switch settings (covered more in Chapter 4) to be made to configure it for use, and you subsequently change such resources in Device Manager, you have to go back to the physical hardware. Pull the card or other device to reset the jumpers or switches to correspond with the settings as you changed them in Device Manager.

NOTE **If a problem with the device is reported by Device Manager, the Device Status report may provide an error code. For a list of Device Manager error codes, please see Appendix E.**

Utilities for Assessment

For all versions of Windows, there are various utilities that can scan your system and report on type of devices (including amount of memory) installed, along with what resources are being used by what hardware needs.

These can help you get an overall picture of what hardware you are running and what resources you have both in use and available, which you need to make informed decisions about what you add and how.

Please bear in mind, however, that these report utilities are rarely perfect. On one PC system a few years back, I happened to test reporting utilities by running them on my 486/66. Some of the utilities read my real hard disk size, while others realized I was using disk compression to store more data on the same-size drive. My tidy little Trident 1 MB video adapter was reported to be various different things, but rarely seen accurately for what it was. One utility informed me my CD-ROM drive was plugged into my second IDE channel, when my 486 was one of those few with only a single IDE channel available; the CD-ROM was actually plugged into the proprietary IDE interface provided on my SoundBlaster 16-bit sound card.

So reference the information you get from reporting utilities with any documentation you may have for the hardware, what you can eyeball both outside and within the case of your PC, and what other resources tell you to help establish a larger, truer picture of your system.

MSD (MSD.EXE—MICROSOFT DIAGNOSTICS)

MSD is the old DOS-based diagnostic program Microsoft used to make available to its users to help troubleshoot a problem. It is a system information cataloger that spells out what type of display you have, what basic hardware is connected, and how much RAM is installed. It also provides IRQ settings and more, to provide a single-screen analysis of what makes up your PC's configuration.

MSD is freely distributed and was packed with older versions of both Windows and DOS. You can still find copies floating around the net for download as well.

OTHER MANAGEMENT PACKAGES

Also, popular management packages like Norton Utilities and Helix's Nuts and Bolts provide a comprehensive system information report as part of its feature set. But remember to choose one specific to your operating system for best results and most accuracy in reporting devices and resource usage correctly.

SHAREWARE AND FREEWARE

There are also shareware packages such as CoolInfo99 by Luke Richey, PC Diagnostic Company's Tuff-Test (and Tuff-Test Lite), and Ultimate Systems' Hardware Info Pro, just to name a very few, to help do the same thing.

Here are just a few shareware and freeware options for checking system information under all Windows versions:

FC

For File Comparison, FC is a DOS-based command that allows you to compare the rough stats of two files to see if they match in size, date, and more.

Windows 98's WinDiff

WinDiff is a graphical program that also does file (and folder) comparisons, identifying differences between two files or folders.

Dr. Watson

Check your Windows directory for Dr. Watson, a trouble-tracking program available for the Windows platform since the fairly early days. (Windows 98 offers Dr. Watson as an option under Start|Programs|System Tools| System Information Tool (MSINFO).) When you run it, it takes a snapshot of your system whenever some type of system fault occurs. Additionally, it summarizes what drivers and programs are loading and interrupts software faults, while documenting what caused the fault and the conditions in which the fault occurred.

Obviously, there is a benefit to using Dr. Watson to help identify problems as part of any troubleshooting you may do, but you may find it useful to familiarize yourself with the type of information this utility tracks before you run into difficulty.

WINDOWS 98'S MSINFO SYSTEM INFORMATION UTILITY

MSINFO acts as a sort of central information clearing house, presenting the type of data you might find collectively in Device Manager and so on, and offering it up in one easy-to-read set of screens (see Figure 3.9). Beyond that, MSINFO provides a host of tools to help you learn what your system is loading, using, and doing, which is both helpful for your immediate understanding and in situations where you may need to troubleshoot system difficulties.

The main screen when you first open MSINFO (under Start|Programs| Accessories|System Tools|System Information) is divided into three major sections, with subsections beneath. You may choose to display the information in Basic, Advanced, or History modes.

These three main sections are entitled Hardware Resources, which provides information on system resources and configuration; Components, which details devices attached to the system; and Software Drivers, which supplies details what software components are loading.

Following are items listed under Hardware Resources:

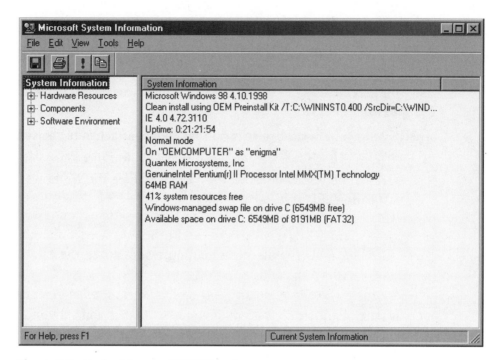

Figure 3.9 Device Manager/MSINFO main screen.

◀ *Conflicts/sharing.* Offers details about IRQ and other resources that are in conflict or are being shared, including PCI devices that permit such resource sharing (detailed in Chapter 4).

◀ *DMA.* Reports on Direct Memory Access resources, including what is in use and what is available to be utilized.

◀ *Forced Hardware.* Looks at devices that have been specifically or manually set (hence, forced) outside of the normal Plug and Play configuration; this can be very useful to check during trouble-shooting.

◀ *I/O.* Features a long list of devices and their related I/O address ranges to which they are assigned.

◀ *Memory.* Gives a summary of assigned memory ranges for the PC's hardware devices.

◀ *Components.* Data is listed by device, applicable Registry key related if any, driver and driver date, IRQ and resource information, and more.

◀ *Multimedia.* Lists audio and video CODECS plus CD-ROM drive.

◀ *Display.* Provides information on the PC's display hardware.

◀ *Input.* Details information on input devices, like your keyboard.

◀ *Miscellaneous.* Gives information on miscellaneous devices, such as tape units.

◀ *Modem.* Provides details on the modem attached to the system.

◀ *Network.* Stores network information (for those not on a traditional network, Winsock may be listed here for Windows communications on the Internet).

◀ *Ports.* Provides COM port details.

◀ *Storage.* Lists storage devices such as the floppy drive.

◀ *Printing.* Gives information on any printers attached.

◀ *Problem Devices.* Reports any difficulties related to these devices, if any.

◀ *USB.* Provides data on any universal serial bus attachments

◀ *History.* Gives a complete history of the system as related to System Information.

◀ *System.* Stores information on things like PnP Enumerator, PnP BIOS, and so on.

Following are items listed under Software Drivers:

◀ *16-bit Modules.* Gives 16-bit driver data

◀ *32-bit Modules.* Gives 32-bit driver data

◀ *Running Tasks.* Provides information on tasks running (what you can view in Task Manager)

◀ *Startup Programs.* Reports on what programs load on startup

◀ *System Hooks.* Details hooks

◀ *OLE Registration.* Includes .INI files and Windows Registry

Under the Tools menu in MSINFO, you will find the following tool choices:

◀ *Windows Report Tool.* Automated utility to allow you to send a report automatically to support engineers; copies necessary information about your PC and system setup to complement the report.

◀ *Update Wizard Uninstall.* Allows you to undo (or revert to a previous version of) any system tools, patches, or drivers you may have updated on your Windows system; previous versions are retained in a special folder to help you reverse a problem update and return your system to normal.

◀ *System File Checker.* Performs a test to verify the integrity of your operating system files and automatically replaces corrupted, damaged, or missing ones as necessary from the original install CD-ROM.

◀ *Signature Verification Tool.* Security/integrity tool that verifies the "signature" or validity of special files bearing such signatures to make certain they have not been violated by file tampering.

◀ *Registry Checker.* Checks your Windows Registry each time the PC boots, and if it identifies a problem with the current Registry, it replaces the Registry's files with the last known good copies of them.

◀ *Automatic Skip Driver Agent (ASD).* Permits Windows 98 to skip drivers that have presented difficulties during previous computing sessions (useful in troubleshooting).

◀ *Dr. Watson.* As discussed before, more of a troubleshooting tool, but the information provided can be useful in helping you acquaint yourself with all that is running.

◀ *System Configuration Utility.* A sort of automated troubleshooter that tries to help reduce variables during a problem that requires your attention while also backing up key files; aids you in trial-and-error work.

◀ *ScanDisk.* Performs a scan of the hard disk, looking for both logical and physical errors.

◀ *Version Conflict Manager.* Lets you restore backed up copies of files or programs when an update wreaks havoc with your current setup.

Additional Resources for Planning and Implementation

CHECKING MOTHERBOARD AVAILABILITY

Before you buy anything that needs to be seated in the motherboard's expansion slots, you need to find out what room is available there already.

Some PC motherboards have more expansion slots than others, purely by design. One consideration many make when upgrading a motherboard, in fact, is the number of available slots and how they're designated (how many PCI slots, for example, over how many ISA, since these are the two most commonly seen today). It is, after all, possible to run out of physical expansion slot room to install new hardware before you run out of resources to handle that hardware, and those resources aren't plentiful either.

If you're unfamiliar with the space under the case, try to find your make of motherboard, with an accompanying diagram or photograph (look at the manufacturer's Web site), before you open up your case. There you should find PCI versus VLB versus ISA slots noted, and you can also check on other considerations, like memory banks.

But what the manufacturer's diagram won't show you is how your motherboard's expansion slots are populated, and what you can fit into what is already there. For that, you need to pull the cover and eyeball.

CHECKING HARDWARE COMPATIBILITY

I run an office that uses a mix of machines running different flavors of Windows, from 3.1x all the way up to Windows NT 4.0, with Windows 98 just added. This is great for testing, or for working on something like this book where I need to span Windows generations, but it doesn't make for a whole lot of fun interchanging some types of hardware between machines in my office.

What it means is that for every piece of hardware I own, I have to check to make certain I have drivers to run it under a particular version of Windows. Yes, you can interchange drivers to some extent (as you will see in Chapter 6), but you will get your best results working with a driver written specifically for your piece of hardware running under your version of Windows. My HP 660 Cse printer is a great example. It's not crazy about Windows 3.1x and it's an exercise in frustration to make it work perfectly in Windows NT 4.0, but it is happy as a clam operating in Windows 95 and 98.

Associates of mine, with larger offices and more hardware, sometimes organize this information into spreadsheet form, so they can tell easily what can be moved where with little accommodation. This is a case where

USB and FireWire could make a lot of sense for minimizing special considerations due to their ease of swapability.

The bottom line is this: Check before you buy that a piece of hardware specifies it supports your version of Windows. Do not assume that when a product says "will work with Windows 3.1 and up," it means you will have a driver specifically supporting Windows 95/98 or Windows NT. Manufacturer Web sites often contain better information than what you will find on a product's exterior labeling and should be consulted before purchase. If the specifications don't list it, check the manufacturer site's download area for the presence of drivers for the hardware device, which specify your Windows version.

The README.TXT file included with Windows often lists hardware known to have compatibility issues when running under that version of Windows. Consult it when you first upgrade Windows and again when planning future purchases or other additions to your system. Likewise, the Microsoft Knowledge Base at *http://support.microsoft.com/support* offers information on known problems between hardware (and other items, such as applications, drivers, and more) and Windows and should similarly be consulted.

Windows NT 4.0 provides a Hardware Compatibility List (HCL) to help you make hardware decisions based on known compatibilities or incompatibilities.

Backups

Before you begin any work, while you have a system fairly optimized and running well, you need to perform a backup. During an upgrade or any hardware changeover process, things may go wrong. You may need to go back to the last working configuration you had for your PC to start over during a particular thorny conflict just to save time.

There are three major types of backups people commonly refer to when talking about making a copy of your data for later restoration if a crisis hits:

◀ *Full.* A complete backup that makes a copy of all the files on your system and stores them via a backup medium for possible later retrieval.

◄ *Differential.*—Performed in between full system backups, with its function to copy only those files that have changed since you last backed up your hard drive(s).

◄ *Incremental.*—Similar to a differential backup, but it does not over-write the previously backed up copies of files (configuration files for Windows, for example); it just adds updated copies, which is useful for tracking how changes may have influenced the develop-ment of a problem.

How often you back up depends on your needs. Commercial opera-tions may do full system backups once a day or more, while smaller busi-nesses and casual users may do these once a week or once a month, along with more frequent, smaller backups of important, modified files.

Let me jump on my soapbox for just a moment here. Do you know when most people realize how important a backup of files is? When they lose a hard drive or develop serious drive-based irregularities or a virus, and they need to install a new hard drive or reformat an existing one. This is way too late, of course. In my experience, it may take several crises, per-haps even a time when serious money is lost because you can't access work on a system, to get people to implement backing up as a regular part of their computing life.

And before I jump off the soapbox, let me add that considering the size of today's hard drives, many who are backing up are doing so to backup media too small to be practical. If the backup procedure is a major pain, you are far less likely to do it.

Many people using Windows 95 and beyond are still employing floppy-based backup techniques. Floppy backups were unwieldy back when most of us had 100 MB or less hard drives. To try to back up even a half gigabyte hard drive (and many of us now use 2 to 8 GB drives) to floppies is preposterous. One bad floppy in the series and you're dead. You will have gone to all this work for nothing, because you won't be able to salvage.

My advice is to take some of the cash you are saving with the excellent prices on large hard drives today and use it for a decent backup medium to protect your work. For between $100 to $250, you can afford a reasonable tape backup unit or a removable disk medium (like super floppies) storing between 100 MB and 1–2 GB. For substantially more money, you can get something like a high-capacity DAT drive. Writeable CD-Rom drives are becoming an increasingly popular choice for home/small business users. Do your homework into options that fit your usage and price range.

Yet do remember when evaluating and pricing, the more you have to change the medium during the backup process, the less likely you are to perform the backup. Don't go too cheap, too small, or too slow. If your data is important, be willing to spend a bit more than if you expect only to do backups of key files and programs you would need if you had a crash or needed to swap hard disks.

Boot or System Disks

Boot or system disks help you boot your system from the floppy drive if something is preventing the hard disk or disk-based operating system from loading. These really should be created well in advance of an emergency and kept updated as necessary. If you need justification why, imagine this: It's 2 a.m. and you have precious little time to finish a report or other deadline by 9 a.m. While you're working feverishly, you get a lockup that forces you to reboot. Think about the panic you will taste in your mouth when, much to your chagrin and inconvenience, the PC won't boot. Without a boot disk, you may be locked out of your PC and unable to resolve the problem. It happens; trust me on this.

CREATING BOOT DISKS BY WINDOWS PLATFORM

Boot disks are critical. When you need them is usually not the best time to realize you need to make them, because you may be unable to do so. Make these ahead of time for every PC in your home or office, and every different operating system you have. It's far better to boot with a boot disk prepared with the same operating system you have on your PC than one made with even another version of the same Windows platform.

Also, you should always have at least two copies on hand, because if there is a problem with one, you can fall back on the other. Once you do have them, label them appropriately (OS/version/boot disk) and store them safely. Failure to do so will aggravate any problems you experience during a crisis itself.

`TIP` Floppy disks do not last forever. Exposure to harsh conditions (beverage spills, dust, sunlight, or higher-than-normal temperatures) and just wear and tear can all contribute to a boot disk that won't boot. Make duplicate copies and refresh these on a regular basis to achieve best results in resolving a hardware problem or other emergency.

It's a wise idea to scan your system for viruses *before* you make a system boot disk, so you don't unwittingly pass along something like a boot sector virus. You should also check the floppy first, by trying to read it from Windows File Manager (3.1) or Windows Explorer (95/98 and NT), or by typing the following from a DOS command prompt:

```
DIR A:
```

This helps you be sure that it doesn't contain files you mean to keep, if it is one already formatted and in use (or to check if you don't recall). An unformatted floppy will give you a drive error, since it cannot be recognized by your operating system until it is formatted. Unfortunately, a bad floppy will also give you a read error, so remember to check even system disks that appear to format fine. A format that appears to struggle with the diskette (most noticeable by a slow format or excessive noise coming from the floppy drive) should not be relied upon as a system disk or, really, for any other purposes either. Toss it.

CREATING BOOT DISKS FOR USE WITH WINDOWS 3.1

Windows 3.1 itself gives you two different ways to make a boot or system disk that includes the required DOS system files (COMMAND.COM and the two hidden files, IO.SYS and MSDOS.SYS). To make a system disk in Windows 3.1, open File Manager, and pull down the Disk menu. Select either [Disk—Make System Disk] or [Disk—Format Make System Disk] option and insert a floppy into the floppy disk drive. The difference between these two options is this: The former allows you to add bootable capabilities to a previously formatted floppy (which you may pack with other rescue utilities), while the latter formats a diskette—erasing all data that may previously exist—as well as makes it into a system disk.

You can also use DOS itself to make a system disk. To do so, from the DOS command prompt (best to do in DOS itself rather than as a session in Windows):

```
FORMAT A: /u /s
```

where */u* informs DOS to remove any formatting already applied to the diskette and */s* prepares the diskette as a system or boot disk.

NOTE When creating a DOS 6.x boot or system disk to use in relation to Windows 3.1x, keep in mind that Windows 3.x File Manager does *not* create a complete MS-DOS 6.x boot, which needs to contain IO.SYS, MSDOS.SYS, COMMAND.COM, and DBLSPACE.BIN or DRVSPACE.BIN—depending on the version used. If you use DoubleSpace or DriveSpace disk compression on your Windows 3.1x PC, you will have problems booting the compressed drive unless you manually add the correct .BIN file. To do so, from the DOS command line, type:

```
COPY C:\DOS\DBLSPACE.BIN A:
```

or

```
COPY C:\DOS\DRVSPACE.BIN A:
```

CREATING BOOT DISKS FOR USE WITH WINDOWS 95/98

You can make a boot disk from DOS 7.x in Windows 95/98, as indicated above. To format in Windows itself, load Windows Explorer, right-click on the floppy icon, and choose Format. Please remember to check the box labeled "Copy System Files," because you need these to boot. Then test your boot disk.

CREATING BOOT DISKS FOR USE WITH WINDOWS NT 4.0

Two programs—Winnt.exe and Winnt32.exe—enable you to create a set of Windows NT 4.0 boot floppy disks. These work not just for NT installation but also for use in conjunction with your Windows NT Emergency Repair Disk (ERD). You will find these in the /I386 installation directory on your NT 4.0 CD-ROM.

Two switches are available for use with these programs:

◀ /O switch creates a set of boot or system floppy disks that you can use to perform either a Winnt.exe or Winnt32.exe installation. Importantly, it allows you to create these floppy disks without installing Windows NT.

◀ /OX switch creates a set of boot floppy disks to perform a CD-ROM or floppy disk NT installation and is identical to the disks included with the Windows NT package in CD-ROM or floppy format.

NOTE Because of the size, scope, and complexity of Windows NT, it is critical that you make the Emergency Repair Disk (ERD) when prompted to do so. Only it and a supported backup unit like a tape drive stand in the way of recovering from complete disaster or data loss in a serious situation caused by either hardware or software.

SWITCHES FOR INVOKING WINDOWS WHEN YOU USE A BOOT DISK TO BOOT

A series of switches may be used with each version of Windows to boot it into a particular mode or with particular options enabled or disabled, for help in troubleshooting.

FOR WINDOWS 3.1, THESE SWITCHES INCLUDE:

```
WIN [/3] [/S] [/B] [[/D:[F] [S] [V] [X]]
```

where these switches mean:

/3 tries to force a recalcitrant Windows to load in 386 enhanced mode.

/S forces Windows into standard mode.

/B starts Windows while also creating a file called BOOTTXT.LOG that records error messages the boot process has encountered.

/D is used with the following subswitches, which are useful in troubleshooting a scenario in which Windows refuses to start up properly:

:F turns off 32-bit disk access; useful for diagnosing a problem with corrupted data or inability to access a drive using 32-bit disk access.

:S prevents Windows from using the ROM (read-only memory) space between F000:0000 and 1 MB as a breakpoint.

:V forces the ROM routine to handle interrupts from the hard drive controller instead of Windows itself; worth a try if you cannot access a drive.

:X keeps Windows from including the adapter area from a range of memory Windows scans to look for unused space; try this if you hit a memory conflict you can't diagnose otherwise.

Here is an example of how you would load Windows using these switches (in this instance, attempting to force Windows into 386 enhanced mode while running a boot log):

```
WIN /3 /B
```

For the use of switches with Windows 95/98, it's a bit trickier, since 32-bit Windows boots automatically and not by running a command from the DOS prompt or at the bottom of the AUTOEXEC.BAT. You can set your PC up to boot not directly into Windows but into a boot menu (the same one you see if you hit the F8 key as Windows is launching) . You can then choose the Command Line option from the menu, and from Windows with switches from that prompt.

Switches available include:

```
WIN [/D:[F] [M] [N] [S] [V] [X] ]
```

where the subswitches beneath the sole /D switch include:

:F   Same as Windows 3.1

:M   Starts Windows 95/98 in Safe Mode for troubleshooting

:N   Same as Windows 3.1

:V   Same as Windows 3.1

:W   Same as Windows 3.1

The following switches can be used to specify how Windows NT (WINNT.EXE) is invoked during its Setup process. These include:

WINNT/B or WINNT32/B—utilized for setups without a (working) floppy drive, copying files to the hard drive making it in effect the boot drive disk

WINNT/W—bypasses enhanced drivers/driver issues for Windows NT setup

WINNT/U—switch used for unattended setup (counterindicated in a machine you're trying to troubleshoot through a Windows NT setup)

WINNT/T: or WINNT32/T—indicates temporary setup files are being directed to a specific drive: is used for specifying a drive on which temporary setup files are placed

TIP   Typing WIN alone gives you a list of the default options.

WHAT ELSE TO INCLUDE ON YOUR BOOT OR SYSTEM DISK

A boot disk can make all the difference in resolving an emergency or a conflict severe enough to keep Windows from booting. However, you need to think about what else you may need to include in a PC emergency kit besides the basics of a boot or system disk with its operating system files. You may need enough extras that your boot disk actually becomes a set of disks; this is largely because program sizes today make it extremely difficult at times to fit all you need onto one diskette—that is, unless you have an LS-120 drive, which stores 120 MB and is configured as the boot "floppy" drive. This issue about program size makes it important for you to wisely choose what to include based upon what files or programs you think you will absolutely need if a crisis arises. Don't include anything more than you absolutely need, but if in doubt, you may want to add something just in case.

Examples of other things you may need or want to include are as follows:

◄ System configuration files, edited if necessary to reflect the floppy drive location; remember, however, that you must have on the boot disk any files or drivers you reference in the configuration files.

◄ Related to the first, if you need to access your CD-ROM to install or reinstall your operating system, you need to have your DOS or real-mode CD-ROM driver (make sure it is loaded in the CONFIG.SYS) and MSCDEX.EXE (loaded in your DOSSTART.BAT or AUTOEXEC.BAT copy on the floppy) included among the system configuration files. If you don't, you might get locked out of using the CD-ROM.

◄ Virus scanning software; locates ones with an encapsulated version small enough to run from a boot disk.

◄ Disk image files, if you have them, to recover in the event of a hard drive crisis.

◄ Disk preparation utilities, like FDISK for creating a DOS partition on the hard drive and FORMAT, to prepare the hard drive for use, along with SYS.COM, which copies system files. Powerquest's Partition Magic, if you use it, might be included instead.

◄ A small text editor, so that you may edit configuration files as necessary (and it's almost guaranteed to be necessary).

◀ Many programs, particularly those written to aid in emergency situations, have an option to create an emergency disk version of them to use in conjunction with your boot or system disk. Check your utilities for these options, and store emergency disks you make safely, labeling them properly.

◀ Include others, too, like any additional programs such as diagnostic tools and the restore component of backup software you may use that may not create its own emergency disk for use.

◀ SCANDISK.EXE is recommended.

If you don't have a program that automatically stores CMOS settings for you, you may want to create a text file detailing all your current working CMOS settings, which you can reference from the boot disk in a catastrophe.

Other utilities such as a copy of PKUNZIP if you need to decompress ZIP archived files, and MEM.EXE (to provide you information about conventional memory and how the drivers are loaded in DOS or real mode).

WHAT TO DO IF THE BOOT DISK DOESN'T BOOT

OK, you have your boot disk and you have the situation in which you need to use it, but lo and behold, you find your system won't boot off of the boot disk. There are two common causes for this. One is a defective boot disk itself (as mentioned, they go bad, so you should have multiple copies that you update and replace with fresh ones regularly). If you don't have another copy, you need to try making a boot disk from another PC available to you, or ask a responsible friend or associate to provide you with one (try to ascertain that this person is using the same operating system type and version as you are).

The second likely culprit is that your system BIOS is set to ignore the floppy drive and boot directly from the hard disk itself. This is often employed as a means to speed up the boot process, so the PC doesn't spend time looking for a boot disk in the floppy drive. However, not all BIOSes support this option. Go into CMOS and check for this option and change it, as necessary. Then try a reboot to see if the boot disk is recognized this time.

Viruses can sometimes also result in an unbootable system or system disk. To best rule out this option, you need to employ virus scanning of your system on a regular basis and have a microversion of a virus scanner on floppy for emergency use. Many of today's motherboards incorporate virus scanning for the BIOS level, as well.

Adding Cards and Other Hardware

TYPES OF CARDS YOU MAY ADD

Many types of add-on cards are available in the marketplace currently, with more variety—as well as updated features to current ones—on the horizon all the time. Types of cards you may add include the standard ones, like video and sound and internal modems. You also may need or choose to add:

◄ I/O cards (these, for example, give you access to additional COM ports—though do not increase your number of IRQs to handle them)

◄ Controller cards (including SCSI)

◄ Interface cards (scanners usually need these; some CD-ROM drives and other equipment do as well)

◄ Video capture cards (for capturing still images from video)

◄ Memory cards (allow you to expand memory if your memory slots are exhausted but you need more RAM)

◄ TV and radio tuners (add TV and radio capabilities to your PC)

OTHER TYPES OF HARDWARE

Most of what we talked about in the previous section related to PC expansion adapters or cards you install into the PC motherboard's expansion slots with the cover off. As you know, a number of devices install outside the PC, without the need to remove the cover. These include printers, gaming devices like joysticks, speakers, scanners (though SCSI- and ISA-based scanners require adding a controller into the expansion slots), pointing devices, keyboards (including MIDI keyboards for music), cameras, and assorted other peripherals.

Some of these require interrupts either directly or indirectly (e.g., the mouse needs an interrupt, the printer plugs into a parallel port that automatically has an interrupt assigned to it, the keyboard's interrupt is preserved, and a camera won't require one), while others do not.

CONFIGURING FOR NEW ADD-ON CARDS

If you have ever done it before, you know that adding a new card or other piece of hardware usually isn't that difficult. Many aspects of it, however, can conspire to make it a more troublesome project than it has to be. Poor or poorly translated documentation (or missing entirely), inaccurate or insufficient specifications on the product or the PC you are installing the hardware into, and poor quality assurance at the factory are all factors in tough installs.

One bonus today is that more and more hardware companies, as well as other PC industry vendors, are making technical information freely available on their Web sites. Often, but not always, the Web site-based technical information exceeds the printed material you may receive packed into new equipment you purchase. These sites also usually have a listing of frequently asked questions (FAQs) that may cover information you need, as well as a database of problems and solutions that you can search. It's very common for updated drivers and related utilities to be offered on these sites as well. You may want to bookmark or add to your Favorites list major vendor sites (see Appendix B, "Online Sources for Hardware Help").

Before you begin, be aware that it's hardly unusual to get a new piece of hardware with an already-outdated driver. The product may have been sitting on a shelf while two, three, or even four updates to its driver are made. Because the new driver may correct for known problems and improve stability, it's a good idea to check the manufacturer's Web site or FTP area for the latest driver before you install the new hardware. You may get both a better driver and save yourself the trouble of installing one driver and then needing to replace it shortly thereafter.

You *do* need to read the documentation for the device you are installing, because it may specify settings or issues you need to know before you physically deal with the hardware. Failing to read it before an installation may result in time lost trying to troubleshoot a setting you missed or a conflict predicted.

With that said, here are the basics steps used in installing an add-on card or adapter:

1. Properly shut down your PC, then turn it off and physically disconnect it from its power source.

2. Remove the case (some cases may permit you access to the expansion slots and drives through a drawer that slides out of the case).

3. Before you remove the card from its antistatic bag, remove the dust cover (metal bar) in the back of your PC that corresponds to the slot you intend to install the card into. Keep the screw in a safe place to mount the card in place.

4. Double-check that you have all the physical settings, jumpers, or switches duly in place (the fewer times you have to pull the card to recheck it, the more you reduce the risk of injury to the card).

5. Observe proper grounding procedures (by wearing a grounding belt or wrist strap, or by simply touching both hands to the metal casing around the PC's frame), and then attempt to seat the card into the slot properly, per any special instructions in the documentation. Never force a card into place, because you may not damage just the add-on card but the PC itself.

6. Once the card is properly seated, secure it in place in the slot using the screw.

7. Restore power to the PC and boot it up. Depending on the type of device, Windows should automatically recognize it and install its driver. If not, you may choose Add New Hardware to manually select and install the device driver needed for the new card.

8. If included, run any installation software that accompanied the new hardware, but again, you need to read the documentation in case it warns of any conflicts.

Note that I left off mention of returning the PC's cover before reconnecting the power to see if the PC recognized the hardware. My personal preference when installing a new adapter card or internal modem, for instance, is to leave the cover off until I know the new device is installed and working properly. Then I return the cover to its proper, secured place over the components. This means that I don't have to pull the cover off again if I need to check the physical seating of the card or adapter in its slot, or change it to a different slot, or double-check the settings on physical jumpers or switches (covered in Chapter 4).

If you don't mind a few extra turns of the screwdriver if there is a problem, you can return the cover as soon as the new card or other hardware is installed.

CONSIDERATIONS IN CHOOSING SCSI OVER OTHER INTERFACES

SCSI (Small Computer System Interface) has a reputation both for being very good and very difficult to introduce to a PC for the first time. This is why I want to take a few moments to discuss it, since SCSI takes a bit of advance thinking-through and requires attention to detail to configure properly.

First, let's look at some facts concerning SCSI. In the old days, there was a clear division between the normal MFM (and, later, IDE) hard drives installed on most PCs and the high throughput capability of SCSI. The cost differential between the two made more casual computer owners—who also heard the rumors of difficulty in configuring—steer clear. SCSI stayed largely in the domain of power users and corporate computers, who demanded serious performance advantages in the transferring of data. SCSI isn't limited to hard drive transfer technology either; you can find a full range of SCSI devices, including CD-ROM, backup units, and scanners.

One of the prime benefits of SCSI, particularly over older IDE drives, is that it utilizes the CPU far less in handling data. Also, all SCSI controllers use a form of bus mastering or other technique to achieve that lowered CPU need, a faster spindle speed, and traditionally, SCSI drives were offered with longer product warrantees (they also cost more initially).

Times change, however, and so has hardware, as I related in Chapter 2. The introduction of faster and faster EIDE (Enhanced IDE) hard drives—so-called by Western Digital, while other drive manufacturers call them Fast-ATAs—reduced some of SCSI's larger advantages. Then the evolution of Ultra DMA drives—an enhanced version of ATA/IDE—brought about doubled current burst data transfer rates up to 33 MB/s with potentially faster disk read/writes. Older, slower SCSI implementations like SCSI-1 operate at a much slower bus speed of 5 MB/s, with a bus width of just 8 bits. It's not until SCSI-3, Fast Wide SCSI that bus width jumps to 16 bits, and not until SCSI-3, Wide Ultra SCSI that the bus speed revs to 40 MB/s (even faster ones, like SCSI-3, Ultra2 SCSI and SCSI-3, Wide Ultra 2 SCSI, move this up to 80 MB/s). The price differential between SCSI and these better generation EIDE drives has narrowed considerably as well.

The bottom line is that if you decide to go with high-end SCSI, you should still appreciate better overall performance. But if your choice comes down to less expensive, lower end (older) SCSI and enhanced IDE, performance differences may be far less noticeable.

SCSI really isn't much more difficult than standard drive interfaces, as long as you remember two basic rules: (1) you don't select conflicting drive IDs on devices, and (2) the bus is properly terminated.

Probably the most troublesome and error-prone element of incorporating SCSI is encountered when adding a device to an existing SCSI chain. (SCSI devices chain or link together off an adapter.) A seeming majority of SCSI ID conflicts manifest themselves here and are responsible for oddities such as making one drive appear as seven different drives or causing two devices to simply disappear.

Virtually every make and model of SCSI adapter offers a different method of displaying the drive IDs at boot, although most of them include a graphical interface for Windows 95/98 and Windows NT that will permit you to see what IDs are active and in use. Unfortunately, what it does *not* tell you is if the IDs are in conflict with one another. Such ID conflicts are usually best resolved by thoroughly checking each device (per its manufacturer's specification data) and then making certain that no two devices use the same ID.

You may find it a lot easier to avoid such ID conflicts by determining which IDs are already in use *prior* to installing a new device. You can do this either via the graphical interface program accompanying the unit, as I touched on before, or by checking in Device Manager. You are then better prepared to try to assign the new device to an unused ID.

However, it may be worth noting that there are a few older devices still in regular use that will only work if they are set to specific IDs, such as 0 to 2. Also, if you are planning to boot from the SCSI device, your boot device must either be the highest or the lowest numbered ID—and this depends entirely on the SCSI adapter itself. Finally, you need to be aware that it can be most difficult to attempt to boot a SCSI device if an IDE device also resides on the system. Why? Because the PC's BIOS automatically routes (software) Int13 to the IDE bus, and that is what is required to boot.

Information changes with each type of SCSI adapter. Adaptec adapters usually recognize device ID 0 to be the boot drive, while Future Domain considers device ID 6 to be the boot (ID 7 is usually reserved for the adapter itself).

One other trap a friend recommends avoiding for the uninitiated involves having both internal and external SCSI devices. Since most SCSI cards ship with the termination already implemented on the card (both ends of the SCSI bus must be terminated), placing both external and internal devices on the same system means extra work. The terminator must be removed from the card, and both ends of the bus must be terminated instead.

Termination problems are trickier. The reason is that there are many different ways a bus can be terminated. Sometimes it is with the resistors plugged into a device; sometimes termination is accomplished via jumpers or settings on the physical device itself; sometimes it is implemented with a dongle plugged onto the cable. You need to determine which method is correct for your situation, largely through trial and error and by checking out information from the manufacturer and other resources.

To use SCSI, you must have three elements: the SCSI drive itself, a SCSI card adapter (SCSI-1, Ultra SCSI, Ultra-Wide SCSI, etc.), and a SCSI device and appropriate cables meeting the guidelines for that particular SCSI standard that is manufactured by firms like Adaptec, Future Domain, NCR, and Symbios Logic. All major operating systems discussed here support SCSI use (Windows 95/98, for example, support SCSI and SCSI 2 adapter types, Windows 3.1 overcomes some earlier SCSI problems but isn't the best platform, and Windows NT supports it better).

One tip for those first setting up SCSI adapters in Windows 95 or 98: Not all SCSI adapters are supported, so if Windows doesn't list yours as a choice, you may hit a bit of a wall. Also, before you install the Windows protected-mode drivers for your SCSI adapter, Microsoft Knowledge Base recommends that you be certain your adapter is working fine in real-mode configuration. This means that drivers are loaded in the DOS-based CONFIG.SYS and/or AUTOEXEC.BAT files and that they're being recognized properly in DOS or real mode first.

To install a Windows protected-mode SCSI controller driver, simply use the Add New Hardware option from Control Panel. If Windows cannot detect your adapter, you can try manually adding it if your adapter is on the supported list. If your adapter is unsupported, Windows won't be able to load protected-mode drivers and you're stuck in real-mode unless your adapter manufacturer offers a solution.

NOTE Since SCSI drives tend to run faster, they also have a tendency to run hotter, so to preserve the life of your equipment and prevent random to worse failures, observe proper cooling techniques. For more information on PC cooling, see Chapter 13.

A Fast Look at Ultra DMA

Since I touched upon Ultra DMA in the section on SCSI, let me provide a few more details here. DMA mode drives are an extension of direct memory access, which serves as the foundation for bus mastering technology. Because of their capacity to directly access memory resources for hard drives or other bus mastering-compatible peripherals on a PC bus without demanding huge allotments of the CPU's time, some people view them as emulating SCSI capabilities. Since bus mastering is built into these drives, you don't have to enable it. It definitely boosts transfer rates over traditional IDE, which transferred at a much slower 16.6 MB/s. Also, it uses Cyclical Redundancy Checks (CRCs) to help maintain the integrity of the data during transfer.

Be aware though that your overall PC won't function twice as fast with an Ultra DMA device since all it doubles is the drive transfer speed. You may appreciate between a 5 to 10 percent performance jump overall because of the transfer boost as long as your system is equipped to work with UDMA drives. Support for ultra DMA has been around since the Intel 430TX PCI and the Intel 440LX AGP chipsets. You can also achieve support by adding an Ultra DMA PCI adapter/controller card to older systems.

To use Ultra DMA drives on your system, you must have the following:

◄ Ultra DMA-compatible BIOS (contact your motherboard manufacturer or its Web site if you wonder if yours does).

◄ An Ultra DMA-capable motherboard chipset like the ones mentioned above or a PCI Ultra DMA adapter; again, check with your manufacturer if you have questions regarding yours.

◄ An Ultra DMA device such as a hard disk or CD-ROM.

◄ An Ultra DMA-aware device driver that supports the operating system you will load this driver into.

CHAPTER 4

IRQ, DMA, and
I/O Essentials

Included in this chapter are the following topics:

◀ Overview of these three critical system resources

◀ Understanding "bus" types

◀ IRQs and their assignment

◀ DMA channels and their assignment

◀ I/O and its address assignment

◀ How to see what you are using and where

◀ How to implement changes to system resource configuration

Hardware devices need system resources to communicate properly with the PC itself and the operating system to get the attention they need to operate. Resource assignment for devices is how this whole process is kept orderly, as requests for attention transmit along the bus—very much like a system regulating vehicular traffic through a busy downtown area.

Here's an example: Through proper device and resource assignment, the system knows that IRQ7 is assigned to LPT1, which is a parallel/printer port. When you install a (first) printer to your system, it plugs into the parallel port, which is assigned to use the specified IRQ. When the printer needs the attention of the central processing unit (CPU), also known as the processor, it signals through LPT1 to joggle IRQ7, which alerts the interrupt controller. The controller then assigns this signal a priority, based on what else may be happening with other devices, then sends the signal along to the processor, which juggles this demand along with all the others. The

CPU then responds to the device, backtracking along this same route along the bus. This prevents the CPU from erroneously notifying your modem, "OK, print page 2."

But who or what decides what resources get assigned to what device? There, the answer gets more complex because, in truth, the system does, the hardware does, and you can to some extent, too. Some assignments are predetermined by standard PC bus architecture and are hard-coded, meaning you cannot adjust them easily, if at all. These include certain system devices, a PS/2 mouse, and the video adapter (usually), as well as the floppy, the keyboard, and the primary IDE controllers.

Other devices tend to want or need a specific resource of those not hard-coded. The MIDI channel on some sound cards will want IRQ5, for instance, though so too may COM3 or COM4 or a modem using either of these, additional printer ports (IRQ7 is demanded by your first printer, remember), a tape drive accelerator card, old XT hard disk controllers, and certain network cards. The same DMA channel, let's say 3, could be requested of an ECP-enabled parallel port (ECP stands for Extended Capabilities Port), an SCSI host adapter, a tape drive accelerator card, an old hard disk controller, a sound card, and some network cards.

Likewise, similar demands may be placed on the same ranges of I/O addressing, and on the memory area in which these demands are noted and handled by many devices. Other devices tend to accommodate around these, taking whatever resource assignments are still available to them. This means juggling, because one thing you almost never hear is, "Wow, I can't believe I have so many system resources remaining!" Many people running a very standard setup for today—including both 2D and 3D video adapters, a modem for Internet communications, a printer, a scanner, a sound card and the obligatory keyboard, a pointing device such as trackball or mouse, a floppy drive, and a hard drive—may be lucky to have just one or two IRQs left to assign in adding any other hardware to the system.

As you read, bear in mind that system configuration and hardware resource assignment can be more of an art than a science, because you have to weigh priorities and needs against what you have left to use. Coming up with a workable solution around these limitations is where the art comes in.

Modifying Hardware Settings

There are three primary ways to modify how a newly added piece of hardware is configured for use on your PC, which can include which interrupt request, which I/O range, and which DMA channel this hardware uses when properly installed. These are physical hardware settings, software-based configuration (SoftMenu), and Plug and Play handling.

PHYSICAL HARDWARE SETTINGS

Physical hardware settings are mostly used in older ISA-based adapters but are still found today even on some Plug and Play hardware. Jumpers and switches were how hardware devices were configured for specific system resources (use this IRQ, set this feature to off, for instance) before the birth of Plug and Play technology.

Many devices still offer these switches and jumpers, and I frankly prefer a device that does include the ability to resort to hardware "forces." Occasionally, if I experience unusual difficulty in installing a PnP device, I will jumper it (which removes it from PnP mode and forces it into default ISA standard mode) to get the results I want faster: a device configured to the IRQ I demand instead of the one the system insists it should use.

Jumpers are simply two parallel-mounted pins that compose part of a circuit on the device itself. There are variations: Some jumpers exist in a single row, and you must jumper two side-by-side numbered pins. Small black (usually plastic) covers called shunts can fit over the top of a jumper, as needed.

If a shunt is placed over the top of the jumper so that it covers both pins, the circuit is closed, and the result is known as "jumpering." A shunt can be removed by simply pulling up on the shunt, and installed by fitting it carefully over the pair of pins making up the jumper. If a shunt is placed over just one pin, the circuit remains open (and it's the standard way a shunt for a hardware device is left so you can still find the shunt later to use as needed while not closing the circuit). If both pins remain freely standing, without a shunt, the circuit is open and no jumpering has occurred.

Each jumper or set of pins has a unique function, turning something on or off. This is where you not only need a copy of the hardware device's documentation, you need to read it to find the function of each jumper and whether it should be set to on or off. Don't guess.

Also still seen, but more rarely these days, are DIP switches. These can either be common slide switches or what is sometimes referred to as "rocker switches," which act much like jumpers, to turn something on or off. A switch set usually contains 4 to 12 switches, which are usually poorly labeled, if labeled at all. Those that are labeled may read ON/OFF; 0 or 1, where 0 indicates off and 1 is for on; or O/C for open or closed.

The unique combination of which switches are set to ON and which to OFF directly bears on how the device is configured to work when installed in your system. Again, you need to consult your documentation to see how the device should be set depending on your needs and what you want enabled or disabled.

Check for jumpers and switches *before* you install a card or adapter into an expansion slot, because pulling them out again to check is a hassle you don't need to bear. Also, make a note of the default settings for the jumpers and switches, so that if you need to go back later (perhaps long after you have lost your documentation), you have a place to start.

SOFTWARE-BASED CONFIGURATION (SOFTMENU)

SoftMenu is included with many types of controllers and adapters to change configuration settings via keyboard with the same overall effect as if you had jumpered or changed switches on hardware manually.

This is usually part of an installation (aka Setup) program provided with some hardware. Run it, configure or reconfigure setting options provided in the setup program, and these changes are then written to a special programmable component of the hardware device known as an EPROM.

PLUG AND PLAY HANDLING

In Play and Play, your PnP-capable BIOS and operating system help configure devices and assign resources on an as-necessary basis.

In today's PCs, which are usually a mix of Plug and Play and non-PnP devices, much of the configuration is done automatically as part of the process before a PnP-supporting operating system like Windows 95 or 98 loads. Before you can even get into Windows 95/98's Device Manager, your modem on a COM port is recognized to use one set of system resources, your printer through its LPT/parallel port another, your sound card a third, and so on.

FORCED HARDWARE SETTINGS

Also, as you will read later in Chapter 7's section on PCI, the computer's BIOS will decide whether individual available interrupts are made available to PCI or older ISA hardware (true for VESA local bus, too) through settings you may adjust in CMOS. There will be times, however, when you may need or want to force a particular device to use a particular set of system resources (IRQ, DMA, I/O) apart and aside from how your system tries to juggle them during the PnP enumeration process. Again, enumeration is discussed in Chapter 7, but briefly, it is the process by which non-PnP devices are acknowledged for using their set resources and the system tries to assign PnP devices around them.

This process is known as a forced configuration and can be done easily in Windows 95/98 through Device Manager, as well as in Windows NT 4.0, by altering the settings assigned to a particular device. Needless to say, you need to take care in this, making sure you don't assign this device to resources already being used by something else. Doing so would likely create a hardware conflict.

The Details of System Resources and Their Assignment

INTERRUPT REQUEST OR IRQ

Just as its name implies, this resource interrupts the PC's brain, also known as the CPU or processor, to let it know a piece of hardware assigned to that IRQ needs attention. These interruptions inform the busy CPU that something attached to the PC needs to print, to transfer, to play a warning sound, that a key has been pressed, or that the mouse has been moved, for example. The interrupt controller is the device that monitors and manages these interruptions. Physically, an IRQ is simply a wire on the PC bus.

While earlier PCs were limited to just eight IRQs, numbered 0 to 7, modifications in the late 1980s (the EISA bus) introduced another eight, which are cascaded into the first string of IRQs by using one of them (IRQ2) as a plug-in outlet of sorts. You either cannot assign anything to IRQ2, or anything you do assign is actually handled on IRQ9. In many cases, you can assign either IRQ2 or 9 to a device, but if you assign both, a conflict will arise. This leaves 15 IRQs to work with, in theory.

In practice, however, there are fewer because some IRQs are used by the system itself to handle the timer and the clock, the COM and LPT ports, both the floppy and hard disk controller, the math coprocessor (and even if you don't have one, the IRQ isn't wired in, meaning you cannot assign anything to use its IRQ, which is 13), and one for a PS/2 mouse (which you may be able to reclaim later by changing jumper settings on the motherboard). This setup alone leaves you with just four IRQs available for use. You also need to know that most of the available IRQs fall into the high range, above IRQ7, and may not be assignable with some types of hardware. This is why careful planning and configuration are key to meeting your system demands.

TIP Always remember that you will never be able to assign devices properly to IRQs 0, 1, 2, 8, and 13. No physical wiring exists for the interrupt to permit an external device, such as an adapter card you may install, to use them. They're retained instead for system use only (and no wires prevents you from trying to reclaim them for your own greedy hardware needs).

The bitter pill about IRQs—besides the general one-device-per-IRQ rule—is that once they are used up, they are used up. There is no add-on card you can get to give you additional IRQs, which is part of the reason advanced planning is stressed in this book. When you have limited resources, you have to optimize; to do that, you have to plan carefully how best to configure your PC to get everything you want connected.

I mentioned that it is possible, though tricky, to share an IRQ, so let me explain. Certain operating systems such as OS/2 are rather particular about resource assignments and the "one per customer" rule. DOS and Windows, however, can be rather forgiving at times about setting up a mouse and a modem on the same IRQ, or a scanner and a printer set up likewise, sharing an IRQ off the same parallel/printer port. Sometimes, they forgive blindly, allowing a situation like a serious conflict to arise and exist for a bit before you realize it is there.

But they forgive only so far. As long as you have only one device using that shared IRQ at a time, you can squeak along. The instant you use both, problems ranging from warning messages to lockups and crashes may occur. Or you may only be able to boot up next time into Windows "Safe Mode" or "MS-DOS Compatibility Mode" on Windows 95 and Windows 98 PCs until you resolve the conflict to Windows' satisfaction (see Chapter 5 on troubleshooting).

To avoid the hassle and headaches, avoid sharing an IRQ where at all possible. However, PCI devices do permit the sharing of system resources, including IRQs, as is discussed further in Chapter 7 under the section on PCI.

INTERRUPT PRIORITY

IRQs operate on something of a priority system, which is more important in some situations and for some devices than others. By *priority*, I mean that those with a higher level of priority (the lower the number, the higher the priority) should be recognized for attention faster than low-priority ones.

Priority, however, does not usually play a major consideration with hardware you may install these days. So you only need to worry about it in those instances where priority may matter, which should be listed in a device's documentation or technical specifications. Those craving every little notch of performance they can raise are welcome to investigate what priority order of IRQs may gain them by switching device assignment around. This could be more trouble than its noticeable results, however.

Also realize that the priority order gets messy, because the bridge for IRQs 8 to 15 plugs into IRQ2. So while IRQ0 has priority level 1 and IRQ1 has priority level 2, the priority level for IRQ3 jumps to number 11.

Table 4.1 shows the listing for which IRQs are handled where in the priority chain.

One of the most common hardware areas where problems related to interrupts occur is COM ports. Think about it though: This is one area where you don't want difficulty, because what you are most likely to run from your COM port assignments are a modem for Internet and other dial-up communications, along with your pointing device like a mouse. These days, neither is exactly optional.

Most PCs can support up to four COM ports, which sounds almost like

TABLE 4.1 IRQs and Their Priority Levels

IRQ#	IRQ Priority Level	IRQ#	IRQ Priority Level
0	1	8	3
1	2	9	4**
2	Not assigned	10	5**
3	11*	11	6**
4	12*	12	7**
5	13*	13	8
6	14*	14	9**
7	15*	15	10**

* Can be used with 8-bit or 16-bit devices
** Requires 16-bit devices only

more than you need. This is true only until you realize that only two COM ports can be used simultaneously. Why? Simple. Even if you have four COM ports, you only have two IRQs supporting all four, meaning that two (COM1 and COM3) share one interrupt (usually 4), while the remaining two (COM2 and COM4) share the other (usually 3). If you end up assigning three or four COM ports, you move into a classic hardware conflict situation, where only one will work if any, and you find that some software, application, and even hardware doesn't take well to being assigned to COM3 or COM4. This was more true in the past (original PCs only allowed for two physical communications port), but it continues to be seen.

Time and again, a new user online will come to me upset that his or her mouse won't work, and 90 percent of the time when I check, I find that the person's mouse is on COM1 and the modem set to COM3, which won't work. Assigning one to COM1 and one to COM2, or one to COM2 and one to COM3, should. If a problem is still seen, I suggest swapping the two assignments (say, move the mouse from COM1 to COM2, and the modem from COM2 to COM1). Some devices just prefer one over another, and a simple swap sometimes clears up a problem such as this.

Today's PCs usually provide two COM ports (one may be provided by an internal modem that packs its own—externals do not), which are always active by default. In order to turn a COM port off availability, you usually need to remove a jumper or change a setting. Also, some modems end up wanting to install to IRQ2, which can work, because anything assigned to IRQ2 (except on a PC/XT, which only has eight IRQs) is automatically shifted to use IRQ9. But if you also assign something else to

IRQ9 (thinking you have two IRQs to work with and not just one), you will create a hardware conflict.

Additionally, many devices gravitate to the first eight IRQs (0 to 7), avoiding IRQs 8 to 15 (and even if the device supports them, their drivers or associated software may not). IRQ5, for instance, is often hotly pursued by sound cards, network cards, and more. As mentioned elsewhere, most sound cards are less forgiving at being moved than other devices. IRQs 7, 9, and 12 are also common areas in which to see device conflicts; IRQ9 because many devices that will use higher IRQs seek out 9, and IRQs 7 and 12 because they are typically assigned to other system devices, namely the LPT1 or first parallel port and a PS/2 mouse, respectively.

Typical symptoms of an IRQ hardware conflict may be either constant and extreme, or intermittent, and may demonstrate themselves in:

◄ "Noise" or other issues related to sound card performance

◄ Crashes, lockups, and fatal exception errors without other explainable cause

◄ PC forced into Safe Mode or MS-DOS Compatibility Mode (see Chapter 5)

◄ Lockups during use with a specific device, like a printer or sound card

◄ Atypical mouse behavior, including sluggishness and "jerky" motions

◄ Intermittent device failures, often resolved on rebooting

◄ Printer sending only garbage or no output at all

◄ Error messages at bootup

RECLAIMING IRQS NOT USED ELSEWHERE

As you may have noticed, there are a few IRQs that could potentially be up for grabs if you're not actually using the hardware typically assigned to them. One is IRQ12, the one assigned for PS/2 mouse style support. If you're using a USB mouse or trackball, or a serial mouse or trackball, you have the option of trying to reassign IRQ12 to something else (check modifying hardware settings earlier in this chapter).

Another one you may not think of can reside on (usually older) sound cards. SoundBlaster sound cards and some clones used to provide an IDE controller onboard to provide an interface to which you could plug in the CD-ROM drive for use (on systems already packed to the gills or where no secondary IDE channel existed, for example). If you own one of these cards, and you are not using the IDE controller built in, just disabling this device in the hardware profile won't reclaim the IRQ (and other resources which may be assigned to it). You may need to jumper the sound card (consult documentation) or change CMOS settings for your BIOS to reclaim the IRQ (often but not always IRQ10) for other use.

Additionally, if you have LPT2 tying up IRQ5 (remember, that's a popular one), but you do not have a second printer or other device needing LPT2, you want to free up IRQ5. If LPT2 is mounted on the motherboard itself (not common but possible), you need to jumper the motherboard (check the motherboard's documentation) to disable it; if LPT2 is provided through an add-on I/O card, look for the appropriate pins to jumper on the I/O adapter itself.

Table 4.2 lists devices and typical problems associated with each IRQ.

Direct Memory Access, or DMA

Direct memory access channels are another way of attempting to take the hardware load off the processor, to allow your processor to do the more critical things it needs to do more efficiently. Specifically, it is concerned with higher speed-type data transfers either from something like an adapter card or a hard disk or other mass-storage device to memory. CD-ROM drives may use them, as well as tape backup units and anything else data-intensive.

DMA can also move data—shipped in blocks—between different locations within memory. This circumvents the need for a lot of unnecessary CPU time being diverted to handle such transfers. Because DMA is a high-speed channel, these transfers can be done much faster without the processor's active involvement.

There are either four or eight DMA channels, though most PCs today offer eight, which are numbered 0 to 7. Granted, this is not a lot, but thankfully, many devices don't require a DMA channel, so open channels don't have as many competitors as say, IRQs.

TABLE 4.2   IRQ Devices and Typical Problems

Interrupt Request (IRQ) by Number	Device Standardly Assigned to IRQ by Number	Common Problems Associated with Use
0	System timer	Completely unavailable for external assignment by user
1	Keyboard controller	Unavailable, as above
2	Programmable Interrupt Controller (PIC) for IRQs 8 to- 15	Since the bridge connecting IRQs 8 to- 15 into the first interrupt controller is located here, anything assigned to IRQ2 is moved to IRQ9.
3	COM2, COM4 (modem or mouse)	Since both COM ports share an IRQ, you cannot assign devices to both COMs 2 and 4 without raising possible conflict.
4	COM1, COM3 (modem or mouse)	Since both COM ports share an IRQ, you cannot assign devices to both COMs 1 and 3 without raising a possible conflict.
5	LPT2	If not used for a printer, many things like to try to grab this assignment, including sound cards. Frequent site for resource conflict.
6	Floppy drive controller	Unavailable
7	LPT1	Trying to assign something else here can cause problems with standard print functions when you have one printer.
8	System clock	Unavailable
9	Unassigned	See IRQ2. You can use IRQ2 or IRQ 9 for assignment, but not both. One of the preferred IRQs for network cards.
10	Unassigned	While available, not all devices, particularly older ones, will work when assigned to a IRQ9 or above.
11	Unassigned	See IRQ10
12	Motherboard (PS/2) mouse port	You may be able to reclaim this if not using a PS/2 mouse.
13	System math coprocessor	Unavailable, nor does an interrupt wire exist to allow the IRQ to be used if it were possible to redirect it from supporting the math coprocessor.
14	Hard drive controller	Since this standardly provides system drive control, this is not a wise one to attempt to modify.
15	Unassigned	See IRQ10

Instead, DMA channels are reserved for use by data-intensive hardware such as a hard drive, backup units, or a CD-ROM drive. To a limited extent, sound cards also use DMA to send data from sound files out to be played by your PC's speakers. However, one of those channels, DMA channel 4, is already in use as a plug-in place for channels 5 to 7 (much like IRQ2 serves for the second string of IRQs previously mentioned). This second set of channels was introduced with the EISA bus (formerly, the ISA bus on PC/XTs had just four, numbered 0 to 3). Another, channel 2, is in use by the floppy disk controller, unless you run a system without a floppy drive.

This leaves channels 0, 1, 3, 5, 6, and 7 available to you. But wait, DMA 0 is involved with memory refresh, so you can assign nothing to it. So you are reduced to a maximum five possible DMA channels to assign for use. Again, as with IRQs, it is within the realm of workability to share a DMA channel, but it is rarely the easiest or best solution. The most significant drawback to sharing a channel, besides possible resulting transfer oddities, is that when a problem does arise from a DMA conflict, it can be notoriously difficult to track down. The failure isn't occurring because of a loose cable or a poor connection you can eyeball easily. Plus you may not remember—or even during setup, failed to consciously note—that you have DMA channels sharing.

There is an additional limitation: 16-bit cards only may use channels 5 to 7, while a surprising number of 8-bit cards, such as older SoundBlaster sound cards, remain in daily use. With channels 0 and 2 excluded, only DMA channels 1 and 3 are available to the 8-bit cards (16-bit cards also work on these same channels), and you can only use them if they're not already in use by something else, of course. While 16-bit channels can handle up to a 128K block of data in one DMA operation, 8-bit channels only work with up to a 64K block per operation. Note, too, that PCI devices don't utilize standard DMA channels, while EISA, ISA, VLB or VESA local bus do.

DMA is controlled by a chip (8237A or an equivalent) integrated into a larger chip included in the vast majority of PCs. Each channel is itself made up of two different signals:

1. *DRQ*—The DMA request signal (as in "get me this")
2. *DACK*—The DMA acknowledgement signal (as in "here it is!")

Please note: If you have an add-on card with jumpers specifically for setting these signals, be sure that both DACK and DRQ are set to the same number, or a problem will ensue.

DON'T CONFUSE TYPES OF DMA

You also need to know that there are two types of DMA frequently discussed, called *first-party DMA* and *third-party DMA*. Standard DMA, the kind we have been discussing, is also called third-party DMA, because it's using a third entity, the PC's physical DMA controller, to handle transfers between whatever other two parties are sending and receiving these transfers.

First-party DMA, better known as bus mastering, relies not on the physical DMA controller but on the peripheral itself to control these transfers. How the peripheral accomplishes this is through the addition of faster and more intelligent DMA circuitry than the old ISA-designed onboard DMA controller, built right into the peripheral's hardware. One example of this is the high-speed DMA-33 or mode 3 hard drives. You will find that some video cards, network cards, and higher-end SCSI cards now use this technology as well. You can read more about bus mastering under the PCI section in Chapter 7.

Table 4.3 shows assignments, devices, and bus lines for DMA channels.

COMMON DMA CHANNEL ASSIGNMENT PROBLEMS

Very much like IRQs, DMA channels are assigned on a one-per-device basis. You can share them between two devices not needed to work simultaneously, but it's tricky and not the best solution. Also, many devices are inclined to try to find assignment on DMA channels 0 to 3 (the original 4), only two of which are standardly available for such assignment. In fact, very few hardware devices will allow themselves to be forced to use the upper channels, of which only 5, 6, and 7 are available to start. If you have a lot of 8-bit devices requiring DMA channel assignment, this can result in a supreme headache. Even with 16-bit devices, it's not always or usually easy.

The good news is that not every device will need a DMA channel to help assign resources in order to work. When you have to use a device that will require one, it may be worthwhile to check around and ask, "hey, will

TABLE 4.3   DMA Assignments, Devices, and Bus Lines

DMA Channel Address	Standard Assignment	Typical Devices Using the Channel	Type of Bus Line Provided
0	Memory refresh	Best not to use to permit memory refresh	None
1	Unassigned*	Sound cards (using low DMA assignment), network adapters, ECP parallel/ printer ports, SCSI host adapters, voice modems	8/16-bit**
2	Floppy drive controller	Besides floppy, tape accelerator cards	8/16-bit
3	Unassigned	Sound cards (low DMA), network adapters, ECP parallel/printer ports, SCSI host adapters, voice modems, tape accelerator cards, old XT hard drive controllers	8/16-bit
4	DMA controller	None possible since it provides the bridge between the first set of DMA channels (0 to- 3) and second (4 to- 7)	None
5	Unassigned	Sound cards (needing high DMA), network adapters, SCSI host adapters	16-bit
6	Unassigned	Sound cards (high DMA), network adapters	16-bit
7	Unassigned	Sound cards (high DMA), network adapters	16-bit

* "Unassigned" means available unless your PC has assigned something else to this
**16-bit bus lines means that those DMA channels are only accessible to 16-bit hardware devices, while 8/16-bit means these channels are accessible to either 8-bit or 16-bit, whichever needs it

this piece of hardware take an assignment to DMA channels 5, 6, or 7?" The answer may be found in the technical specifications for the specific device on the manufacturer's web site or by asking around on online newsgroups among users already using the same equipment.

Input/Output or I/O

If input/output is defined as the actual transfer of data to and from the processor and anything attached to your computer, such as a printer or external tape drive, then think of an I/O address as simply the designated spot along the PC's communication lines for that transfer of data to take place. I/O can be difficult to work with for many reasons. One is the same problem encountered with IRQs and DMA channels: It is best to have one device per assignment. While there are more I/O addresses to go around than IRQs or DMA channels, orderly assignment, as well as keeping track of them all, presents a real stumbling block. Another is that I/O addresses are expressed in hexadecimal notation, while most of us don't do hex conversions in our heads. This is not only cumbersome, but makes us more prone to errors because we may not readily spot a bad or already used I/O address.

To make things more confusing, only the first byte of the I/O address is often referenced rather than the full address range. For instance, a COM1 serial port may be located at hex address range 3F8-3FF, but all you may see is 3F8. From that alone, how do you tell the I/O address range's size? How do you tell it's not conflicting with the range of another device's address? If another device is coming in to use a range starting before 3FF, the first byte-only address will not permit you to see that easily.

Beyond this, I/O address space is sized to fit the need. Some devices need to transfer a great deal more data than others. For instance, a network or SCSI card with its large data demands will need a larger-sized I/O address space than a mouse or a keyboard. Most, however, use an address space of 4, 8, or 16 bytes, while the range spreads from 1 to 32 bytes. If you don't know for certain the size of the range to start, and you only have the first byte of the I/O address to reference, troubleshooting conflicts when they arise—and they will—is something of a logistical nightmare. Add to this that some of the I/O addresses are reserved for system use only and should never be assigned to a device you are adding.

It's also vital to understand that some devices don't have multiple I/O addresses at which they can work, while others offer some flexibility in assignment. COM1, for instance, *always* occupies hex address range 3F8-3FF, while a sound card that wants to use address 220 may permit resetting to a different address and operate perfectly.

TIP Sound card/adapter assignments are tricky for several reasons. One is that a sound card is actually a complex of devices (input, output, MIDI, etc.) that need to work in unison. Another is that DOS games and some DOS-based drivers may not like finding a sound card assigned to anything other than the standard default system resources it was designed to use. Where possible, consider moving or modifying other devices and the system resources they use *before* you try to coax the sound card through such an adjustment.

Many devices, but not all, use I/O address ranges in their proper configuration and use. These include video and sound adapters, SCSI host adapters, network cards, drive controllers, and COM and LPT ports.

I/O COMMON PROBLEMS AND COMMONLY USED ADDRESSES

The good news is that you have a great deal more options to work with when trying to assign I/O address space than with trying to fit devices into a limited set of IRQs or DMA channels. But when you have address ranges of varying sizes and this much flexibility to assign addresses, you are going to hit many more snags when you have to work through a resource conflict. It's not quite as easy as noticing you have two devices assigned to IRQ7.

As noted above, it's fairly typical to know the starting I/O address range but not the end of the range for a particular device assignment. If another assignment is made to an address that starts before the end of the previous address assignment, you will hit a resource conflict, whether or not it is obvious by behavior on your PC.

If you're confused, consider this analogy. Say you own a business and venture to the post office to rent several postal boxes for business mail. The post office assigns you P.O. boxes 16 to 24, and that's where all your business mail should plug into. This works fine until the next person comes in and rents a series of mailboxes, and the post office gives him or her mailbox numbers 23 to 30. Your mailboxes will overlap with theirs, and confusion can result. You will get their mail sometimes, and they yours, and you may have a serious mess on your hands until you get the post office to sort this out and reassign mailboxes properly, so that the other person gets P.O. boxes 25 to 32 instead.

Resource conflicts surrounding I/O addresses won't be so easy to work out, so you may have to play with range assignments a bit to overcome a problem. And don't assign a new I/O address without knowing what your other devices use. A list of common address ranges with their corresponding devices is provided in Table 4.4.

One common problem is network cards, which may use a wide variety of address and range sizes. Another is SCSI host adapters, which really have no standardized I/O address they should shoot for assignment on. They can really change from vendor to vendor (Adaptecs tend to start at 330, while Trantor looks to 350). Here's another case where you need to

TABLE 4.4 Common Address Ranges and Corresponding Devices

I/O Address	Typical Device or Component
000-00Fh	Controller for DMA Channels 0-3—don't assign
T010-01Fh	System use—don't assign
030-03Fh	
050-05Fh	
090-09Fh	
0B0-0BFh	
0E0-0Efh	
020-02Fh	Interrupt controller #1 (IRQs 0 to -7), system use—don't assign
040-04Fh	System timers, system use—don't assign
060h and 064h	Keyboard controller (and PS/2 style mouse—they can share because you won't use the mouse simultaneously as you type a key), speakers
080-08Fh	DMA page registers
0A0-0AFh	Interrupt controller #2 (IRQs 8 to- 15), system use—don't assign
0C0-0CFh	Controller for DMA cChannels 4 to- 7, ranged as 0C0-0DFh, bytes 1-16
0D0-0DFh	Controller for DMA cChannels 4 to- 7, ranged as 0C0-0DFh, bytes 17-32
0F0-0FFh	Floating- point unit (FPU), math coprocessor
100-10Fh	
110-11Fh	System use—don't assign
120-14Fh, 140-15Fh	SCSI host adapters
170-17Fh	Secondary IDE controller, master drive assignment
1F0-1FFh	Primary IDE controller, master drive assignment
200-20Fh	Joystick port, system use—don't assign
220-22Fh	SCSI host adapters, sound cards
240-24Fh	Network cards, sound cards
260-26Fh and 270-27Fh	Network cards, sound cards Plug and Play devices, LPT2, LPT3
280-28Fh	Network cards, sound cards
2E0-2EFh	COM 4 (serial)
2F0-2FFb	COM 2 (serial)
300-30Fh	Network cards, sound card MIDI ports
340-34Fh	SCSI host adapters, network adapters
360-36Fh and 370-37Fh	Printers (by way of LPT assignments), network cards, tape accelerator cards, secondary IDE channel's slave drive, if exists
380-38Fh	FM synthesizer component of some sound cards
3B0-3BFh and 3C0-3DFh	VGA video adapters (formerly monochrome, CGA, and EGA)
3BC-3BF	LPT3
3E0-3EFh	COM 3 (serial) port, tertiary (third) IDE controller, tape accelerator card
3F0-3F7h	Floppy disk controller, slave drive for primary IDE controller
3F0-3FFh	COM 1 (serial)

read the documentation as well as the online technical specifications for help in assigning these properly, then double-check to make certain that the range they need to use is not being shared with other devices.

Tips to Help You Plan

Until you do this for a bit, it's going to be hard to remember which system resources are standardly available, which are predesignated to use a specific resource assignment (to support things like the keyboard controller or the floppy drive controller) and which you have already used for other devices. This is why doing a summary of resources ahead of time can cut down frustration later on.

You can also use a table like Table 4.5 to identify which system resources are routinely used by which device.

Compiling Your PC's System Resource Profile

As I suggested in Chapter 3, I think it's a wise idea to actually make a record of which device uses what resources. Do this once, keep it updated, and you have a quick reference sheet to consult before you buy a hardware device that may not fit into or work in your PC given the resources you have available.

I just got a new PII in here, and I haven't had time to check everything out. Before I bought a system, I checked to make certain the motherboard in the machine would have some expansion slots left to work with so I can add adapters and other hardware as needed. I knew I didn't need a lot of available ISA slots, because one factor in buying the PII was to say goodbye to some of my ISA-based dependency. I wanted AGP to carry video, and PCI and USB to carry the majority of the other hardware I need to run beyond the basic system.

Knowing I would be fairly busy, would need to switch quickly throughout various Internet applications as well as Microsoft Office, and would print and scan a good deal, I made certain I had 64 MB of PC100 RAM (on a BX motherboard). One thing you don't want to do is increase your

TABLE 4.5 System Resources of Various Devices

Type of Device	Device	IRQ Used	DMA Channel Used	I/O Address Range Used
System	Reserved for system use	0, 2, 8, 13	0, 4	000-0FFh (excluding 060h and 064h), 100-12Fh, 20C-20Dh, 270-277b
Input devices	PS/2 mouse	12	N/A	060h, 064h*
	Keyboard. controller	1	N/A	060h, 064h*
	Joystick	N/A	N/A	200-207h
Parallel/Printer ports	LPT1	7	1,3**	378-37Fh, 3BC-3BFh
	LPT2	5	1,3**	278-27Fh, 378-37Fh
Serial ports	COM1	4	N/A	3F8-3FFb
	COM2	3	N/A	2F8-2FFh
	COM3	2 or 9, 4, 5, 7	N/A	3E8-3EFh
	COM4	2 or 9, 3, 5, 7	N/A	2E8-2EFh
Modem	—	2 or 9, 3, 4, 5, 7	1, 3***	Same as COM port assignment
Video adapter	Standard VGA	11, 12	N/A	3B0-3BBh, 3C0-3DFh
Sound adapter	—	3, 4, 5, 7, 9, 10, 11, 12	1,3 also 5, 6, 7	220-22Fh, 240-24Fh, 260-26Fh, 280-28Fh, also 300-301h, 330-331h, also 388-38Bh
Storage	Primary IDE controller			
	Secondary IDE controller			
	Floppy drive controller			
	SCSI host adapter			
	Tape accelerator card			
Networking	—	9, 10, 11, 12, (15)	1, 3, 5, 6, 7	240-243h, 260-263h, 280-283h, 2A0-2A3h, 300-303h, 320-323h, 340-343h, 300-363h
PCI devices	Individual PCI devices	9, 10, 11, 12	—	Device dependent (see documentation)

* Shares resources with a device not being used simultaneously, like keyboard and mouse

** If used as ECP (ECP stands for enhanced capabilities port or IEEE 1284, a faster printer port standard more commonly in use the last 2 years, which is bidirectional)

*** If voice modem only

downtime by bottlenecking your system with too little RAM for all you need to do.

OK, since I want to inventory what I have and what is being used for each device, I need to chart that. But I also may want to provide the date (and version, if provided) of the driver for the device, and any comments I need to make relative to special requirements of a specific device. So, based on the information I compile from Device Manager, from the System Information (MSINFO) tool, and from Dr. Watson, I can come up with the chart in Table 4.6, showing my resources used and by which devices (a few details are missing for brevity).

Now, I don't want a WinModem and have plenty of spares, and this listing will help me have the information on hand to assign the resources needed (around its COM port assignment) to substitute. I also have a record of what existed prior to any change I make (in this case, swapping out the modems).

The same is true for the writable CD-ROM drive and the network card I plan to add, plus I anticipate moving the printer, the mouse, and the modem off of traditional connections and onto USB ports.

OK, what does this tell me? Well, if I know that between the system itself and my add-on hardware, I'm using IRQs 0, 1, 2 (out because I'm using 9), 4, 5, 6, 7, 8, 9, 10, 11, 12, 13, 14, 15. So unless I add a lot of USB hardware under the USB controller using IRQ5 or juggle PCI sharing an IRQ, I have just one IRQ available to me for any additional add-ons: IRQ3. Ouch. But by using a standard modem as opposed to a voice modem, I may be able to reclaim the extra IRQ needed by the voice capability of the modem; I could also move my pointing device to USB and try to recapture IRQ12 for my use elsewhere.

On DMA channels, I fare a little better. Besides DMA channels 0 and 4, already in use, I'm only using channel 2 (for the floppy drive controller) and 1 for the legacy sound card, leaving me with potentially four open channels.

You may want to do something very much like this for yourself, as demonstrated here and talked about in Chapter 3. A worksheet to start from is included in Appendix C, but you may want to make your own to factor in any special information or notations you know you want to make.

TABLE 4.6 Device and Resource Chart

Device	Make/ Model	IRQ#	DMA Channel	I/O Address	Driver Date/ Version	Comments
Modem	Lucent V.90 voice	10		De00 DE07 Dc00 DCFF	5-11-98	
Mouse	PS/2	12				
Keyboard	Standard 101 key	1		0060 0060 0064 0064		
Video				03B0 03BB 03C0 03DF	6-05-98	
Sound card	SB PCI 64	11		DA00- DA3F	5-11-98	
Sound legacy	SB	07	01	0530 0537 0330 033F 0220 022F 0388 038B	7-16-98	
DVD/CD-ROM					5-11-98	
Floppy controller		06	02	03F0 03F5	5-11-98	
Hard disk controller	Primary and secondary	14 & 15		01F0 01F7 03F6 03F6	5-11-98	
Universal serial bus		05			5-11-98	
Media processor	Mpact	09		03B0 03BB 03C0 03DE	6-05-98	
LPT1		07		0378- 037F	5-11-98	
COM1		04		03F8- 03FF	5-11-98	

What to Do When You Spot a Resource Conflict

There are three primary steps in dealing with a hardware system resource conflict as defined here so far:

◀ Assessing what system resources are in use by which device

◀ Identifying which devices and resources are in conflict

◀ Modifying the settings for the device and its resources so that the conflict is resolved.

We will tackle this in detail in Chapter 5 on troubleshooting.

Troubleshooting Practicum

Included in this chapter are the following topics:

◄ Essential concerns and techniques in troubleshooting

◄ Identifying and resolving fatal errors

◄ Using configuration files and logs in troubleshooting

◄ Creating boot disks

◄ Clean booting versus single-stepping through boot

◄ Troubleshooting through Windows Protection Errors at boot

◄ Troubleshooting in/out of Protected Mode/MS-DOS Compatibility Mode

◄ Ways your PC helps you identify problems

Almost as vital as solid configuration management to PC productivity is a solid body of troubleshooting techniques. What differentiates true skill at troubleshooting from haphazard "let me try this and this" is the approach or methodology. You put together as many facts as you can—what facts you can't prove are clearly labeled assumptions—then you take the time to analyze this data to see what it tells you. Only then do you proceed, and only then do you start to "monkey around" with the setup. Almost any other course results in lots of unnecessary wheel spinning.

Checklist of the Dos and Don'ts of Troubleshooting

◄ Do have boot or system disks and emergency recovery disks on hand, in working condition and equipped with necessary additional files, like a driver and MSCDEX.EXE to run your CD-ROM, if needed.

◄ Do have a regular backup plan so you can recover any data lost during a crisis.

◄ Do turn on logging in programs, when provided the opportunity, so that you may use these in conjunction with other system logs to track down where a pesky error is originating.

◄ Do take care to note error messages that appear on the screen during bootup, along with error messages appearing when Windows first loads (if it does). Noting what they report may hold clues to the problem(s) you have.

◄ Do use resources like technical pages for a product located at the manufacturer's Web or other online site, as well as information databases like the Microsoft Knowledge Base, to give you suggestions for ways to resolve the dilemma.

◄ Do use Safe Mode as a means of troubleshooting hardware and other problems in Windows 95 and Windows 98.

◄ Do use a clean boot combined with a minimal configuration to minimize drivers and memory used in troubleshooting a hardware or other issue.

◄ Do reread documentation accompanying a product; important switches or considerations may be noted there.

◄ Do scan for viruses using an updated virus scanning program to eliminate an infection as a possible source of problems.

◄ Do simplify your work by eliminating—before you troubleshoot—any programs or special software that reside in the background, new hardware add-ons, management utilities, special function monitors or screensavers, or anything nonstandard.

◄ Do remember the old adage: FIFO (first in, first out). When problems arise, look at the most recent thing installed or added, however minor or unrelated it seems, then try removing or disabling it to see if the situation is corrected.

◀ Do eliminate any excessive extra connections to reduce the variables; if a PC is part of a network, for example, and that machine alone is experiencing difficulty, disengage it from the network and test it as a standalone.

◀ Do remain aware of warranty and hardware purchase return policies; while some issues are worthy of spending time troubleshooting, others may be resolved more time- and cost-effectively by returning or replacing the unit in question.

◀ Avoid trying to overclock on a system already experiencing difficulties; if you overclock a stable system and experience strange errors, draw back on the overclocking or return the system to its original configuration until it is stable again.

◀ Avoid beta software without taking precautions; remove the beta if you cannot quickly resolve an issue that develops, or troubleshooting can be far more difficult.

◀ Avoid creative or highly specialized configurations until you get a problem under control, and then add back elements one at a time.

◀ Avoid aggressive BIOS tweaks and superoptimization techniques during the troubleshooting phase.

◀ Avoid adding any additional hardware or software until a current situation is resolved satisfactorily.

◀ Avoid trying to troubleshoot when you are too tired or frustrated, since you are too prone to heap mistakes on top of mistakes and think you checked something you may not have checked thoroughly.

◀ Never assume. One of the biggest pitfalls in attempting to successfully troubleshoot a hardware issue is that we naturally make certain assumptions (it's properly seated, I'm sure this is a rated capability with my motherboard). These may be reasonable guesses, but they are not indeed facts. Yet somehow we transmute these assumptions into facts and build a whole foundation of problem resolution around them. Precious time is lost, and everything you do subsequent to forming the assumption may be in error. Prove the assumptions right or wrong before you proceed.

I was reminded of this last checklist item recently when helping a relatively new technical support person fault-isolate why her new video card would not work. Somehow, when she presented her information to me, I made the jump to assuming that if she bought an AGP (advanced graphics port) video card, her system was based on a LX or BX motherboard type that implements the AGP port. It took an hour of banging my head before I asked her for the exact make and model of her motherboard so I could surf over to the manufacturer's Web site and check the specifications out for myself. Nothing in those specs indicated AGP, and it turned out to be an older motherboard that does not offer an AGP socket. I sent her back to exchange her AGP card for a PCI version, and success was achieved.

Perhaps as much as 80 percent of the time, especially with hardware, difficulties we encounter happen immediately or shortly after a change. This change may be an installation, a removal, or even what appears to be a minor modification. If you know your PC was working fine until just about the time you performed that small change (or had an incident happen, say a system lockup during a bad electrical storm), this is strong indication that change or event is responsible for your present grief.

Less typically, but hardly uncommon, some changes will cause a slow degradation of performance or ability. For example, after upgrading your operating system, you may have a decent video display to start, and then notice a slow but steady decline in overall visibility and/or a reciprocal increase in error messages or blue screen lockups. This is usually corrected by obtaining and applying an updated video driver engineered for the upgraded operating system.

Thus, one of your first considerations when a computer crisis arises is, "What have I most recently changed?" Look at the following items:

◀ Any new software or utility updates added, especially system management utilities, driver-laden applications, and more.

◀ Changes to your configuration files, such as tweaks to achieve better conventional memory in DOS, or adding or removing a DOS based driver; don't discount anything as too minor until you check it out.

◀ Changes to the Registry or other system files performed while using RegEdit or SysEdit.

◄ Changes to your hardware: replacement, removal, or addition. Review what was installed or modified in the process; more may have changed than you think.

◄ Outside influences (major power events like a bad electrical storm or power surge; a physical relocation of the hardware—say moving a PC from one desk to another even in the same office—which may have unseated or damaged components; another user with access to your PC).

Before You Get in Too Deep

Before you launch into an aggressive troubleshooting mode, it's time to take a deep breath, perhaps grab coffee or a quick break, then come back and think about the problem again. Identify all the behaviors you can spot and consider what clues this may give you to what may be wrong.

Then—don't laugh—recheck things you are sure are already correct. If the nonfunctioning hardware device has a power cord, make sure it's plugged into a working outlet supplied with power. Make sure a board is properly seated in the PC itself. Try to narrow down anything obvious you might have missed before. Triple-check that all cables and wiring are properly secured, and that the device is turned to the ON position, if there is an ON/OFF switch, or that it displays a green or red LED ready light.

Considering that these obvious failures account for a majority of initial "hardware won't work" issues, you can never simply assume you did it perfectly the first time. You could save a serious amount of time spent troubleshooting tiny details only to discover a simple visible switch was missed or a cable is loose. Don't make a 3-second fix turn into a 3-hour or 3-day excursion.

This is also the reason I strongly advised you to prepare before performing an upgrade or performance tweaking, and so on. If you are informed and prepared, you are more likely to check the details, because you were aware of the detail work ahead of time. You won't be blindsided by the obvious.

Working Though Blue Screen Errors

Now that we've looked at the basics of troubleshooting, let's take some of what we discussed and apply it to one of the more annoying and hard-to-pinpoint Windows problems. Blue screen errors are named for their royal blue error screen—and are accompanied by an often-cryptic error message. These grab control of your display and usually force you into a reboot. They are also referred to as BSOD or "Blue Screen of Death" errors, since getting one may kill what you happen to be doing in Windows for the moment.

More often than not, these errors indicate a possible device or other hardware conflict. Rare observances of these should not cause undue concern, because a very low incidence points to a temporary issue probably resolved after you boot your system again. It's when they occur with increasing frequency, particularly after some type of upgrade or other change to your system, that demands a closer look.

Microsoft Knowledge Base, which I often use as a primary trouble-shooting information source along with manufacturer Web sites, recommends you take these orderly steps to try to resolve the blue screen errors:

1. Since this can indicate a conflict with the video card itself or its video driver, you need to look here first. Go to Device Manager and examine resources used, giving careful attention to any warnings or errors encountered. You also may want to check with your video card manufacturer's Web site to determine if a fresher driver for it is available for download and subsequent application.

2. When blue screen errors arise during a setup of the operating system or other installation, try removing the video driver from Device Manager prior to or during installation, and then reinstall it afterwards.

3. Scan the event log for possible conflicts noted.

NOTE The event viewer should list an error message for each device that failed to start. If two or more devices failed to start, double-check Device Manager for device conflicts—it's less likely to be dead hardware.

4. Try removing any applications or data files you initiate to load upon Windows bootup. These can be found by selecting Start|

Settings|Taskbar, then choosing the Startup Menu tab (in Windows 95/98 and Windows NT). This tip works well for other situations besides blue screen errors, such as working through boot sluggishness or Windows hanging soon or immediately after the launch is complete.

5. Check to see if the file WIN.INI exists. If present, it should be found in the Windows System directory. Load it into a text editor or SysEdit, then look for programs that load in the lines RUN= or LOAD=. Delete these or put a semicolon (;) or REM (for remark) statement at the beginning of the line so it will not be processed.

   Look at the version or dates on BIOSes for essential hardware such as your motherboard, or SCSI or other controller. Then cross-reference this against the manufacturer's Web site to see if an upgrade is necessary or available. Many types of BIOS are flashable, which means they can be updated using a software program.

6. Use Device Manager to seek out conflicts based in the IRQs, I/O addresses, or DMA channels. Modify settings as necessary.

7. Verify and recheck that your hardware is properly installed. This is particularly important with hardware like SCSI devices.

Undoing Optimization

Certain techniques are recommended for optimizing the boot speed of your PC with Windows. While these can significantly cut down on load time, and while we all want faster response, you should consider reversing the options provided below to help you more appropriately evaluate your system during troubleshooting. These optimization techniques include:

◀ Disabling the floppy drive seek option in the PC's CMOS

◀ Removing the boot delay in CMOS, if your BIOS provides this option

◀ Enabling either the QuickBook or QuickPOST features that are provided on some recent types of PC motherboards, which forces the PC to bypass some of its usual tests performed during boot

◀ Tuning and trimming Registry (tweaking some settings, removing old or unnecessary entries)

◀ Trimming Startup, which removes unnecessary programs from launching as soon as Windows loads

The Basics of Resolving Device Conflicts

The exact resolution of almost any device conflict amounts to covering your bases to make certain each device (with some notable exceptions) is assigned exclusive or at least unfettered access to a particular resource, be it one DMA channel, one interrrupt request, or one I/O address range. Additionally, you need to make changes throughout so that each part of your PC—Windows and Device Manager, the physical hardware itself, and any programs used in conjunction with that particular hardware, plus any relevant initialization files—all report the same thing, with no variation.

Here's a common situation: A COM or LPT conflict arises because two devices have the same COM or LPT name or are assigned to the same resources. Let's say you have a mouse and a modem, and they are both configured to work off of COM1. Logic tells you only one of the devices can live and work there successfully. So you have to reconfigure the second one to another name (like COM2) and another resource, like a different IRQ.

To make sure all links in the hardware chain are set to "read" the same way for these devices, you would:

◀ Change the position of a jumper to reflect the change in COM ports, if necessary, or

◀ Alter the settings of a DIP switch to reflect this, if necessary, or

◀ Run a program that will "soft" switch, which resets via keyboard a setting on the device just like you physically altered the position of the jumper or modified the DIP switch settings, and

◀ Make the appropriate changes in Device Manager, making certain the mouse is on COM1 using the appropriate resources, and the modem is now on COM2, using the appropriate resources.

Understanding Device Contention in 32-bit Windows

As defined by Microsoft, device contention refers to Windows' ability to arbitrate requests for the use of devices attached to it (often a serial or

COM port) by more than one program. Also, by definition, at least one of these programs in question is not Windows-based.

Previous versions of Windows did not really care about this issue and happily released devices to whatever entity demanded them with only a short (2-second) time delay. But 32-bit Windows—particularly Windows 95 and 98—is by nature picky about what uses which and when. It won't, unless forced, permit one of its programs to use a serial or COM port that has previously been assigned to a non-Windows-based progam running in its own virtual machine (VM or enclosed session) until that virtual window was closed and forgotten.

This can be altered by modifying a section of the SYSTEM.INI file. This line in the [386enh] segment of SYSTEM.INI:

```
Com <n> AutoAssign=<x>
```

where *<n>* is the serial or COM port number and *<x>* is a value ranging from –1 to 1000, allows you to manipulate 32-bit Windows' default settings for releasing this port for device use. Set the value to –1, its default setting, and Windows will behave as programmed, refusing to release the COM port until whatever program running in a VM properly closes and releases it. It's tuned to this default, in part, to aid programs like MS Fax that demand the ability to auto-answer a phone line, for instance, plugged into a device there. Dial-up Networking Server needs this setting as well.

In 16-bit Windows 3.1, this setting defaults to AutoAssign=2, which gives you that 2-second buffer before the port is released for use. While you can assign a value of 2 in Windows 95 and 98, you can't do so and run a 32-bit communications program such as HyperTerminal (often used to help troubleshoot a modem problem), or you'll hit problems. You may be told that another program is using the selected telephony devices, or you may receive an error message stating that Windows cannot initialize the serial or COM port in question.

One recommended fix is to set the value assignment in SYSTEM.INI to:

```
Com<n> AutoAssign=0
```

which allows Windows and MS-DOS, for example, to hot swap a serial port between themselves for use by their respective programs. The 0 value tells Windows to allow no delay in releasing the port. This works, but you may hit another snag if both programs try to issue commands simultaneously to the device attached to this port, so implement judiciously.

What occurs in the process is this: Each and every time a Windows- or MS-DOS-based program reports to Windows that it needs to use a specific port, Windows runs a check to see if the port is available. If it is indeed available, Windows authorizes its use, and the port is readily passed off to the requesting program. If the port is in use, Windows (if still using the default value of –1) simply refuses to authorize the port's use until the program queries again after the virtual machine using the port is distinctly finished.

Remember to seek out clues in resolving device conflicts. Consider this: If you add a new piece of hardware (and this may apply to software as well) and find that it does not work, you don't have to just yank the new hardware out. Stop and look first. Do you see something that was working fine during your last session that has suddenly ceased working during this session? If that's the case, it may not be that the new hardware is broken or incompatible with your PC or its configuration. More than likely, you have a conflict rather than a true failure. Scout around in Device Manager and work it out.

Quick Changes in Device Manager for Checking and Resolving

To modify/change a device's Resource settings:

1. Boot Windows 95/98 in Safe Mode (as described later in this chapter).

2. Choose Start|SettingsControl Panel, then double-click on the System icon.

3. Click on the Device Manager tab to open the Device Manager properties page, as illustrated in Figure 5.1.

4. Find the device causing the conflict. The device list should already be open and displaying the questionable device if Windows itself detected the problem. This is usually delineated by a red exclamation mark.

5. Highlight the device, then click on Properties to show the properties information for the device in question (see Figure 5.2).

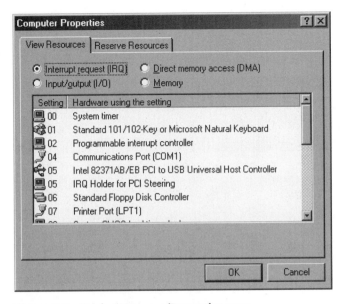

Figure 5.1   Device Manager/Properties page.

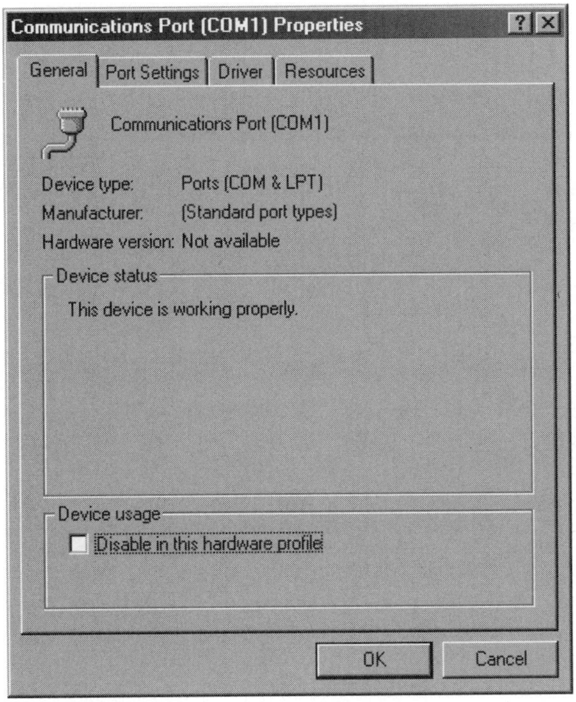

Figure 5.2   Properties page for device.

6. Click on the Resources tab to show the device's Resources information.

7. Click on the Use Automatic Settings checkbox to clear it, if selected.

8. Using the documentation or product manual, any information gleaned from other resources such as the manufacturer's Web site, and such, modify the resources assigned to the device, conforming to what you learned about IRQs, DMA channels, and I/O address spaces in Chapter 3. Make certain the changes you make here don't conflict with resources assigned elsewhere, or you will create a new issue.

9. First close the Resources property tab, then close Device Manager.

10. Shut down and restart your PC; check to see if the changes were implemented and are functioning properly.

A shorter-term bandage is to temporarily disable the device. This is a stopgap measure to let you get Windows back up, (hopefully) allowing you to work until you have the time to spend addressing the problem at hand. The downside, of course, is that you won't have access to whatever that particular device is or does. When you're ready to really try to fix the device's setup in Windows, you can reenable it.

To disable a device in Windows Device Manager:

1. Choose Start|Settings|Control Panel, then double-click the System icon, and click on the Device Manager tab.

2. Once in Device Manager, double-click the category name you need to work with, then double-click on the device listing.

3. From the General tab beneath, click the Original Configuration (Current) checkbox to clear it, as illustrated in Figure 5.3. Click OK.

4. Shut down and restart the PC.

When Windows loads, reenable the devices disabled above. Remember though to enable in the following order:

1. COM ports

2. Hard disk controllers

3. Floppy disk controllers

4. All other devices

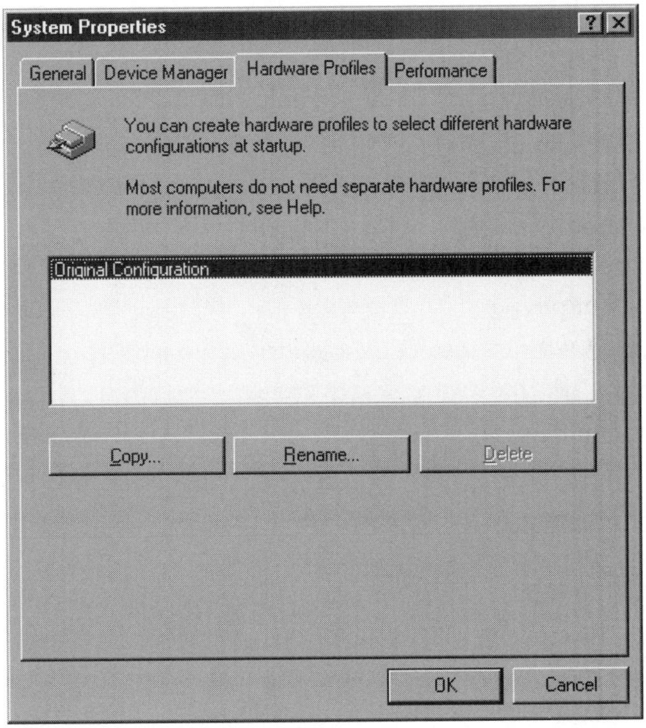

Figure 5.3 Device Manager/Disable Device/Original Configuration.

To enable a device, return to Device Manager as indicated above, then:

1. From Device Manager, double-click the category name, and then double-click the appropriate device in the list.

2. Choose the General tab, and click on the Original Configuration (Current) checkbox to select it. Click OK.

3. With the properties for each device open, click on the Resources tab, then review each to make sure no conflicts are noted in the Conflicting Device list.

4. Shut down and restart the PC normally.

Sometimes, a device simply needs a fresh copy of its driver to go from a dysfunctional to a working state again. This is a pretty simple and clean solution, and it doesn't hurt to try this early on. However, you do have to remove the copy of the driver you're replacing or refreshing to be sure the reinstall will "take."

To reinstall a device driver in Windows 95/98, you:

1. Bring up your PC with Windows in Safe Mode (see directions coming up).

2. Choose Start|Settings|Control Panel, then double-click on the System icon.

3. Select the Device Manager tab to show the Device Manager window.

4. Identify the hardware device whose driver you want to replace or refresh from the hardware list presented, highlight it, and click Remove. When asked if you wish to proceed, click Yes (or Cancel to stop the process).

5. Windows is designed to redetect such devices automatically after you remove the drivers, so power down and reboot in normal operating mode. Windows should detect the device as new and try to install the correct driver for it (be prepared to provide a disk or CD-ROM containing the driver if you know it is not available in the hardware list).

   Should Windows fail to detect the device, go to Control Panel, invoke the Add New Hardware wizard by double-clicking on its icon, and then following its prompts to install the hardware into Windows.

6. If the product or hardware device was packed with its own Setup program, don't forget to run this software (usually by clicking on Start, choosing Run, and then typing in the name of the file to execute) as well. Failing to do so may result in an inability to fully customize the device per its intended use or a failure to install DOS drivers for using the hardware (like a CD-ROM drive) in DOS mode.

You may also use Device Manager to force Windows not to load drivers or allocate any resources for a specific device. To do so:

1. Choose Start|Settings|Control Panel, then double-click on the System icon.

2. Choose the Device Manager tab, select a device, and then click on Properties to view its resource information.

3. Choose the General tab, and click the Original Configuration (Current) checkbox to clear it. Click OK.

This clears out the resources assigned to that device, and Windows won't load drivers for it. You can use this to put a device "on hold" while you troubleshoot, for example.

TIP **Remember, where Device Manager is requesting that you update a driver, all that may be necessary is removing the current driver from Device Manager, shutting down then rebooting the machine, and letting Windows "find" the device and its driver anew.**

As you work, however, you need to be aware of some fundamental truths. One is that not all devices are fully truthful in reporting what resources they are using in Windows. Because of this, Windows may not be able to smartly discern that a conflict is happening at all, or to see the extent of a conflict it can identify. Plus, Device Manager may not report to you everything you need to know to resolve a conflict, because you don't have all the data you need to work with.

For this reason Device Manager and its data should be just one of the tools you use in troubleshooting a conflict. Logs, configuration files, and other utilities may yield clues for issues not readily illuminated in Device Manager. You also need to check any errors that you do see in Device Manager against its list of error codes and suggested resolutions. You can find this information in Appendix E of this book.

Also, don't be alarmed if different devices have differing property tabs. Some devices have more information to report than others, so some devices may have two tabs, while others have three or four. So don't assume there is a problem when one device has less than another.

The basic rule is that if Windows can successfully detect a particular device, it should automatically assign the proper resources for it. Subsequently, the device should work perfectly. Yet situations arise whereby what Windows automatically establishes as settings for a device are not the best ones to use. You might need a different basic configuration, for example, to get a device to work the way you need it to. If you don't have an alternative basic configuration available in Device Manager, you may want to insist Windows not use the default automatic settings and instead use what you

TABLE 5.1 Symbols to Aid in Device Manager Troubleshooting

Device Manager Error Symbols	What Symbol Indicates
Black exclamation point in yellow field	Indicates problem with device that may or may not keep it from working; includes problem code for each device with the symbol.
Red X	Indicates a present but disabled device, with no protected-mode driver loaded for its use.
Blue "I" on white field	Shown on device resource in Computer properties; indicates device is not using auto settings ("Use Automatic Settings" not selected for this device), but is forced (user assigned specifications); if proper resources are assigned, device should work fine in this state.

specify. To do this, you need to click on the Use Automatic Settings checkbox to disable this option (unchecked), then select Change Setting, and after specifying the appropriate resource, provide the values you want to use.

Remember, too, if necessary you can reserve a specific resource in Device Manager. To do this, click on the Computer listing in Device Manager, then choose Properties. You have then two tabs, reading View Resources—which shows resources allocated under Plug and Play and on PCI bus PCs—and Reserve Resources. Select the latter, and reserve for exclusion the resource (setting) desired.

Table 5.1 shows the error symbols that occur in Device Manager, along with their descriptions.

More on Troubleshooting with Configuration Files and Logs

Look back at the configuration files we discussed in Chapter 3, because it is possible that a driver or program located within the DOS-based files (remember, Windows 95/98 don't require them) or the Windows .INI files may be creating or contributing to problems you are experiencing. To troubleshoot the CONFIG.SYS, remove any nonessential drivers (like support for a DOS-based sound card). However, if you don't know what a driver or other entry does, do not remove it until you find out. You should also remove any form of caching referenced, like FASTOPEN or SMART-

DRV (which may be located in AUTOEXEC.BAT instead). If you are using DOS and Windows 3.1x, verify that you have at least these entries set to these values:

```
FILES=60
BUFFERS=20
STACKS=0,0 (for DOS 3.3 and later, only)
```

To troubleshoot the AUTOEXEC.BAT, remove any nonessential programs like virus scanners, calendars, auto reminders, and such; check and remove (if found) any duplicate path entries; and verify (if present) that you are pointed to an existing, valid directory in the setting pointed at in the line SET TEMP=.

You also may want to boot with a very minimal CONFIG.SYS that loads just HIMEM.SYS and EMM386, to help narrow down the likely suspects in a problem. You can do this simply by remarking out any unnecessary things in AUTOEXEC.BAT (place a REM or a semicolon at the beginning of a configuration file entry line to prevent that line from being read during the boot). Remember, *minimal* means just enough to get you running. Also remember to save your changes, so they will be acted upon during the next boot.

Bear in mind: The more you load, the more variables you need to fault-isolate (a hopefully intelligent means of using trial-and-error to isolate a problem to a particular cause) later.

IF YOU THINK AN ISSUE LIES WITH SYSTEM.INI OR WIN.INI

Sometimes conflicting settings, syntax errors, or old messes in Windows .INI files can create a problem. To isolate whether either of these files is giving you grief, here's a method to test:

1. First, rename the SYSTEM.INI file located in the Windows directory/folder to SYSTEM.TST (or other appropriate name).

2. Copy, without renaming, the SYSTEM.CB file located in the Windows directory to SYSTEM.INI.

3. Use SYSEDIT or a text editor such as Notepad to open the SYSTEM.INI file and add this line to the [boot] section:

   ```
   Drivers=mmsystem.dll
   ```

4. Save the change.

5. Rename the WIN.INI file located in the Windows directory to WIN.TST (or other appropriate name).

6. Shut down and restart your PC.

Should this method work, your problem is narrowed down to whatever was listed in these old .INI files, now saved with the .TST extensions (or other appropriate name). You need to go through these with a fine-toothed comb if you want to see what the differences are that may account for your difficulty.

If changing these files doesn't work, even if you step through the boot process (as described shortly), you can try loading Windows in Safe Mode (also discussed later in this chapter), then change your current video driver to the standard VGA driver.

NOTE In the process of copying the SYSTEM.CB file to replace SYSTEM.INI, it is possible that you find your mouse or other pointing device will stop working. If this happens, you need to add certain lines to your new SYSTEM.INI file to rectify this:

In the [boot] section, add:

```
Mouse.drv=mouse.drv
```

In the [386enh] section, add:

```
Mouse=*vmouse, msmouse.vxd
```

IOS.LOG, found in Windows 95/98, is created by the I/O Supervisor (IOS) when it tries to determine whether it's possible to safely install a 32-bit (non-DOS) driver. If any of your drives are running in MS-DOS Compatibility Mode, you should locate the IOS.LOG in your Windows directory and examine it to see if it provides any details which may be useful.

The IOS.LOG contains several sections of details, including:

1. An IOS takeover summary that may report incompatible or problematic drivers as well as errors and error codes

2. A summary of all drives that are using real-mode mapper (RMM) for disk access

3. A listing of each device driver found in the DOS-based CONFIG.SYS. Each driver is listed in the following format, though not all lines may be present in your IOS.LOG:

Driver name: <filename>

Character driver

Block driver controlling nn unit(s)

Driver info (followed by hooks and addresses)

CONFIG.SYS line number: nnnnnnnn

Hardware interrupt hook map

4. A listing of all terminate-and-stay-resident (TSR) programs in AUTOEXEC.BAT, with their names, AUTOEXEC.BAT position, and hardware interrupt hook map provided

TIP   **If you start seeing a lot of errors referencing IOS or the IOS.LOG, you may want to check who made your CPU. In some cases we have seen, changing from an AMD to an Intel CPU can resolve long-standing IOS issues.**

BOOTLOG.TXT

This text-based log provides a summary of what happened during the startup process for Windows. While it is created when you first install and set up Windows, you can also turn it on during subsequent sessions to help track problems you may experience.

You can turn on boot-logging in two ways: by pressing function key F8 when you see "Starting Windows" to bring you to a boot menu where this is an option, or by running WIN.COM with the /b switch (switches are discussed later) from the DOS command line.

What you will discover in BOOTLOG.TXT is information about the Windows startup process logged sequentially (in the order events occur), divided into five basic sections. A loadsuccess= entry followed by a specific driver or program indicates the item loaded properly, while a loadfailed= notation will tell you that a virtual device driver (.VxD file) did not load. These sections are divided into the following categories:

◀ Loading real-mode drivers

◀ Loading VxDs

◀ System-critical initialization of VxDs

◀ Device initialization of VxDs

◀ Successful VxD initiation

◀ (include sample BOOTLOG.TXT file)

Not all entries will immediately fly red flags to help you spot trouble; instead, you need to closely examine the log to check that an initialized device or component met with success. For instance, if you see a line beginning DynamicInitDevice=<name>, without also finding an accompanying statement reading DynamicInitSuccess=<name> (where the name of the device or component is the same as the DynamicInitDevice subject), you can identify a VxD that is not loading when it should. The same is true with the entry Loading Device=<name> if not followed by a LoadSuccess=<name> when the names match.

USING HARDWARE LISTS AND TOOLS

Never omit reading the README.TXT file or similar documentation that packs with your Windows operating system. The reason is simple once you realize that hardware notes, often pertaining to specific types and models of add-ons like Diamond video cards or Seagate tape drives, for example, may be noted there. Also, switches may be suggested, troubleshooting techniques offered, and other useful data given.

Besides this, the Microsoft Knowledge Base and other technical information databases on the Web provide hardware lists for various operating systems. Windows NT 4.0 always offers a Hardware Compatibility List (HCL) where the types of PCs and add-on hardware supported under it may be found. For Windows 98, check HARDWARE.TXT, which lists issues related to Plug and Play, as well as specifics on known problems or issues with devices like scanners, modems, tape drive detection, ISDN drivers, as well as offers possible workarounds for overcoming issues.

Then there are utilities that can make our work easier, too. These include HWINFO.EXE, Microsoft's hardware diagnostic tool built into Windows 98, which provides an alternative view of the same information available by running Microsoft's System Information tool, MSINFO.EXE. What HWINFO offers is a color-coded information reference to help you identify values or issues with hardware devices (and it works with software, too). Figure 5.4 shows HWINFO.

You have the choice of several views in HWINFO, including all devices (the default view), current devices, drivers with problems, file verify, and the resource summary. The color codes are identified as:

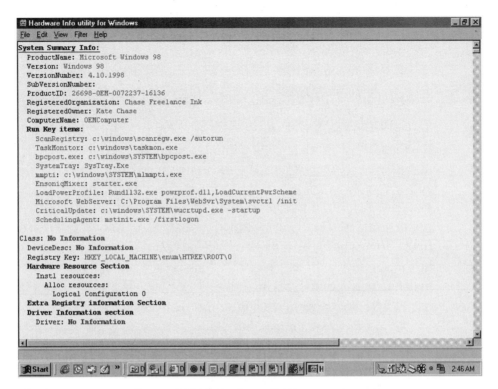

Figure 5.4 HWINFO (from MSINFO) Hardware Resources main screen.

◀ Bold blue is coded for warning information

◀ Bold red for error information/messages

◀ Dark Red shows Configuration Manager information

◀ Green presents all keys from the Windows Registry

◀ Pink shows file attributes information

RESTORING ORIGINAL CONFIGURATION FILES

If you have reason to suspect a single, specific, and recent modification to your PC hardware profile may be responsible for your current difficulty, you should attempt to restore your backup configuration files. Then test or otherwise evaluate your system to see if this resolves your problem. However, please remember to make a backup of the current set of such files you are now using before you reinstall a previous set. This way, if restoring the backup doesn't work, you can return to the set of configuration files in use when the problem first cropped up.

USING MSINFO OR MSINFO32.EXE (WINDOWS 98 ONLY)

Like HWINFO, MSINFO/MSINFO32 is a utility provided in Windows 98 to collect information about your PC and its configuration. It functions both to assist you in getting the facts you need to overcome a problem with your system, as well as to offer menu access to other tools and utilities you may find helpful in troubleshooting. Critical information is provided in a pretty straightforward, at-a-glance format. Most important, it offers a status of drivers being used by your PC and Windows, and provides a running history of device drivers installed. This is the kind of detail work that can make a difference in tracking down a particularly murky error message.

MSINFO32 reports its data in three categories:

1. *Hardware resources.* See below
2. *Components.* Includes a listing of hardware itself, indicates problem devices, gives the driver history and BIOS information, and provides Windows 98 and system configuration data
3. *Software environment.* Includes DOS drivers, real-mode device drivers, kernel drivers, and more

Let's take a moment to see what necessary data you can view under MSINFO32's Hardware Resources section, the main screen of which is presented in Figure 5.5.

The Hardware Resources section is divided into several subcategories, which include:

◀ *Conflicts/sharing.* Details identified conflicts between ISA devices, IOS resources that are shared by PCI devices, and more

◀ *DMA.* Details DMA resource information for your system

◀ *Forced hardware.* Details user-specified hardware information (for example, when you need to force a sound card to use specific resources instead of the ones Windows tries to push it to take), as well as information on PnP devices that you can use in troubleshooting resource conflicts

◀ *I/O.* Details I/O address resource information for your system

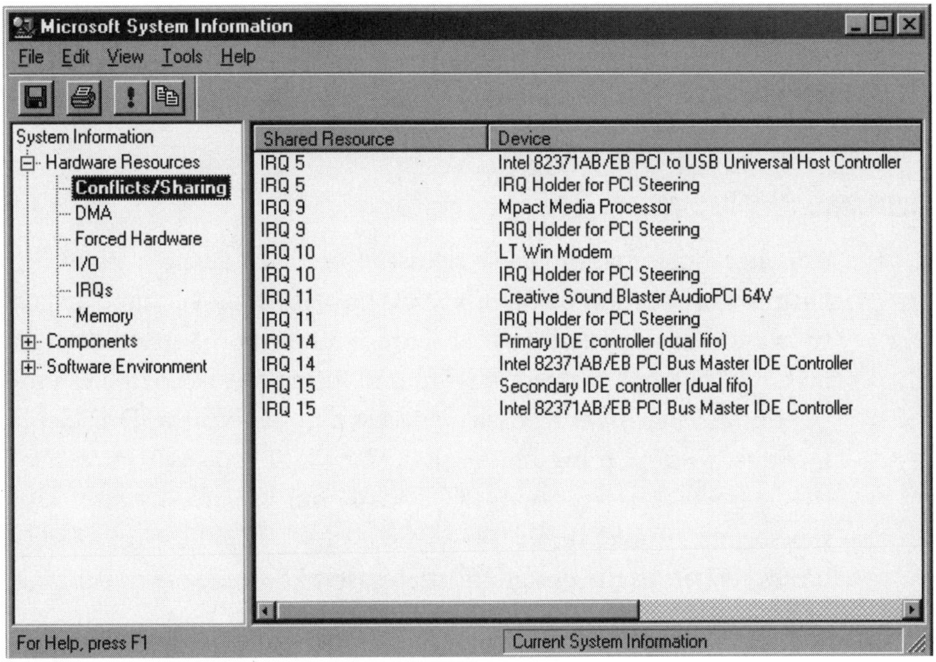

Figure 5.5 Hardware Resources in MSINFO expanded.

◀ *IRQs.* Details the interrupt request resource information for your system

◀ *Memory.* Details memory address ranges currently utilized by devices

Additionally, you can use MSINFO32's menu to launch other programs provided by Microsoft System Information. These include:

◀ Windows Report Tool (WinRep)

◀ Update Wizard Uninstall

◀ System File Checker

◀ Signature Verification Tool

◀ Registry Checker

◀ Automatic Skip Driver Agent

◀ Dr. Watson

◀ System Configuration Utility

◀ ScanDisk

◀ Version Conflict Manager

To run MSINFO32, select Start|Programs|Accessories|System Tools|System Information. You can also execute it by selecting Start|Run, and typing MSINFO32.EXE in the Open dialog window.

WINMSD (WINDOWS NT 4.0)

This is a Windows NT-based version of the older, DOS-based Microsoft Diagnostic program (MSD.EXE) we mentioned in Chapter 3. Its purpose is to tell you what your PC packs in and out of its NT 4.0 configuration, and it should be implemented in troubleshooting hardware issues under NT.

But as Microsoft Knowledge Base reports, WinMSD has some imperfections, too. One big one is that WinMSD reports the wrong interrupt (IRQ) for PCI devices on a PC, which conforms to the Intel Multiprocessor Specification (MPS) v1.4. MPS is itself a specification by PC manufacturers related to the design of Intel-based PCs capable of running multiple processors.

This occurs because WinMSD extracts its information about the resources used directly from the MPS interrupt table, while MPS v1.4 itself uses a revised format to show PCI devices. What results is that WinMSD reports the PCI interrupt signal value as the source bus IRQ instead of reporting the correct interrupt as the source bus IRQ.

Table 5.2 shows an example noted in Knowledge Base, based on a computer conforming to MPS v1.4 specs that is using the MPS hardware abstraction layer (HAL):

To fix this problem on MPS v1.4-capable NT PCs, you need to use the normal uniprocessor (single processor) hardware abstraction layer to rectify the conflict and then revert to MPS HAL. In order to get NT to use the uniprocessor HAL and kernel files, you need to:

1. Copy HAL.DLL and NTOSKRNL.EXE from the Windows NT master CD-ROM or from a Windows NT Service Pack folder if installed to a temporary directory/folder of your choosing.

2. Rename HAL.DLL to UNIHAL.DLL.

3. Rename NTOSKRNL.EXE to UNIKRNL.EXE.

4. Copy the original HAL.DLL and NTOSKRNL.EXE to the 96systemroot96\winnt\system32\ folder.

TABLE 5.2   Errors in WinMSD Reported in Windows NT 4.0

Devices	Vector	Level	Affinity
I8042prt	1	1	0xffffffff
I8042prt	12	12	0xffffffff
Serial	4	4	0x00000000
Serial	3	3	0x00000000
E159x	32	32	0x80718ce0
Floppy	6	6	0x00000000
Sndblst	178	5	0x00000001
Aic78xx	40	40	0x00000000

*Note:*The interrupts for E159x and aic78xx PCI devices are not correct.

5. Remove the Read Only attribute from the BOOT.INI file. Do this from a command prompt by typing:

```
Attrib -s -h -r <system root> \boot.ini
```

where *<system root>* is the device in which your boot files are located. (Hit Enter after typing the line.)

6. Load a text editor. Modify the [operating systems] section of BOOT.INI as follows:

Multi(0)disk....\WINNT40="Windows NT Service Version 4.00"
Multi(0)disk....\WINNT40="Windows NT Version 4.00 [UNI-HAL]"
/hal=unihal.dll /kernel=unikrnl.exe

NOTE Do not wrap final line to second line.

7. Save changes, shut down, and restart Windows NT.

8. Choose Windows NT Version 3.00 [UNIHAL] from the Windows NT 4 boot menu.

9. Once Windows NT 4.0 is loaded, run WinMSD.EXE tool again to view the correct interrupts for your PCI devices.

NT 4.0 PERFORMANCE MONITOR

Performance Monitor is a performance status-reporting utility included in Windows NT 4.0. When you find yourself up against a situation that is affecting overall performance of your NT system, it may be wise to turn logging on in Performance Monitor to give you another tool in determining system behavior.

To invoke this logging:

1. Load Performance Monitor, pull down the View menu, and select Log.

2. Pull down the Edit menu, then choose Add to Log. The Add to Log dialog box lets you specify two settings: Computer and Objects. Computer allows you to specify the name of the local computer or a remote computer you wish to log information on; Objects lets you add counters for those things you choose to measure in troubleshooting a problem (examples include process and processor, memory, system, paging file, and more).

3. Highlight those Objects desired and select Add.

4. Pull down the Options menu, and select Log.

5. Under File Name, assign the log a name (be specific so it doesn't get lost in other reports and logs).

6. From the bottom of the window above, note the Update Time option. Use it to increase the interval timer higher than 15 seconds if you expect to perform a log over a longer period of time. This prevents you from returning to a humongous log file you have to review.

7. Click Start Log when you are ready to commence logging

To then stop and review the log:

1. From Options, choose Log, then Stop Log.

2. Under Options again, select Data From and Log File. Select the radio button beside the Performance log field, then find your log file.

NOTE Choosing File|Open will not open this file for viewing.

3. When the log file is open, add the objects and counters that you monitored, and do this for each view needed. If you don't, the log file's data may be unavailable for you to return to for review.

SINGLE-STEPPING VS. CLEAN BOOTING

There are two methods implemented in standard troubleshooting to over-come problems during the boot/Windows load process: single-stepping and clean booting. *Single-step* means to go item-by-item through the booting process so that you are prompted before your system processes each line of the CONFIG.SYS file. If you say Yes, it loads the line; if you say No, it does not. This can help you control a driver you suspect of causing a problem from loading, and you can more easily read error messages generated by the running of a particular line.

To single-step in Windows 95/98:

1. If you are already running a boot menu, boot the PC and choose the option that permits you to run the CONFIG.SYS line by line (in Windows 95/98's own boot menu, this is Option 5

   or

   If you don't ordinarily run a boot menu, press Shift + F8 as soon as you see the message "Starting Windows," This breaks out of the launch and brings up the boot menu. Select Option 5.

2. Proceed to respond Yes or No (Y or N) regarding whether to run each line, as prompted. If you are using disk compression like DriveSpace, it is here that you have the option of whether to load the driver for it, but you're only prompted to do this if DriveSpace (or its predecessor DoubleSpace) is installed on your system.

NOTE Once the CONFIG.SYS is stepped through, the AUTOEXEC.BAT file is processed normally (nonstepped), if you respond Yes to the prompt to execute it.

A clean boot, on the other hand, allows you to completely bypass your DOS drivers and configuration files altogether. This can be useful some-times, but it has limitations. Anything you need to operate in DOS—drivers for your mouse and your CD-ROM, for example—isn't loaded. Nor do the memory managers EMM386 and HIMEM. Conventional memory will be affected, too.

To clean boot in Windows 3.1:

1. Boot your PC.

2. As soon as you see "Starting MS-DOS," press the F5 key (please note, this is only available in MS-DOS 6.x), which prevents the configuration files from being processed.

3. From the DOS command prompt, you can either edit your configurations files using something like DOS 5.0 and later versions' EDIT.COM, or you can try executing or removing any program you normally run in the AUTOEXEC.BAT file you feel may be wreaking havoc. You can also run Windows manually with any of the switches, detailed earlier in this chapter.

But you face limitations here, in addition to the ones I mentioned previously. You can't test device drivers, because those usually cannot be executed from DOS itself, and you may need to point to directories on your PC normally found in the PATH= statement in the AUTOEXEC.BAT, because your system won't know to try to find them without the PATH=.

To clean boot in Windows 95 or Windows 98:

1. Reboot the PC.

2. From the boot menu, if configured, choose Option 7 (Safe Mode Command Prompt Only), which bypasses the files in question, or choose Option 3 (Safe Mode), which also bypasses the configuration files but loads Windows in Safe Mode, if possible.

   or

   If your system is not configured to automatically bring up the boot menu, press F8 when you see "Starting Windows..." then choose Options 7 or 3, as indicated above.

TROUBLESHOOTING FROM WINDOWS SAFE MODE

Windows 95 and 98 allow you to boot in a special mode known as Windows Safe Mode. It's meant to help you get past certain boot problems temporarily while giving you access to your system to make changes. It's definitely well-suited for working with several hardware-related issues, but other reasons include:

◄ Observation of repeated of PC "hangs," where the PC seems locked in a prolonged waiting state

◁ Loss of some to a serious amount of Windows functionality

◁ When Setup hangs during the first reboot after it's commenced

◁ Presence of various (perhaps seemingly unrelated) error messages

The advantages of Safe Mode is that it can bypass some of the usual suspects in why such problems occur. For example, using Windows in Safe Mode:

◁ Ignores the DOS configuration files and any programs they may load

◁ Can bypass Registry damage

◁ Ignores issues with troublesome drivers

◁ Substitutes a driver for a standard VGA video adapter instead of the video board-specific driver your PC normally loads (and video drivers can be responsible for many of the issues described)

Once you boot into Safe Mode, you should be able to access the Control Panel to check system resources, check drivers and update or remove them as necessary, modify device property settings, and do other changes. Be aware that there are three types of Safe Mode you can employ:

1. Safe Mode itself, which boots Windows but loads only essential, safe drivers to overcome certain conflicts.

2. Safe Mode with network support adds real-mode support for both your network (if you have one) and network interface cards (NIC). Drivers used here are very limited, so plan accordingly.

3. Safe Mode Command Prompt ignores your DOS configuration files and boots not to Windows but to the DOS 7 command prompt.

NOTE You need to be aware that Device Manager may look slightly different in Safe Mode, so become familiar with how Device Manager stores information before you use Safe Mode.

Occasionally, you can get into a situation where you find that despite your best efforts, you cannot get Windows to start up even in Safe Mode. When this occurs, the likeliest suspects are as follows:

◁ A serious hardware conflict preventing even Safe Mode

◁ Some setting in the file MSDOS.SYS needs to be modified

◀ A virus of some type

◀ Incorrect current CMOS settings

◀ A video problem that requires a change of drivers to VGA.DRV or VGA.VXD from the Windows installation CD-ROM

If all else fails, your only recourse here is to try installing Windows to a new folder.

TROUBLESHOOTING THROUGH WINDOWS PROTECTION ERRORS IN WINDOWS 95/98

One of the more ominous greetings you may receive right after Windows 95 or 98 loads is either one of these:

```
When initializing device (device name) Windows Protection Error
```

or

```
Windows Protection Error
```

It not only sounds bad, it can be a bit elusive in ferreting out, since a host of things could be responsible. Basically, it's warning you that before it loaded, it encountered a serious error that resulted in a failure to load a virtual device driver.

One likely candidate is a physical I/O or memory address conflict, and this should be ruled out early on, using the techniques already mentioned for working with Device Manager. If no conflict is seen, consider these possibilities:

◀ *Plug and Play BIOS function is not working properly.* May need CMOS checked, may need BIOS upgrade, may need motherboard replaced.

◀ *A virus or other damage-causing event has infected and/or corrupted. COMMAND.COM or WIN.COM.* Virus scan or check these files and replace as necessary.

◀ *Wrong settings in CMOS are wreaking havoc, usually related to built-in peripheral devices (hard drives, cache settings, etc.).* Evaluate them and adjust accordingly.

◀ *The Windows Registry has become corrupted or damaged.* See Chapter 8 on the Registry.

◄ *Malfunctioning system cache or memory.* May need replacement, if possible.

◄ *Conflict between a real-mode and a protected-mode driver vying for control.* Isolate which and remove or adjust one.

◄ *SYSTEM.INI file is loading a driver for which a protected-mode driver has already been loaded.* Evaluate SYSTEM.INI and modify as needed.

◄ *Perhaps irreparable failure of the motherboard.* Replace mother-board.

To narrow down the source of the problem, first try booting Windows in Safe Mode. You may see the error disappear as soon as you load Safe Mode.

If it is not resolved, or returns when you reboot into normal mode, and your PC is Plug and Play enabled, it may be wise to try a fresh reinstall of Windows using the following command:

```
Setup /p I
```

If still not resolved, verify your BIOS settings, paying close attention to anything normally turned on or off that is now reversed.

Should you still not find resolution, you may want to try installing a clean copy of Windows to a new, empty folder on your hard disk. Run Setup, then select Custom Installation. Do *not* allow Windows Setup, however, to detect the hardware connected to your PC. Instead, select only a minimal hardware configuration to launch with, to include the mouse, the keyboard, and the standard VGA video adapter. Should even this fail, there's a hardware failure occurring, which you must locate and repair or replace.

Microsoft Knowledge Base notes that a VxD generating an error can be any VxD, either one installed by default or through a third-party (.386) driver that is loading in the SYSTEM.INI file. If you can't figure out which it is through other clues, you want to initiate a BOOTLOG file, which you can then review to see which driver was the last driver to initialize. This is more typically a driver problem than an actual hardware failure.

Also, it is possible to receive a Windows protection error when you first restart Windows 95 or 98 immediately after installing a program or making a configuration change to your computer. This could resolve by itself on the very next boot. You may not want to make serious adjustments until you try this, though it may be that the changes made invoked a driver, or a switch setting that Windows found too incompatible to cope with, and these need to be evaluated, as instructed above.

TROUBLESHOOTING PROTECTED-MODE DRIVER ISSUES

You may run into a situation where Windows will only load if you choose No when prompted whether to load all Windows drivers. Here's the work-around to try to get back from this:

1. Launch Windows in Safe Mode.
2. Use your right mouse button to click My Computer, then click on Properties from the menu that appears.
3. From the Device Manager tab, you may then disable any devices from the following categories:
   Display (video) adapters
   Hard disk controllers
   Mouse
   PCMCIA (PC Card) socket
   SCSI controllers
   Floppy disk controllers
   Keyboard
   Network adapters
   Ports
   Sound, video and game controllers

THE ROLE OF HARDWARE PROFILES

It's always wise to make a copy of the Registry files, as discussed in detail in Chapter 8, before you use Safe Mode to do anything like a Registry modification, if that's where your errors point you toward.

TROUBLESHOOTING MS-DOS COMPATIBILITY MODE ON HARD DISKS— WINDOWS 95 AND WINDOWS 98

If you notice a slowdown in drive performance, try checking under the Performance tab in System Properties. You may find it reports that one of more of your drives is running in MS-DOS Compatibility Mode. This could indicate it's simply in use by the file system or virtual memory, but it can also spell a problem.

You may also be greeted by an error message stating:

```
Error: Compatibility Mode Paging reduces overall system performance
```

MS-DOS Compatibility Mode can happen for a few different reasons, which include:

◀ *A serious resource conflict between the hard disk controller and some other hardware device installed to your system.* You need to check your system resources to see who is using what then reassign resources accordingly.

◀ *Your hard disk controller was not recognized by Windows.* This could be because it's nonstandard or proprietary, doesn't have the right driver, or the controller (or its connection) is bad and needs replacement.

◀ *The controller was removed from the current configuration/profile in Device Manager.* This could be caused by a problem that cropped up during the last boot or last work session.

◀ *The Windows protected-mode driver for the hard disk controller is either corrupted or missing entirely.* Needs replacement.

◀ *Windows detected 32-bit program protected-mode drives on an unsupported configuration or incompatible or unsupported hardware.* This is one to call the manufacturer on.

◀ *Windows balked because an "unsafe" device driver, a memory-resident program or TSR conflict, or a virus that is hooked to the INT21h or INT13 chain (responsible for booting drives) is interfering prior to Windows loading.*

MS-DOS Compatibility Mode can be troublesome to overcome, because as seen above, so many things can be the source of the problem. So you need to step through the process, evaluating conditions as you go. Here are some methods for resolving this, as presented in the Microsoft Knowledge Base:

1. First, double-click on the System icon in Control Panel, choose the Performance tab, and determine which drive(s) is running in Compatibility Mode and if it gives you an indicator why.

2. Second, check to make sure the controller for the drive in question is listed in Device Manager. If it isn't, try installing by double-clicking on the Add New Hardware icon in Control Panel. If you still can't find the controller listed, try running the Add New Hardware wizard again. This time, don't let Windows try to detect what you have. Instead, manually select the controller from the list given. If yours isn't provided in the list, contact your controller manufacturer immediately to find out if there is a protected-mode driver or even a Windows 3.1x 32-bit disk access driver available you can try to use instead.

3. If the hard disk controller is showing a Red X, this means it's been removed from the current hardware configuration/profile. To get around this, look under Properties for this controller in Device Manager, then click the checkbox that corresponds to the current hardware profile.

4. If the hard disk controller listed in Device Manager shows instead a yellow exclamation point, the problem is a) a hardware conflict of some sort involving IRQ, DMA, or I/O resources with those of another hardware device, b) under File System properties, the option "disable all 32-bit protected-mode disk drivers" is selected, or c) the protected-mode driver is missing or corrupted.

   To change a), you need to resolve any hardware resource conflicts, as previously instructed.

   To change b), you need to uncheck the "disable all 32-bit protected-mode disk drivers" option by going to Control Panel, double-clicking on the System icon, choosing the Performance tab, and then selecting File System (this option is listed on the Troubleshooting tab beneath File System properties).

   To change c), double-check to make certain the protected-mode driver is indeed present and located in the Windows\System\ IOSUBSYS directory. If it is not, you need to get a copy there. If it is present, you need to check to see whether it is working properly and loading by running a BOOTLOG. If this log shows an Init Failure/Load Failure message for the driver in question, the driver may be damaged and need replacement. But if it shows an InitComplete-Success message, you need to jump to the IOS.LOG, mentioned earlier. Remember, this log runs whenever a drive is forced into MS-DOS Compatibility Mode. Carefully evaluate the first few lines for an indication of why the driver may not load.

5. Next, look at your SYSTEM.INI file to see if a Mh32bit.386 driver is being loaded, such as device=mh32bit.386 (this can indicate that a driver for an incompatible drive like the MicroHouse EZ-Drive has been found but its driver has not been removed during the Windows Setup).

6. Contact your drive manufacturer for support on dealing with their drives in MS-DOS Compatibility Mode. It's possible that you can get protected-mode, 32-bit disk access by getting a protected-mode driver from the manufacturer, or by disabling any extra features on the controller itself such as caching, special operating modes or transfer rates (for ESDI, IDE, or SCSI), or system BIOS (IDE only).

TIP The IOS.INI file contains a list of drivers judged safe by Windows and loaded. It should be identical to drivers and programs found in CONFIG.SYS and AUTOEXEC.BAT—from which the list is compiled—along with their corresponding protected-mode driver.

For examples of troubleshooting various types of hardware devices, read Chapter 11, "Troubleshooting the Dirty Dozen."

CHAPTER *6*

Particular Issues in 32-Bit Operating Systems

Topics in this chapter include the following:

◀ Understanding the integration necessary in 32-bit Windows

◀ Issues with device-specific 32-bit drivers

◀ NT and device drivers

◀ Issues with OEM hardware and nonstandard hardware

◀ Issues with the Windows Registry

◀ Issues with a multiboot environment

◀ Coming trends: Merced and the 64-bit operating system

Consider this a midway chapter, where a summary takes place of what has been covered, along with a refocusing of what we need to fully understand before we are done. Also, since the majority of people reading this will undoubtedly be using Windows 95/98, as opposed to 16-bit Windows 3.1x or Windows NT 4 (or 5), this contains a good deal of information specific to these operating system versions. Windows 95/98 expands on much of what we saw in Windows 3.1x, and then the rules get a bit more complicated once we move to Windows NT.

Because Windows is an integrated operating system, every component must have the same set of facts (this printer is attached, that IRQ is unavailable, use this modem as the default, Internet Explorer 4.0 is installed as the Internet connection software) in order for Windows—and you—to be able to work properly. As we delve deeper into hardware configuration issues in the remainder of this book, you will see that even hardware installations under Plug and Play sometimes require you to check one or more areas for consistency of information. Certain PCI bus devices and processes, for example, may require not only addition to the system through the operating system's PnP interface, which is fairly automatic, but also adjustments to CMOS to alter BIOS settings (acknowledging the presence of bus-mastered drives or specifically assigning an IRQ to PCI rather than ISA). You may also need to double-check the resources assigned under Device Manager, and you may need to edit the Windows Registry to make changes for a deleted driver or an added option that the Registry didn't adjust by itself.

It's not at all that uncommon, for instance, to find that a modem you have previously removed and replaced with another still has its driver acknowledged and loading in the Windows Registry. You may not notice because the new modem is functioning perfectly (which means you're just wasting Registry space), or you may notice because Windows gets confused and tries to handle either both devices or neither of them.

Unfortunately, the system still relies on you as master conductor to make sure all the bases are covered, and part of the reason why a few specific concepts—like backups, Registry care, and removing "automatic" settings for things during troubleshooting—are getting hammered on in this book. The better you can familiarize yourself with your total system—BIOS, hardware, and operating system—the better control you will be able to exert.

Proper Installation and Deletion

Here, we're going to walk through both software and hardware considerations, since if you muck up a software removal badly enough, it will impede your ability to use the hardware. With software, the rule is simple: Don't just delete a program as we sometimes did with earlier versions of Windows. Applications and programs don't usually install themselves as freestanding entities (and if they do, they are generally DOS programs). A record of their existence and loading needs may be written to several different .INI and other configuration files, as well as to the Windows Registry itself. Even when you follow the rules, you may still be left having to prune residual components of a long-deleted application out of your system. Why? Some software is written better than other software, and some programs establish a lot fewer "hooks" in the operating system than others. If you have many hooks, you have many things to try to unhook to make an application completely vacate the premises upon removal.

With hardware, you need to make certain that when you add a device, every component of your system that needs to know about its existence does, and is configured properly for its use. Likewise, when you remove the device, you also have to make certain that all these elements again know of its absence, and that no leftover drivers or indicators or stray references remain behind to confuse Windows.

SOFTWARE

When you add software to Windows 3.1x, it's a fairly simple process—if the program or application's installation routine was written well. These routines will sometimes load Windows, if it's not already loaded, hook the software into Windows' initialization files so Windows is aware it has a new program onboard, and then set itself up with an icon in the proper Windows group (Applications, Games, and so on).

In Windows 95 and 98, you can add new programs one of two ways, which hopefully will accomplish the same result (forgive me, spending my entire adulthood with PCs has left me cynical). The first is just launching the install program (often named Setup or Install) by double-clicking on it from Windows Explorer. You can also select Open from the File menu, then provide the location and filename, or you can choose Start|Run and then supply the same information. Any of these will do the trick in most instances. The actions initiate a process where the files (if more than one is stored in a single compressed file format, which is what is commonly done) are expanded and copied to a fresh directory/folder or subdirectory. If the directory or folder you want to install the program to does not exist, the installation program handles making it. Then links in and to Windows configuration files are created to record the program's existence, and finally, the program is added to the menu of programs available when you click on the Start button and select Programs.

The second way to install a program is by using the Add/Remove Programs option in Windows Control Panel. Just double-click on its icon, then

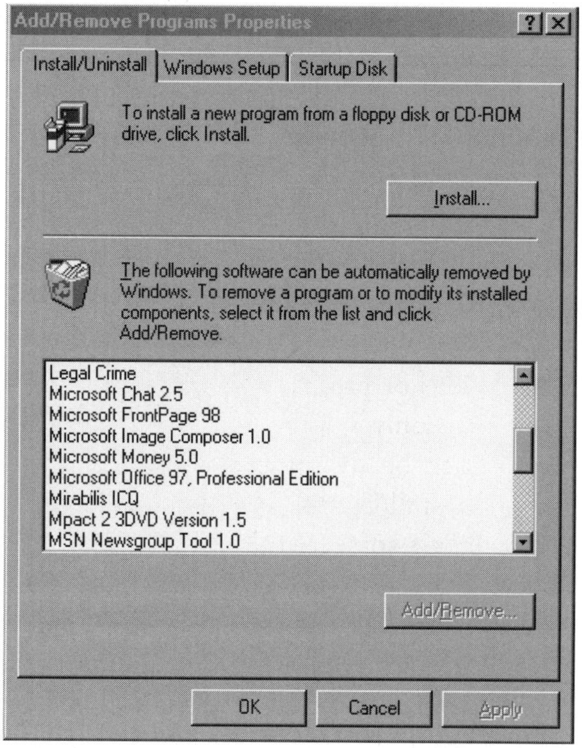

Figure 6.1 Add/Remove Programs/Install/Uninstall screen.

choose the Install/Uninstall tab, shown in Figure 6.1. Where it says "To install a new program from a floppy disk or CD-ROM drive, click Install," do so. Then provide the appropriate medium containing the program or application to install. Many recommend this as the preferred method, since it removes some of the variables present in depending on another software publisher's install routine.

Bear in mind, however, that only 32-bit programs and applications will install themselves in a fully Windows 95/98 compatible way. Either 16-bit, Windows 3.x, or DOS programs will usually *not* be available either from the Add/Remove Programs list under Control Panel or reside in the Programs list available once you click on the Start button. You have to manually remove these if no uninstaller routine is provided with the program or application (check the documentation for specifics). But the potential exists that something related to this program may have found its way into your Windows Registry and may scream an error later on, post-removal, when Windows tries to acknowledge something no longer present.

If what you need to install or reinstall is a component of Windows itself—Dial-up Networking or Multimedia, for example—you want to double-click on Add/Remove Programs in Control Panel, then choose the Windows Setup tab instead of Install/Uninstall, then select the component(s) you want to install. You can also *remove* components from this screen.

To remove 32-bit applications or programs other than from the Windows Setup screen, which covers only Windows operating system components, again, simply double-click on the Add/Remove Programs icon in Control Panel, and select the Install/Uninstall tab. Find the program you want to remove in the list (there are some that will not be there, like poorly behaved Windows-based software and 16-bit programs originally written for Windows 3.1x) and highlight it. The Add/Remove button will become available. Click on it. Windows will confirm that you want to remove this program. If you are sure, choose Yes (or No if you are not). Windows will then attempt to remove the program and any traces that remain in the operating system.

You may, however, receive a message stating that not all components could be removed. Sometimes, this will not be a big deal, because some little traces may not affect Windows performance or generate later error messages. But other times, they lead to random error messages of files or drivers or components not found. When this occurs, you need to begin tracing through the Registry (more information is provided later in this chapter and in some detail in Chapter 8), configuration files like SYSTEM.INI, and so on to root them out and remove them.

So what happens if you get into a situation where you deleted the program or application without removing it first? In my experience, the best thing to do is go to the Add/Remove Programs icon in Control Panel and try to remove the entry from there, as explained above. You may get an error message telling you this is impossible to do. If so, try installing again the program you are trying to remove, and then use the Remove option under the Add/Remove Programs icon in Control Panel. Reinstalling it should reunite links to the program with the program itself, and the results should be a lot cleaner when you try to remove it the correct way.

HARDWARE

When you add or remove hardware, it basically becomes your de facto job to check to make sure it's installed properly, that all references to its resources are correct, or all traces of its existence are removed.

Issues related to Drivers and Hardware

The arrival of Microsoft Windows 95 and 98 brought certain standards to hardware drivers really not present before. Windows NT 5.0 will extend those standards farther still. One reason for this, of course, is the introduction of Plug and Play support into the operating system. PnP hardware, as I'll cover more deeply in Chapter 7, packs encoded information identifying it to the system as part of the attempt to allow the hardware to be recognized and configured appropriately. This is one of the features that distinguishes a PnP device from non-PnP.

Yet the device and the operating system need an interface between them to work properly. This interface helps take the normal operating as well as special features of a particular device and translate them, if you will, into information that can then be used by the operating system in interacting with the hardware. Before PnP and Windows 95/98, drivers tended to be more hit-or-miss. By this, I mean that the major general rule for them in use was that they let the device be operated mostly as desired within the Windows (and DOS) environment. Some of these drivers worked very well and some of them worked extremely badly.

Because Windows (and DOS) had no idea really what you were installing, it had to rely upon what you—and the device driver—told it you had connected. If you didn't manually add a driver for something you installed, it was like you had never installed anything at all; it wouldn't be seen when you attempted to access it, and it certainly would not work. This method also allowed a less knowledgeable user to install the wrong driver. From a tweaking perspective, this could work out great because it means that, if necessary (and it if worked), you could fool Windows into thinking it was using a driver for the product you installed when you were actually using a competing product's better driver. Thus, you could easily buy a cheap clone of a name brand laser printer and forego the clone maker's sloppier driver in favor of the name brand's superior one that gave you nicer performance with a few dollars saved.

For that matter, previous versions of Windows and DOS would let you install not only the wrong driver, but also the wrong device totally. You could theoretically install a modem driver when what you really needed to install was a printer. You might get annoying error messages and the modem setup didn't work nor, of course, did the printer. But for the most part, you could still work.

TIP Windows 3.x drivers have the .386 extension ending their filenames, while Windows 95/98 virtual device drivers use .VxD as their file extension. The "x" in VxD is a variation replaced by the type of device driver it is. For example, a virtual printer driver would end in the three-letter extension .VPD.

PnP helps make Windows smarter, however. So when you install a modem on a serial or COM port, Windows should be able to tell that you have a modem on a serial port. Even if you try to forcibly add a printer instead, Windows will keep pestering you that it's found a new modem on a COM port and wouldn't you *really* like to install it now. There are exceptions when you have to walk Windows through to recognizing a device, but that may often be because of a poor driver, poor information about the device itself, or nonstandard hardware not strictly intended for use with a 32-bit PnP-aware operating system like Windows 95 and 98.

Another headache with Windows 3.x-era drivers was that they were statically loaded and were memory hogs, using up vital resources all the time Windows was in use. The release of Windows 95 in August 1995 brought with it universal device/minidriver architecture that finally made it much easier for hardware manufacturers to provide better and better interpreted information about the precise type of device and its features. A universal device driver is much like it sounds: a rather generic type of hardware device driver that tries to cover the basic needs of all the types of devices within its class, be it sound or video adapters, printers or modems. If it's a modem you're installing, a universal driver will meet the basic needs of a modem driver, allowing it to dial out, for example, in a Windows application like HyperTerminal or Dial-Up Networking.

But if the modem has some nice extra options like voice/speakerphone capability or special error correction, the universal driver ignores those. It's not programmed to try to make the modem do any more than the basics of what most other modems can do, such as follow the rules for AT commands. A minidriver, on the other hand, can tailgate on a universal driver, picking up device-specific features the universal driver could not address. This permits customization to fit the exact components of the device.

Completely new to consumer Windows in Windows 95 were virtual device drivers, or VxDs. These are 32-bit protected-mode Windows drivers that permit Windows to make use of one of the resource components of your PC, such as a piece of hardware or an installed software, in such a way that more than one application can use it simultaneously. This is necessary in a multitasking environment, which Windows 95 represented but was not a full practitioner of.

Unlike Windows 3.x's statically loaded hardware drivers, Windows 95's and 98's load dynamically. This means Windows only loads the ones necessary at any specific time and doesn't waste precious resources on those not needed for a particular task. On a slow or overtaxed machine, you might notice the time and overhead when one is loaded dynamically, but it's better than having resources wasted 100 percent of the time for something demanding resources just 10 percent of the time.

In Windows NT 4.0, you have an additional layer built in between the operating system itself and the hardware it runs on. This is the hardware abstraction layer, or HAL, which is interpreter of sorts between the device drivers for a particular piece of hardware and the central processing unit. HAL acts as a layer of protection in this capacity because it prevents a bad device driver or one simply misbehaving from rendering the whole NT system unstable. This helps keep NT from crashing on you and is part of why NT has something of a reputation as a "bulletproof" operating system (bullet-retardant may be more apt).

But in order to ensure the stability possible with HAL and, in turn, with NT itself, some sacrifices are made, including support for other Windows version drivers (3.x, 9x), as well as drivers written for some devices under earlier versions of NT itself (mostly printer and video drivers). Wherever possible—and even if it means getting to know your hardware manufacturer's tech staff on a first-name basis as you pester them for it—you want drivers for your hardware that are specifically written for Windows NT 4.0. Anything short of this should be considered a short-term bandage that should be treated as soon as possible. It's not that Windows 9x drivers won't work with NT 4, it's that you will get the best and most stable performance with NT drivers for the hardware.

The best way to try to guarantee that you will have NT 4-specific device drivers is to use products listed as supporting them in Microsoft's NT Hardware Compatibility List (HCL). You can find a copy on your Windows NT 4 CD or visit the Web-based listing at *http://www.microsoft.com/hwtest/hcl*. Also, you can find a list of more than 100 products known to be *incompatible* with Windows NT 4.0 by checking out *http://www.conitech.com/windows/ntwanted.html*. Also, familiarize yourself with the manufacturers' Web sites and see what technical data, as well as updated drivers, for NT they offer. Until you do some research, it may pay to *not* purchase a piece of hardware for your NT system until you're sure that the manufacturer directly supports NT 4.0 or you have located a workaround driver for the device.

Partly because NT is not a PnP operating system, and partly because it's NT, which is a more powerful operating environment packed with both more complexity and safeguards, NT won't install at setup all the device drivers you will need to work with it on a regular basis. Among the devices it won't install drivers for are important items such as your hard disk and video, your pointing device, and your network interface card (NIC), if you have one. You can find out more about how these drivers can be loaded in Chapter 9, "OS: Starting Over from Scratch."

A note about OEM versus retail issues in hardware:

While this is not specific to 32-bit Windows, please be aware that there are often serious differences between a full retail version of a product and the OEM, or original equipment manufacturer's, version. The latter may have fewer (or sometimes more) features, proprietary tweaking or settings, and may need different drivers.

OEM hardware is in abundance: Various hardware manufacturers produce specific versions of their product for specific third-party companies. Examples of this might be a WinModem designed by 3Com specifically for use in Dell computers or an Adaptec SCSI adapter produced specifically for inclusion in SCSI scanner packages.

OEM versions often have a price advantage, but they can sometimes be trickier to configure or replace. If you have particular difficulty with an OEM hardware device, you may want to consider trying a full retail version, just to see if the difference means a conflict or inability to operate is overcome. Also, double-check that you are using the correct drivers for your OEM device (and your operating system version), and consult the manufacturer's Web site for any technical suggestions.

NOTE Issues related to the Windows Registry will be covered in some detail in Chapter 8. Do not, by any means, limit your education of the Windows Registry to this chapter, because the Registry is both a very large and complex beast. Most texts can only skim the surface of its fine details and listings.

TIP Keep your modifications tidy. Because information related to the system is indexed into your Registry and .INI files, and we've already talked a bit about the fact that Windows can get confused, it's important for you to double-check your modifications. For example, if you remove a piece of hardware, make certain you have deleted the driver from Device Manager. If you also installed DOS drivers, remove references to these in CONFIG.SYS and AUTOEXEC.BAT. Then use the information you learn in Chapter 8 to look at the Registry to make certain no lingering references to that specific device (or its associated software) linger. If the hardware came with its own software, make certain that is removed as well, using its Uninstall utility or, preferably, the Add/Remove Programs option in Windows Control Panel. In addition, be sure to document changes so you remember them later. This will come in handy if you have recurrent error messages relative to the removed hardware or software, as well as to serve as an example to follow for later changes.

Issues Related to a Multiboot Environment

It seems to be more and more common that people choose to run the more regular consumer-oriented Windows 95/98 interface with the power and stability pretty much inherent in Windows NT 4.0. You may choose to do this as well—even mixing Windows of various types with other operating systems, like the popular Linux, a PC Unix clone.

Certain rules apply to multiple-boot operating systems:

◁ Remember, each device must be installed to each operating system, or it won't be available for use; similarly with uninstalling them.

◁ Existing or possible conflicts should be considered and checked for under each operating system.

◄ Applications must be installed to each operating system to be available in each operating system—but check, since some may not work with all operating systems or operating system versions.

◄ Make certain you have access to hardware drivers for each device under each operating system. For example, if you decide to have a multiple-boot scenario between Windows 98, Windows NT, and Linux and want to use your printer under all three operating systems, you need printer drivers for all three.

◄ While you don't have to store each operating system on its own separate physical drive, you should install each to its own separate drive partition for best compatibility and reduced risk potential.

◄ Meet or exceed the minimum requirements for the greatest of the two or more operating systems you want to make available in a multiple-boot situation; if you take the time to go to a multiboot environment, don't squeeze yourself by barely getting by with your equipment or RAM—do it right from the start.

◄ Research known problems and incompatibilities between the operating systems desired, as well as the hardware and applications you will equip each with, including those at references cited in Appendix B.

◄ Once you have multiple operating systems in place, remember to use only utilities with each designed specifically for use with each individual operating system.

Depending on which operating systems you plan to include on the same machine, you may need a third-party boot management system, such as System Commander, to permit this to work properly.

SETTING UP A MULTI-BOOT BETWEEN WINDOWS 95/98 AND WINDOWS NT 4.0:

For best results, each operating system you wish to install should be installed to its own partition, if not its own physical hard disk (the latter isn't necessary, but it may be more comfortable in the long haul.) If you need to use FDISK to create more partitions, remember that whatever you FDISK is wiped of its data. If you want to protect an existing operating system that resides on a hard disk you need to partition, you either lose the data (it could be restored from a full backup, of course) or use a third-party commercial product like PowerQuest's Partition Magic.

Once partitions are set up, you install the desired operating systems, one to each partition, as you want them designated. Then you need to let the two or more operating systems residing on their different partitions know about each other, so to speak. At least, let the system know at boot that there is a choice of operating systems to make as the PC boots. This is done by editing the BOOT.INI, a file created during Setup and stored hidden in the C:\ or root directory of your master hard disk.
To do this:

1. Launch Windows Explorer from the Start button by choosing the Programs option and selecting Windows Explorer from the menu choices.

2. In Windows Explorer, pull down the View menu, select Options, then click on Show All Files.

3. Check the option Hide File Extensions for Known File Types—this should be unchecked. Click OK.

4. Locate the BOOT.INI file by checking the C:\ or root directory, then highlight it from the list, right click on it, then select Properties.

5. Click the Read-Only checkbox to clear this specification. Click OK.

6. Next, right-click the BOOT.INI file again and select Copy from the option list. Then right-click a blank area of the Windows Explorer dialog box, pull down the Edit window, and choose Paste (of Shift-Insert). This creates a copy of the existing BOOT.INI file and will be so named

7. Double-click on the original BOOT.INI file that will open it for editing.

8. Look for the section of the BOOT.INI labeled [operating systems], and amend it to include both the name and location of all operating systems being used. For example, if you are dual-booting Windows 95/98 and Windows NT 4.0, you would list:

```
C:\Winnt="Windows NT 4.0"
C:\="Microsoft Windows"
```

9. Save your changes, and close the BOOT.INI file.

10. Right-click the newly edited BOOT.INI file, and choose Properties from the menu.

11. Re-check the Read-Only checkbox, then click OK.

When you boot up again, you should have a choice of the operating systems installed to pick from.

SPECIAL ISSUES WITH WINDOWS 98 AND WINDOWS NT ON THE SAME SYSTEM

If you plan to install Windows 98 on a system already running Windows NT 4.0, be aware that Windows 98 cannot be installed *over* NT 4.0. You can reformat and start fresh, or you can set up Windows 98 and Windows NT 4.0 to coexist as dual operating systems.

If you choose the latter, install Windows 98 to a separate partition or hard disk with Windows NT 4.0 already installed. Once installed, Setup automatically adds Windows 98 to Windows NT 4.0's boot menu, which then permits multiple-boot sessions between NT 4.0 and Windows 98.

Windows NT 4.0 should work fine, but if you get an error message on it next time you try to load it, try booting from the Windows NT 4.0 recovery disks. If you choose Repair from the listing, Windows NT 4.0's boot files should be restored. It is also possible that in installing Windows 98, you may get hit with an error message, such as this:

```
Setup has detected that your hard disk has a 64K-cluster FAT partition.
Because ScanDisk does not work on disks with this cluster size, Setup
cannot continue. To complete Setup, you must repartition your hard disk,
format the partition with a FAT file system that has a cluster size of
32K or less and then restart Setup.
```

Microsoft recommends that you instead run Setup using the "is" parameter, as in:

```
SETUP /is
```

This forces ScanDisk not to run, thereby avoiding this problem.

NOTE Windows NT 4.0 doesn't "see" FAT32 drives under Windows 95b/c or Windows 98. This is expected to be addressed in the release of Windows NT 5.0 later this year (1999) or sometime in 2000, and is working under the NT beta as of this writing.

CHAPTER 7

Additional Issues in Adding Hardware

Topics covered in this chapter include:

◀ Fuller understanding of Plug and Play technology and how it affects our hardware installations

◀ ISA considerations

◀ PCI as the newer bus and how it affects configuration and hardware issues

◀ Added benefits to PCI, including bus mastering

◀ Tweaking your BIOS for best PCI bus configurability

◀ Role of Accelerated Graphics Port

◀ The here and now of USB technology, and the future potential of FireWire/IEEE 1394 and Device Bay

In Chapter 2, we walked most of the way through where PC bus architecture has been since the very early days of its design and discussed why we are still stuck with some of the slowness and limitations—particularly because of compatibility issues. Now let's look at the here and now. In this chapter, we'll look at Plug and Play technology and the PCI chipset and bus, then we'll move right through to AGP, universal serial bus (USB), FireWire/IEEE 1394, and beyond.

Plug and Play (PnP) Technology

PC hardware installation is rarely considered a fun job by anyone's estimation, be they novice or seasoned technician. Even if you don't mind wielding a screwdriver and a grounding strap to pull the cover and push or pull on adapter cards, that's only half the battle. Getting both your PC and operating system to recognize the presence (or the absence if you remove something) of a new hardware device has been a drag, as well.

Plug and Play has been around with us for several years, in a slow evolution from before it had an operating system (Windows 95 was the first) to fully support it. It was developed in 1993 in a cooperation between Microsoft, Compaq, and Intel to help set a standard by which adding new hardware would be less of a hassle. By encoding information about the device—who made it, and what it needs to do—and by placing it right on the device, they proposed, they could get a PC to see a device and use it. This would be accomplished through a PC equipped with a similarly compliant operating system and BIOS, and would eliminate the need for special hardware installation routines or more exotic addition of the proper drivers to run the hardware. It would be Plug and Play's directive to try to reduce the user's need to worry about managing system resources and assigning interrupts, DMA channels, and I/O addresses, while keeping them free of conflicts between the various devices installed. (This also means not playing with jumpers and switches on the physical device itself.) The primary direction was clear: Get the newly installed device recognized and operational on the PC without a lot of extra requirements placed on the person doing the installation.

Plug and Play hasn't been our magical savior. We still need to understand some of what resides and functions within our PC's case, and we need to know how to swap equipment in and out properly. Plug and Play just tries to handle the device once the physical installation is complete.

Positive points go to Plug and Play for relative ease of use (if the install goes well the first time) and that it takes care of minor conflicts fairly reliably on its own. But to get best results, you need more than just a PnP-capable device; you need a host of support from other components of your PC environment. Even then, PnP won't work out your tougher conflicts; it leaves that for you to do. Thus, Plug and Play's role has been more of a promising assistant rather than a single great solution.

What makes Plug and Play hardware different is that (as intended) its adapters store information—such as serial number, vendor, other data—in nonvolatile memory that helps a PnP-capable computer recognize it and install it more readily than an unidentified device just plugged in somewhere. Also, whether you realize it or not, PC Card, formerly PCMCIA, devices are examples of Plug and Play devices. These are the small cards, which often look like thick credit cards, standardly used in portable PCs. They install similarly in Windows to other PnP devices.

One last bit of info: If you're wondering whether your BIOS is PnP-compatible, there's a free utility from Phoenix (the BIOS makers) named PNPBTST.EXE that allows you to test your system and report yea or nay. You may be able to upgrade your BIOS to PnP if it's not already, but you need to check with your motherboard manufacturer. Most BIOS firms write BIOS specifically designed for each motherboard manufacturer (with little tweaks or sometimes major adjustments over the generic BIOS release), so the folks responsible for your motherboard are apt to be more of a resource than those who wrote the BIOS itself.

NOTE Not all hardware is PnP-ready. While this technology was starting to be seen in the days of EISA and VLB, PnP was only added to some ISA devices later on. Even today's prevalent PCI devices are not always PnP-capable. If you specifically want PnP hardware, you need to check a product's specifications before you purchase.

COMPONENTS OF A PLUG AND PLAY SYSTEM

Remember that I said that there were three basic ways to change the settings on a piece of hardware: jumpers, DIP switches, or software "soft" controls, which act like you have changed either the jumpers or DIP switches physically. While the latter is the easiest method, you're also committed to keeping the floppy or CD-ROM containing the soft switch software along for the entire life of the piece of hardware.

Plug and Play takes the "soft" control concept one step further. You don't usually have to run separate software to get PnP devices working. They are set up automatically each and every time you boot up your computer. I'll explain that process more below.

There are three elements to a fully Plug and Play PC:

◄ *A Plug-and-Play-capable BIOS.* Some actually perform the initialization of PnP devices automatically, whether or not the operating system used supports PnP.

◄ *A Plug-and-Play-capable operating system.* You need an OS that is cognizant of the special function of PnP devices and that works with other PnP components to permit relative ease of installation and a reduction of conflicts that may occur between PnP and non-PnP hardware.

◄ *Plug-and-Play-ready hardware and drivers.* These must incorporate the technology necessary to allow these devices to be easily recognized and installed.

Now, you can have some elements of PnP in your PC without having all three components present at the same time. For example, you can usually install PnP hardware to a system without either a PnP BIOS or PnP-enabled operating system. You can also have a PnP operating system while running only old ISA cards. Or, you can have two components but not the final third. For best success, however, you need all three in your system. Each component provides a vital part: BIOS lets you set specific resources or handling at the base level of the PC long (relatively) before the operating system loads; the hardware and drivers provide information on what they are and how they should be configured best to work; and the operating system integrates what the other two components provide and delivers it out into a consistent graphical interface with hardware ready to use at a nanosecond's notice from any part of that operating system.

In theory, the more PnP is fully implemented in the operating system, in the BIOS, and in the hardware devices and their drivers, the fewer problems you should encounter. Theories are great, but in practical application, PnP isn't outrageously smart. It tries to do as much of the hardware configuration automatically for you as it can, but in truth, it won't solve messy conflicts between resources. You need to do that. What it does is try to save you from doing everything yourself, but it doesn't do everything for you.

There are other problems with PnP, and some of these actually apply to most devices. One is that a device can only function at its best if the driver supporting it provides all the right information. The best hardware in the world won't outperform bad drivers written for it. Keep this in mind when you purchase hardware: Find out what companies are known for putting out dependable, improved drivers on a timely basis for the products you're thinking of buying.

Another limitation is that PnP can't be superaggressive about seeking out the very best resource variables for your system. There are two reasons here. One is that it has to work alongside other hardware of varying obsolescence, on PC technology designed more than 7 years ago and that minted 7 days ago. It has to work around ISA, EISA, Micro Channel Architecture (MCA), and VESA local bus (VLB), as well as PCI. It also has to work under operating systems that don't directly support its technology (like DOS/Windows 3.1 and Windows NT 4.0) as well as those that do (Windows 95/98, Linux, OS/2). And it must work as reliably on your PC with your specific configuration as it does on someone else's PC with an entirely different configuration.

Even today, there are times when a PnP installation proves far more difficult than the old-fashioned ISA hardware additions, and I resort to jumpering (which takes the device out of PnP mode and into legacy mode) the card to get it to work as I want it to work. This is something you can consider on a particularly recalcitrant installation, but it's recommended that you exhaust usual resources to get it working properly in PnP mode before you move to the fallback position.

WHAT A PnP COMPUTER DOES ON BOOT

First, a Plug and Play-capable PC creates a table of resources available, which includes the system resources (IRQ, I/O, and DMA), excluding any of these needed by system devices like a timer or a controller to function. Next, it performs a dynamic scan of your system to determine which peripherals are PnP and which are not. At the same time, it assigns an ID to each peripheral located.

After this, the PnP PC loads the last-used Extended System Configuration Data, or ESCD, and then it compares the old with the current version. If the old and new ESCD match perfectly, the PC boot continues on its merry way.

The ESCD is a specially allocated 8 KB block of RAM, which is where information about your Plug and Play hardware is stored. To be accurate, more than PnP data is stored here, since it also provides information on non-PnP EISA, ISA, and PCI devices as well. It is found in the upper memory region (the 384 KB area between the first 640 KB and 1 MB of RAM, or E000-EDFF). It is usually located at address E:A000h and E:BFFFh.

But if differences are found, the PnP PC reconfigures ESCD completely. It rescans the table assembled in its first operation, basically ignores any settings in use by legacy or pre-PnP devices, and then uses what resources remain and parcels them out to each PnP device connected. This configuration is then saved (and becomes the ESCD used to compare against the new one in the next boot session), and the boot process to load Windows finishes.

When I said about that the PnP process basically ignores legacy-device resources; I should elaborate. It not so much ignores the settings; rather, it grabs the list of resources needed by legacy devices, assumes these are taken or reserved, and then assigns the PnP devices around these previous reservations.

PnP: DETECTION VS. ENUMERATION

You've already heard me describe detection and enumeration in previous chapters, so let me explain in more detail the differences between them. Hardware detection is the process by which your PC detects or recognizes the legacy or non-PnP devices attached to it. Enumeration, on the other hand, is the process by which your PC identifies the PnP components within your system, including any peripherals attached to PnP buses such as ISAPNP, PC Card (formerly PCMCIA) and PCI devices.

Hardware detection occurs solely when you either run Windows Setup or when you use the Add New Hardware wizard available in Windows Control Panel. It's not a process that is repeated each and every time your PC boots, which is where enumeration comes in. When detection does occur, however, it creates a file in the root directory of the boot drive named DETLOG.TXT (which you should seek out as another tool in hardware troubleshooting).

Unlike detection, enumeration *does* happen every time your PC reboots. It reruns the whole inventory each time your system boots, as well as whenever it detects that an alteration has been made to your PC's hardware configuration. As you can guess, people often say "detection" in referring to hardware when they really mean the process of enumeration.

ROLE OF CONFIGURATION MANAGER

Configuration Manager isn't a program you run but is loaded automatically by Windows 95/98 as part of Startup in the process of configuring the PC, the hardware, and the operating system to work in fairly intelligent unison.

It runs as soon as Windows' protected mode is initiated and operates as a sort of smart coordinator. If there's a PnP BIOS present, Configuration Manager extracts information from it and imports this into Windows, and the operating system coordinates information needed to begin work. If no PnP BIOS is found, Configuration Manager moves on to its next task: enumerating hardware devices and loading dynamic device drivers (static drivers load before protected mode launches), which in turn builds a PnP hardware tree.

PLUG AND PLAY BY OPERATING SYSTEM

DOS/Windows 3.1

Neither DOS nor Windows 3.1x (and remember here, DOS is the operating system of record; Windows is a graphical operating environment sitting above DOS) is a Plug and Play environment. If you choose to add a PnP device to your Windows 3.1x system, you only have a few choices. You may add the PnP hardware as is, and it should install, but as a "soft control," non-PnP device (a PnP BIOS alone may not succeed in helping a PnP device be better recognized under a non-PnP operating system). Or you can add implement a set that is composed of a configuration utility and a PnP-work-alike driver.

ICM is one such set developed by Intel as a generically written configuration management utility and driver—Intel Configuration Manager (ICM) and ISA Configuration Utility (ICU)—meant to provide a solution to using more of PnP cards' features under a non-PnP environment like DOS. Other companies have put out their own versions of this, including Creative Labs, which offers CTCM and CTCU.

Windows 95/98

Windows 95/98 is ready to go for PnP; no modifications are required. However, you need to make certain that (if your BIOS supports it), the PnP option has not been turned off by default in BIOS. If it's turned off in BIOS, the operating system may not be able to do its full job supporting PnP technology. Yet your BIOS may not have a setting for this because the BIOS is set to seek out PnP automatically. Check your motherboard documentation or the manufacturer's Web site if you have any questions. Also be aware that while Windows 95/98 configures and supports PnP devices in

Windows itself and DOS environments, it doesn't cover PnP in MS-DOS mode sessions.

Don't forget that you are still going to be responsible for double-checking the automatic recognition and configuration done by PnP by watching for resource conflicts in Device Manager.

Windows NT 4.0

Now that I've told you the industry wants you to see Plug and Play as a hardware tech's dream come true, let me fill you in on an ugly reality: Windows NT 4.0 does not support Plug and Play. Thankfully, this doesn't mean you're out of the ballpark with all PnP hardware devices. There is a workaround.

Included in the Windows 4.0 drivers library is a PnP enabler driver—Pnpisa.inf—designed to try to help NT detect and install Plug and Play devices. It is neither guaranteed to make PnP a snap to configure on an NT system nor does Microsoft support this driver. But it has helped out in several instances I'm aware of and is in regular use by many NT users.

However, this driver isn't loaded automatically, so you need to manually install it into NT if you want to attempt to make NT PnP hardware-aware. To try it, you need to find the file Pnpisa.inf on your Windows 4.0 CD-ROM in the drvlib\pnpisa\ <processor-type> folder, then:

1. Right-click on the highlighted pnpisa.inf file.

2. Choose Install from the menu that results.

3. Properly shut down and restart your PC.

4. On reboot, Windows NT may report that it has found new hardware devices. These are hopefully your PnP hardware devices missing from the last boot's detection. Future PnP installs may be eased, as well.

TIP For those who dual-boot either Windows 95 or Windows 98 with NT4.0: You may need to turn PnP support off in the BIOS to get a modem set up in NT. But if you do so, remember to go back afterwards and switch the PnP option back on for Windows 95 or 98's use. A friend doing this once forgot to switch the BIOS back and 98 acted like a chowderhead when she tried to get the system to find her printer. Once she remembered and reset the BIOS, all was well.

OPTIMUM PnP RESULTS

For optimum results with Plug and Play technology, there are three kinds of recommendations tendered:

◀ Try to work with a PC equipped with a PnP-compatible BIOS, PnP-supporting operating system, and PnP hardware with their specific device drivers.

◀ Keep PnP device drivers up-to-date

◀ Check Device Manager frequently to scan for possible conflicts created by a new device or newly modified resource configuration, as well as to remove old, unused device drivers that may consume resources for no good reason.

The latter brings up an important point discussed elsewhere. If you choose to simply disable a device driver, it may not return the resources allocated to it for your system to use elsewhere. If you have a sound card plugged into IRQ9, for example, and then choose to disable the driver for that sound card, Windows may continue to assume IRQ9 is taken. This means it won't assign it to another needy device, and you'll be down one IRQ that is connected to nothing.

What occurs is that as Windows 95/98 loads, it looks at the inventory of resources offered up by your PC and activates them on an as-needed basis. This leads us to the next issue, which is that even if you disable the device in CMOS (and in Device Manager), Windows ignores this setting and enumerates and loads the device in preparation for use anyway. Your solution for being completely certain an undesired piece of hardware is not configured to consume valuable resources as though it was supposed to operate is to:

1. Remove the device driver in Device Manager.

2. Disable any setting in CMOS that activates or enables the device and/or its slot (with PCI).

3. Disable the device in the current configuration for Windows. To do this, select Start|Settings|Control Panel. Double-click on the System icon.

4. Select the Device Manager tab, then clear the Original Configuration (Current) checkbox by clicking on it.

5. Click OK.

The alternative to the last part is to physically remove the hardware from the PC. Don't neglect to consult your documentation for any special removal instructions.

Paralleling this, realize that if you are using a PC equipped with a motherboard running a PnP-capable BIOS, it's possible that you will not be able to configure any device within Device Manager that has been disabled in CMOS. Trying to do this may result in an error message in the Status box that reads:

```
The device has been disabled in the hardware. In order to use this
device, you must re-enable the hardware. See your hardware documentation
for details (Code 29).
```

Unfortunately, this can occur even if your version of BIOS permits the preconfiguring of devices for the *next* time. The solution is to enable the device again in CMOS and then return to Device Manager after Windows loads again to configure the device's system resources appropriately.

PCI

Peripheral Component Interconnect, or PCI, was developed as the next step beyond ISA/EISA/MCA, addressing some of their bus limitations as well as punching graphics performance. Unlike the greedy ISA who demands a lot of the CPU's attention, PCI offers up a CPU-independent path for the transfer of signals and data between the processor and the peripherals connected to it. Towards that end, PCI is a fairly high-performance bus with some appreciable gains over earlier PCI bus architectures. But since it still has an ISA bus trailing along behind it, it has to make some accommodations. One of them is that it shares the very same device addressing space model as ISA.

UNDERSTANDING THE RELATIONSHIP BETWEEN ISA AND PCI CARDS IN INSTALLATION AND SYSTEM RESOURCE ASSIGNMENT

OK, the fact that you shouldn't share IRQs has been drummed into you by now, so let's complicate the rules. Not sharing IRQs is indeed the right course with ISA. However, multiple PCI devices *can* share an IRQ—it's one of the advantages of the PCI bus design. But they can only share an IRQ with other PCI devices; ISA devices must live on separate IRQs as a one-device-to-an-IRQ kind of bus. Admittedly though, PCI devices sharing a single IRQ is sometimes easier said than done, although sometimes it can be a breeze.

For example, one of my colleagues has one IRQ auto-assigned to be shared by four different devices: SCSI, video card, DVD decoder, and one more device. When you run out of IRQs on your system and you're using something like a very recent-vintage BIOS combined with Windows 98, they will act in concert to try to assign as many PCI devices to the same IRQ as possible to fit everything in. Doing it yourself may be less successful, and it may require a good deal of trial and error before you find a match that works well. Most agree that it's best, however, to avoid sharing such resources. Don't try to jam a lot of devices on one IRQ if you can avoid it, particularly if you have IRQs left available for assignment.

PCI didn't save us from the old limited hardware interrupt scheme altogether, but it does offer a lot more flexibility than ISA working within the same framework. It also gives Plug and Play systems more choices to work with when parceling system resources out to the various devices that need them.

NOTE EISA and MCA systems also permit sharing IRQs, but since we are mostly left with ISA, PCI, and beyond, this is my focus here.

If your motherboard offers a PCI bus, you have the ability to program some of the 16 (0 to 15) interrupts to use either PCI or ISA mode. What you can't do is make one single interrupt use both PCI and ISA mode simultaneously—this makes sense since confusion would result.

Starting with Windows 95b and continued in Windows 98, Microsoft introduced PCI bus interrupt request (IRQ) steering—it's not available in original release Windows 95 or its subsequent first service release issue. PCI steering allows Windows to dynamically assign (steer) PCI bus IRQs directly to PCI devices. The advantage here is that it gives the operating system room to work in refitting PCI IRQs used at the same time. It also tries to juggle both Plug and Play ISA and PCI system resources around older, non-PnP (legacy) ISA cards. Without PCI steering, Windows can only re-balance resources for PnP ISA IRQs in its quest for getting all devices assigned and operational. What you get from it is an operating system better able to resolve conflicts before they can affect your PC's performance.

PCI BASICS

PCI was the next in line to help conquer our difficulties with the line of small, slow PC buses. It's typically used in conjunction with an ISA bus, which remains for backward compatibility, and tries to work as fast as it can around the slow, old ISA. Your PC's BIOS (if equipped with a PCI bus) allows you to separate out IRQs intended for ISA use only and for PCI use only, as well as set variables for bus mastering (described in detail later in this section), read/write cycles, and more.

The original PCI design allows for a bus speed of 33 MHz, support for both 32- and 64-bit data paths (the first PC bus to allow this) and again, bus mastering, which can help system performance overall. How many devices a PCI bus can handle depends on the types of loads, or physical/ resource demands, placed on it by the hardware itself. Typically, a PCI bus can handle 10 loads per bus, of which the PCIset uses 3, leaving 7 available for hardware additions.

PCI bus slots (there are often at least four slots on a PCI motherboard; this may vary) are usually prioritized by the system itself, and Slot 1 usually gets the highest priority. Thus, it is important that you plan how you populate the bus slots, giving first attention to any devices that need greater priority of system responsiveness and placing them in Slot 1. Peripherals requiring increasingly less priority on the bus should fill the remainder.

One example of this is adding a 3D PCI card for video enhancement to a PCI bus PC with onboard video (video adapter built into the motherboard instead of available as a separate add-on card-style adapter). Should you place this card in a slot other than 1, you may reduce the effectiveness of the 3D add-on. This is because the priority of the onboard video may override a 3D PCI card installed to a lesser priority slot than 1, and the results could be a deleterious effect on VGA-type display.

> **TIP** Don't assume all PCI hardware devices are Plug and Play. Most are, but some are not. Most of the ones that aren't are based on the original PCI standard (PCI 2.0). If you want PnP capability, make sure the products you purchase specifically list PnP support in their documentation (or even right on the product box).

PCI 2.0 vs. PCI 2.1

PCI 2.1 is actually just an advancement to the original PCI bus specifications. These changes led to increased speed (33 to 66 MHz) and much improved bus transfer rates.

PCI STEERING AND IRQ HOLDERS

One of the questions asked most frequently by those newly familiarizing themselves with the information contained in Device Manager is, "What is this thing labeled IRQ holder for PCI Steering?" What it does is act like a reservation or placeholder, telling Windows this IRQ will be used for a PCI device specifically. (Device Manager is shown in Figure 7.1.)

Here's an example of what PCI bus steering does in resolving a system resource issue, provided in the Microsoft Knowledge Base:

◁ Disables the PCI device at its current address

◁ Locates an available interrupt or IRQ (for this example, let's say the device now residing on IRQ 9 needs to be moved to IRQ 10) to act as a PCI IRQ

◁ Assigns an IRQ holder or placeholder to IRQ 10 (in this example)

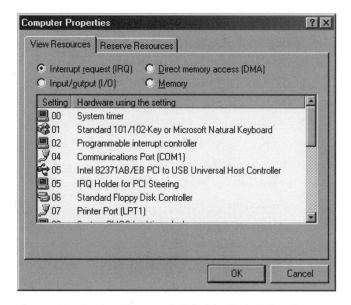

Figure 7.1   Device Manager/IRQ holder for PCI Steering.

◄ Removes any ISA holder placed on IRQ 10

◄ Automatically shuttles the PCI device assignment over to IRQ 10

◄ Reassigns IRQ 9 as an ISA IRQ

To check what hardware interrupts are designated for PCI-only mode use:

1. Choose Start|Settings|Control Panel, then double-click on the System icon.

2. Select the Device Manager tab, then double-click on the System Devices branch.

3. Double-click on the PCI Bus entry, then choose the IRQ Steering tab, which should report either:

IRQ Steering Enabled, or

IRQ Steering Disabled

Various reasons may exist for PCI IRQ Steering to be disabled, including the most obvious: that the Use IRQ Steering checkbox has not been properly selected. In Windows95b (OSR2), PCI IRQ Steering is disabled as the default setting, and you need to manually enable it to use this feature.

It's also possible that your BIOS just doesn't support PCI bus IRQ Steering. If your BIOS is PCI-compliant, it should support bus IRQ Steering. A program entitled PCIDIAG available from the PCI Special Interest Group (known as "pcisig") will allow you to test your BIOS for such compliance. You can check their Website *(http://www.pcisig.com/docs.html)*. Beyond this, you need to contact your motherboard or BIOS manufacturer to see if it's possible to upgrade your BIOS to support both overall PCI compliance as well as PCI bus IRQ Steering.

Also check to see if the Get IRQ table from Protected Mode PCIBIOS 2.1 Call checkbox is *not* selected.

Finally, for PCI bus IRQ Steering to work properly, an IRQ routing table must be provided to your operating system by the BIOS. The routing table contains data on exactly how the motherboard is configured to handle PCI IRQs. If it's missing or damaged, PCI bus IRQ Steering may not be available.

This routing table is critical, because Windows 95b and Windows 98

have to know how the motherboard wires each PCI expansion slot's interrupt pins to the PCI interrupt router's interrupt pins. Every PCI motherboard has at least one and usually more slots along with a PCI interrupt
router. While PCI itself doesn't limit itself to a maximum of four slots,
motherboard manufacturers often do to try to restrict loading problems
that can result from too many devices in too many slots. For each slot,
there are four interrupt pins, which help provide an internal interrupt system for PCI cards and PCI bus slots. These are identified as:

INTA#

INTB#

INTC#

INTD#

NOTE Usually, to keep from confusing these PCI internal interrupts with system IRQs, these
INTs are given letters A through D; however, some manufacturers use 1 through 4
instead. Don't confuse the PCI internal interrupts with IRQs, although there are
situations where specific PCI internal interrupts may be mapped to specific IRQs
(often 9 or 10, if available) if needed.

Similarly, the PCI interrupt router also offers interrupt pins, though not
always of a set number. These are identified as:

PIRQ#1

PIRQ#2

PIRQ#3

...and so on

These INT pins on the slots may be wired with other INT pins from the
same or adjoining slots, and these in turn may be wired to a PIRQ pin from
the interrupt router. Each different chipset offered by different vendors may
vary on which actual PIRQ value is assigned to each interrupt pin on each
interrupt router.

What happens is that the information needed on PCI IRQ routing
specifics is stored in a table, called the PCI IRQ Routing Table, in the
BIOS's ROM. Its objective is to identify the location of the PCI interrupt
router, as well as identify a compatible PCI interrupt router and the IRQs
specifically set to PCI mode use only. It also notes how each slot's interrupt

TABLE 7.1 Format for PCI IRQ Routing Table

Byte Offset	Size in Bytes	Name
TB:0	4	Signature
4	2	Version
6	2	IRQ table size
8	1	PCI interrupt router's bus
9	1	PCI interrupt router's DevFunc
10	2	PCI-only IRQs
12	4	Compatible PCI IRQ Router
16	4	Miniport data
20	11	Reserved
31	1	Checksum
32	16	1st slot entry
48	16	2nd slot entry
(N+1) * 16	16	Nth slot entry

pins are wired together in linked sets, and specifies which link connects to what interrupt pins on the interrupt router.

This information is listed in the routing table using the format shown in Table 7.1.

When PCI Devices Share an Interrupt

As mentioned, PCI devices are unique in that they can share one interrupt (IRQ) among multiple peripherals. When the IRQ is activated, the drive programs for the two adapters or peripherals are examined to determine which is on the bus and needing attention. The first live device found "wins" and is properly loaded to work.

In practical application, trying to accomplish this is not always worth the effort. One of the first things that can hurt your chances with it is a sloppily written device driver that may not permit its PCI device to interact cleanly and nicely with the IRQ. This means it can "burp" and confuse other PCI hardware devices trying to use the same IRQ. Also, every hardware device needs an interrupt handler it works in conjunction with in communicating with the system. When you have one interrupt responsible for multiple devices, you find that multiple interrupt handlers all linked in under that same interrupt. A poorly designed device driver could allow the device to fire an interrupt signal out along the bus prematurely, before the device has been properly linked to an interrupt handler. The operating system then begins scanning down its inventory of known interrupt handlers, looking for one that will identify itself as the correct handler for the device in question. But if no such link has been established before the signal sends, Windows may seize up and crash, unable to resolve the discrepancy.

Another potential trouble spot is that the BIOS may not always perform its proper job shutting down all hardware not required to boot the PC during the POST. Beyond this, either a bad driver or a lazy BIOS can account for a failure to load a device driver for a device it is supposed to include.

While a better driver and a better BIOS should help resolve these issues, they may not be forthcoming for your device or your motherboard. Nor are they something you can readily code yourself.

SPECIAL ISSUES RELATING TO PCI UNDER WINDOWS NT 4.0

Windows NT 4.0's hardware abstraction layer (HAL) and PCI resources sometimes end up doing some strange dance steps together: You end up unsure who is leading, but you have to chuckle over the fancy footwork.

It's not uncommon, for example, to experience difficulty the first time you boot NT after installing a new PCI device. What you see are either pesky system lockups or a failure of the PCI device to operate or operate properly. The cause is often that NT's HAL, when handling the new PCI device, assigned an I/O port address or a memory resource already in use or overlapping into an area in use by another PCI device on your machine. The result is a hardware resource conflict, and the symptoms you see are the lockups or device failures.

You see, although the motherboard's BIOS is usually responsible for configuring and assigning resources needed for PCI devices, NT 4's HAL sometimes rearranges such assignments again as NT itself loads. This can happen because PCI hardware devices are dynamically configurable. The problem lies in the fact that NT gets careless, or at least is "not smart enough" about resources, and may assign overlapping resources to different devices, setting them up for the conflict that you see demonstrated.

This was actually a bigger problem under earlier versions of NT, until Microsoft addressed this with its versions of HAL in NT 4.0 (including

HAL.DLL, HALMPS.DLL, and HALAPIC.DLL). What the fix does is permit NT to read and recognize PCI locking or /PCILOCK, which tells NT *not* to rearrange PCI device system resources as long as the information supplied in BIOS has already taken care of it properly.

If you run into a problem when installing a new PCI device as detailed above, you should:

1. Shut down NT properly if permitted; if not, power off.
2. Remove the newly installed PCI adapter, restore power to the PC, and load Windows NT again.
3. Locate BOOT.INI and modify it to include this line:

   `/PCILOCK`

4. Shutdown the PC, power off, and reinstall the PCI card/adapter.

The problems should be resolved. You can also try putting the PCI adapter into a different PCI slot or changing the order in which the drivers for the conflicting PCI devices load to see if this resolves the problem.

PCI BUS MASTERING

As discussed briefly in Chapter 2, bus mastering is a means of speeding up drive transfer rates, in part by taking a big chunk of the responsibility for handling them off the CPU and placing it instead on the drive hardware itself and your system. The majority of bus mastering is done on the PCI bus, which is why I tackle it here. This is because PCI's performance as a higher-bandwidth bus means more data can flow along it at any given time. Something has to control it. If it's solely the job of the processor or CPU, you're wasting more time than necessary by devoting it to a less critical task.

This is the role of bus masters, to take control of that data flow and leave the CPU out of the work unless the CPU is needed. A chipset contained on the device hardware itself, like a hard disk or CD-ROM drive, is needed to help pull this off. You may hear bus mastering referred to also as "first-party DMA." This is because the flow of data is actually managed by the device involved in the data transfer. But more than one element is needed. After all, there is more than the transfer of data involved here. Something has to control the requests to the bus, also known as bus arbitration.

NOTE Since there are no DMA channels on the PCI bus, bus mastering becomes the way to go to provide this service.

There are two other side advantages packed with the PCI bus related to bus mastering. One is that you can bus master more than one drive/device on the PCI bus simultaneously, which means you can bus master more than one hard disk, or something like a hard disk and a CD-ROM drive. The other is that the presence of a PCI bus lets you configure compatible IDE/ATA hard disks as bus masters, which allows significantly better performance than high-level PIO or programmed I/O modes. (There are five PIO modes, ranging from 0 to 4, with 0 offering a maximum external data transfer rate of 3.3 MB per second, and four I/O modes, which allow up to a 16.6 MB per second transfer rate. I/O modes are only available for various ATA, EIDE, and ATAPI drives.) When you add bus mastering to these drives, you can take them out of PIO mode and into DMA (capable of 33.3 MB per second transfer rates). Remember though that external data transfer rates measure the speed of the interface, which should be slower than the speed of the drive itself.

Also please note that higher PIO modes (3 and 4) are only possible on PCI and VESA local buses, because the ISA bus restricts capacity usually to well under 10 MB per second.

In order to use bus-mastering technology on your PC, you must have all of the following components present on your system:

◁ Bus master-compatible BIOS

◁ Bus master-compatible logic on the motherboard itself

◁ Device drivers incorporating bus-mastering sensitivity

◁ Bus-mastering-capable IDE devices, such as hard disks and CD-ROM drives supporting "DMA Multi-word" modes

◁ Multitasking operating system such as Windows 95/98

All of these components must be present and must be able to work in unison to deliver a true performance gain and to prevent conflicts arising.

Most motherboards feature Intel chipsets FX, HX, VX, TX, LX, and BX support bus mastering, as should their respective BIOSes. Any drive capable of DMA Mode 2 transfers, which includes all Ultra-ATA drives, should support bus-mastering, and you need the appropriate driver (bus mastering uses a special driver all its own for this).

NOTE SCSI drives also bus master through a more integrated process.

Since I mentioned DMA modes, let me cover them briefly here. PIO modes are older and are based on slower drives and a slower bus, like ISA. Now, ISA had a form of DMA, too, but it was a small controller added to the motherboard itself with very little capacity. This form of DMA is also known as "third-party DMA" and would not be at all helpful in handling DMA mode transfers for today's high-speed hard disks.

DMA modes have been introduced slowly to replace PIO modes in IDE/ATA hard disks over the past few years. IDE/ATA drives themselves range from the old and the slow, up through EIDE, ATA-2, Fast ATA, Fast ATA-2, ATA-3, and on to Ultra-ATA, which sports DMA-33 mode. The latter operates at about double the maximum transfer rate of PIO mode 4, or 33.3 MB per second. Most of today's better drives, in fact, support Ultra-ATA's higher-speed transfer operations.

For a listing of the various incremental DMA modes and their capacity (and on what drives), see Table 7.2.

Finally, bus mastering is serious stuff. While more PCs sold today are preconfigured to bus master drives without user intervention, they are often difficult to understand, maintain, and upgrade for many people. If you plan to undertake this for the first time, don't do it casually. Well-implemented bus mastering can seem to seriously speed up transfer times, but poorly configured, it can negatively affect many aspects of system performance. Read any literature from your hardware manufacturers related

TABLE 7.2 Capacities of DMA Modes

DMA Mode	Maximum Transfer Rate Measured in MB/second
Single word 0	2.1
Single word 1	4.2
Single word 2	8.3
Multi word 0	4.2
Multi word 1 (available on EIDE, ATA-2, Fast ATA-2, ATA-3, Ultra-ATA drives)	13.3
Multi word 2 (available on EIDE, ATA-2, Fast ATA-2, ATA-3, Ultra-ATA drives)	16.6
Multi word 3/DMA-33 (Ultra-ATA only)	33.3

to this, check with Intel and others for the most recent bus-mastering drivers, and do your research first. That way, you're prepared for how to recover from a mess if it occurs. Bus mastering is an ideal topic for technical newsgroups and even technical live chats, because you can ask questions, get pointers to excellent resources spelling out the mechanics of the process, and learn from others what techniques and tips they used to implement it.

NOTE As this book was going to press, the first Ultra/66 drives began to appear, but to very few motherboards yet supporting them.

The so-called average PC user may not even notice the performance boost once bus mastering is successfully in place. After all, many don't begin to use their PC to its fullest potential now. Except for the demands the rise in popularity of networks and Internet applications and the availability of more graphic intensive games and more integrated applications have placed on us, many use their PII-350s and 450s to do the very same processes they did on a 486 and Pentium classic. But there are those who do notice, and they want to get the maximum throughput and optimal complete machine performance.

Nor does bus mastering make up for substandard equipment. You still require better equipment for better results, so buying a bottom-of-the-barrel system and hardware that meets the base minimum requirements for bus mastering probably won't be worth the effort. Also, if you are running a Windows system on too little RAM (say, 16 MB when 32 MB is needed, or 32 MB when 64 MB is more fitting), please buy the RAM first. This alone may resolve some problems.

Also, bus mastering isn't indicated for everyone in every computing situation. Even if you use a multitasking operating system, you may be the type who only keeps one or two applications open on your desktop at once. If so, bus mastering would be more trouble to set up than it might be worthwhile, given the way you operate your PC. But even if you use multiple applications at once, bus mastering will only show its true value if one or more of these applications is disk-intensive (a lot of read/writes). Those who run games in DOS or otherwise spend a significant of time in DOS (an environment that task-switches or single-tasks) are also poor candidates for bus mastering.

NOTE For those using Windows 98 with bus mastering, Intel reports that their bus-mastering IDE drivers were not intended for use with Windows 98. In fact, if you attempt to install then under Windows 98, you should get an error message and a halt when the driver installation program detects that you are attempting to install it to a Windows98-based system.

Additionally, Intel reports that those who upgraded to Windows 98 from a Windows 95 system using the Intel BM-IDE drivers may be subject to various subsystem difficulties. This is because the upgrade may "take" successfully, but the Intel BM-IDE drivers remain loaded, creating certain system incompatibilities that may be seen in slowness of drives, and worse.

Those using Windows 98 (as well as Windows 95b or Windows 95c) are advised to enable bus mastering using the native operating system drivers included for this. To enable bus mastering on these systems:

1. Open Control Panel, double-click on the System icon, and choose the Device Manager tab.

2. Highlight the Disk Drives option from the listing of devices, and click on it to expand to the listing.

3. From the listing, double-click on the Generic IDE DISK TYPE 47 entry.

4. Choose the Settings tab, and click on the DMA checkbox to enable it, as illustrated in Figure 7.2, then click OK to finish.

TROUBLESHOOTING WITH BUS-MASTERED DRIVES

The very nature of what bus mastering is and what it does makes this a supremely headache-prone area of troubleshooting. Many components must support bus mastering, and a problem with or improper response or configuration from any one of them—or possibly more than one—can contribute to its failure to work.

There are primary areas, however, you should investigate first:

1. Did you follow directions? If not, try to take the machine back to the point at which you diverged from the instructions. Failing that, take it back to its original configuration, and step through again from there.

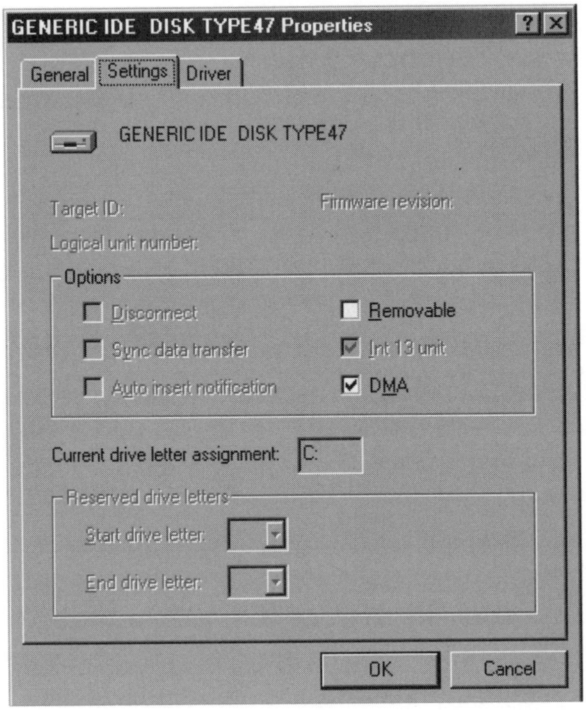

Figure 7.2 Device Manager/disk drives/Settings window.

2. Are all components necessary for bus mastering (as listed earlier) present? Are the drives being bus mastered connected properly and operating normally *without* bus mastering enabled? Recheck the documentation and supporting Web sites for these products to locate any technical papers or FAQs sheets that may explain the reasons for your problem and suggest solutions.

3. Thoroughly evaluate your BIOS settings. Look specifically for entries that disable bus mastering and enable these. Make certain resources are not only assigned to ISA devices. For questions related to what these settings should be to maximize potential for bus mastering, contact your motherboard manufacturer or its Web site.

4. If the problem appears related to a piece of hardware that must work in conjunction with the bus-mastered drives, check its status. Also check to see if the manufacturers of these devices provide any special warnings or setting recommendations for using on a bus-mastered system.

5. Check to see if double buffering is enabled. It's only necessary for SCSI-based systems today (was in wider use before) and should be disabled. To see if you're loading it, open the file MSDOS.SYS with any text editor and look for this section:

```
[Options]
BootMulti=0
BootGUI=1
DoubleBuffer=1
DoubleBuffer set to 1 means it is enabled; set to 0, it means
disabled. Change this value to 0 and save your changes
```

NOTE There is a known issue that PCI bus masters do not always reset when a Control-Alt-Delete reset is used. You need to do a fuller reset if you experience a problem that leads you to believe your bus masters are not being properly reset.

SPECIALIZED BIOS SETTINGS

On a PCI-aware BIOS, various settings within CMOS help you better manipulate and control how PCI (including bus mastering, bus arbitration, and latency), and even Plug and Play and CPU work is handled. Settings there may allow you to either set all Plug and Play devices to be configured and activated when BIOS does its work at boot, or to have Plug and Play ISA devices recognized and analyzed early, but only those required to boot the computer are allowed to activate.

BIOS information and configuration can change slightly (or a lot) depending on its version and manufacture, but let me note a few configuration considerations from a PCI BIOS here.

◁ *Latency Timer (PCI Clocks)*. Controls how long an entity on the PCI bus can hold the bus' attention when another entity has requested it; you may not need to adjust this unless you're experiencing particular problems working the faster PCI with slower ISA devices.

◁ *Slot X Using INT#*. Permits you to specify an INT# selection, usually represented as letters A, B, C, or D (A is the default assumed by the BIOS unless another INT selection is offered).

◁ *Xth Available IRQ*. Maps an IRQ to a specific INT#; if you choose 1st available, the BIOS maps the first available IRQ to the first PCI slot, while a setting of NA means the IRQ in question has been marked for ISA use and won't be available to a PCI slot or INT#.

NOTE If you permit the Automatic Resource Allocation option to be used, you may not be able to set these, and if you do, BIOS may ignore them to configure automatically.

◄ *PCI IRQ Activated By.* Specifies the method (level or edge) in which the PCI bus will recognize the IRQ request.

◄ *IRQ3-IRQ15.* Indicates which IRQs are being used by ISA non-PnP (or legacy) devices; mark one available to allow PCI to take it, or set to Used to reserve one.

◄ *PCI IDE 2nd Channel.* Should be enabled if using the second channel on the PCI IDE card; disabled if not (returns IRQ15 for use).

◄ *PCI IDE IRQ Map To.* Lets you specify your IDE disk controller for configuration (by default, ISA is assumed); with a PCI IDE controller, you can specify actual slot number and internal interrupt (interrupt pin) being used (if for some reason, including troubleshooting, you want to assign no IRQs to PCI slots, let ISA mode be used).

◄ *PCI to DRAM Buffer.* Buffers are more important to PCI than other buses, because PCI is separated from the CPU; enabling this may improve PCI to memory performance by allowing short-term data storage when the destination location is busy handling other things.

◄ *PCI Master Latency.* Helps balance out the time a PCI Master card controls the PCI bus; longer latency gives the CPU more time to work on the bus; shorter time gives the CPU less time (never use 0 as the value assignment or there will be problems).

◄ *CPU to PCI Post Memory Write.* If disabled, the ability for the CPU to perform complete writes is very limited; therefore, be sure it enabled.

◄ *CPU to PCI Write Buffer.* When enabled, allows performance boost by letting the CPU or bus master work even if the destination is busy by allowing it to store data in a buffer.

◄ *PCI to ISA Write Buffer.* Enabled provides best performance, since disabled forces the memory write cycle into slower ISA mode.

◄ *DMA Line Buffer.* Enabled mode permits DMA data to be stored short-term in a buffer to prevent the PCI bus from being unduly interrupted; disabled places system in single transaction mode only, which is far slower.

◄ *ISA Master Line Buffer.* Enabled allows ISA work to continue working at its slower pace, separated from the faster PCI for better overall performance.

◄ *CPU/PCI Post Write Delay.* Lets you set delay time before CPU writes data to the PCI bus.

◄ *PCI Master Accesses Shadow RAM.* Enabled provides better performance, enabling the shadowing of a ROM on the PCI master.

◄ *Enable Master.* Lets you enable a specified device as a PCI bus master.

◄ *Base I/O Address.* Base of the I/O address range from which the needs of the PCI device resource requests are met.

◄ *Base Memory Address.* Base of 32-bit memory address range from which the PCI device resource requests are filled.

◄ *Parity.* Permits PCI device parity checking.

◄ *Residence of a VGA Card.* Specifies in which bus (PCI, VLB or other) a VGA card is located.

◄ *Video Palette Snoop.* Controls a PCI graphics (like a 3D card) adapter's ability to snoop write cycles to an ISA video adapter's color palette registers; disable it if the monitor is connected directly to the ISA video adapter, palette snooping is not an option on your PCI graphics adapter, the ISA adapter uses RAMDAC available on the PCI adapter, or the ISA card is connected to the PCI adapter through a VESA connector. (VGA palette refers to set of colors in use by video adapters with a 256-color mode.)

◄ *PCI/VGA Palette Snoop.* Should be enabled if your system sends MPEG connections though the VGA feature connector on a PCI card (rare), but disabled for most systems.

◄ *PCI Arbiter Mode.* As mentioned, arbitration is the way PCI devices work together to share access on the PCI bus; Mode 1 is the default and should be used unless problems result. Then try Mode 2.

◄ *Stop CPU When PCI Flush.* When enabled, this means the CPU stops doing its thing until the PCI bus is done and flushed of data; disabled is the best option for most situations.

◄ *Stop CPU at PCI Master.* Enabled forces the CPU to stop whenever it detects the bus master operating on the PCI bus; disabled is usually the best option.

◄ *I/O Cycle Recovery.* Enabled allows the PCI bus a recovery period after back-to-back I/O functions; similar to adding wait states.

◄ *I/O Recovery Period.* Sets length of recovery time for the above option.

◄ *Fast Back-to-Back.* When enabled (default), it lets the PCI bus consider CPU read cycles to be PCI burst protocol, which speeds up the process.

◄ *IRQ Line.* Used for informing the PCI bus which IRQ to use for a specific device that requires IRQ service.

◄ *OnBoard PCI/SCSI BIOS.* Used to enable onboard SCSI controller built into a PCIset motherboard for booting purposes.

◄ *PCI I/O Start Address.* Lets you set the I/O starting address for PCI devices; use too if you need to create a block of room exclusively for ISA devices by keeping PCI devices away at other addresses.

◄ *Master Arbitration Protocol.* This is where you set the protocol for which bus master gets access to the PCI bus.

◄ *PCI Clock Frequency.* Lets you set the clock speed of your PCI bus, usually between 0 and 33 MHz.

◄ *ISA Bus Clock Frequency.* Lets you set the clock speed of the ISA bus to a fraction of the PCI bus speed.

◄ *PCI Concurrency.* Enabled tells the system that more than one PCI device may be active at any one time, can allocate memory bus cycles to PCI controller during ISA activity by switching on auxiliary read and write buffering to the chipset; enabled is the default setting.

◄ *PCI Streaming.* Allows the PCI to stream data in larger chunks along the bus than would normally be possible because of CPU considerations.

◄ *PCI Bursting.* Enabled lets consecutive CPU write cycles be treated as PCI burst cycles for better overall performance; disable if it appears to cause problems (also a PCI IDE Bursting option available).

◄ *Preempt PCI Master Option.* Enabled allows PCI bus to be interrupted by important operations of the PCI Master; disabled, the operations wait until the PCI bus is available and then perform.

Unless you are completely confused about how to proceed with BIOS manipulations through advanced CMOS setup screens, you may want to avoid using Automatic Resource Allocations mode, because this leaves the BIOS to make its "best guesses" for you in terms of what your PC and all attached to it will need. These blanket guesses may not always be best for performance and can hinder troubleshooting a problem you suspect may be rooted in BIOS.

My recommendation is to familiarize yourself with your BIOS so you can make intelligent choices in its configuration and device/resource implementation therein. What you learn will give you far greater control over your PC working environment.

ONNOW, PCI, AND POWER MANAGEMENT (ACPI)

OnNow is a computer design initiative whose goal is simple: making it easier for you to control eventually all aspects of your computer. To achieve this, many variables will need to come together. Among these are power management, the "smartness" of the PC in recognizing something not plugged in or removed until after the PC is booted and operational, configuration and system resource issues, actual hardware design, and functionality as well as flexibility of the operating system itself, just to name a few critical points.

Advanced Configuration and Power Interface, or ACPI, introduced into the Windows platform in Windows 95b (OSR2) and continued into Windows 98, is one of the front-line products put forth by OnNow. What it does is nothing short of dynamic. It provides a working interface between the PC's BIOS and hardware, which then interacts with the PC's operating system. This is necessary when you want to create and maintain a cooperative effort to keep "events"—defined as anything that is happening to the overall system—acknowledged and recorded by all components of that system. This provides a smart extension of the Plug and Play system, which previously relied on substantial help from the user and other resources to try to keep track of things.

It's smart because it allows the PC to turn peripherals on or off on demand. Smart, too, because it permits you to turn on the PC by turning on something attached to the PC. For example, you might have a MIDI keyboard or a television attached to your PC. Touch a key on the keyboard or turn on the TV, and your PC roars to life. As we head in the direction of hooking up more traditional consumer appliances like videocassette recorders, video cameras, TVs, stereos, and perhaps even the coffeemaker to our PC—and this is the promise of current PC design trends—ACPI takes on an increasingly key role in how we will get this all to work in unison.

But ACPI is about to leap ahead. The ACPI we have known in Windows 95b and beyond was just a preliminary look at what is coming in Windows NT 5.0, where ACPI becomes the primary interface by which PnP is handled and managed. While Windows 95b, Windows 95c, and Windows 98 required a BIOS specifically designed to be compatible with PnP and ACPI standards, ACPI handles PnP implementation in Windows NT 5.

With ACPI's guidance, Windows NT 5's Plug and Play capability will support:

◄ Both automatic and dynamic recognition of installed (and removed) hardware devices

◄ Coordination and interaction with power management to permit recognition of certain dynamic events—like the plugging in or removal of a peripheral device—as well as permit the system to "go to sleep" after a period of inactivity (which reduces power consumption)

◄ Allocation and reallocation of hardware resources on demand

◄ Loading of appropriate drivers for devices

◄ An interface between the driver and the PnP system itself, which largely consists of Windows Registry information, I/O routines, Plug and Play I/O request packets (IRPs), as well as required driver entry points

All of this contributes to understanding why many are saying that working with hardware becomes far more manageable under Windows NT 5 than earlier versions. Instead of the days of old when your NT-running PC may have worked *in spite* of the hardware attached to it, NT 5 tries to provide an environment more friendly to the user and the hardware when installing a new device.

This also leads the way into an improved method for being able to install and remove hardware at will, whether the PC is on or off—a technology known as Hot Plug PCI.

HOT PLUG PCI

A new technology will be introduced soon that allows you to install and remove PCI hardware devices even while the PC is on and engaged in its work. If this sounds similar to the concept of hot swapping, it is often confused with it. Hot swapping's primary objective was and is to automatically move from one device to another, redundant PCI device in the event that the first device fails, while Hot Plug PCI involves a development of the theme we popularly think of in terms of hot swapping: changing devices in and out at a moment's notice.

Hot Plug PCI uses standard operating system Plug and Play mechanisms and will use ACPI as the operating system's interface to permit you to insert, eject, and otherwise juggle devices from a working PC. Microsoft reports this technology won't be included in the initial release of Windows NT 5.0 but support should follow along in a later service release update to NT 5.

The potential for this is very nice, because traditionally we have to power down our systems, install a device, and then power back up to even allow the ease-of-installation PnP to handle device and driver installation. With this technology, we're looking at being able to decide on the spur of the moment, "OK, I need my external tape drive attached now to run a backup" or "Let me set up my video camera and shoot some live video," and then simply do it, without any appreciable downtime.

Look at this quick rundown of the many processes the integrated Windows NT 5 approach to hardware (and associated power management) once you insert or install a new device into a proper system installation point, like a slot:

◀ The Hot Plug PCI controller or HPPC acknowledges something has *occurred* to the system, sends out an alert, and then other processes determine what the nature of the occurrence—or event—actually was (such as the insertion of a modem in a PCI slot).

◀ The PCI bus receives notification that a device has been inserted into one of its PCI bus slots.

◄ ACPI signals the PCI driver to enumerate the bus to get proper recognition.

◄ This PCI driver then reads the ESCD to properly identify the device now attached and then starts the right drivers to take advantage of that device's particular features.

◄ These proper drivers then ask that the hardware device's particular features be enabled for operation.

◄ The PCI driver then writes back to the ESCD and alerts it to initialize the device for operation per PCI power management (PCI-PM) specifications.

◄ The device's driver then notifies the hardware device itself that it's ready for operation and to go ahead.

PCIX

In September 1998, a cooperation between Compaq, IBM, and Hewlett-Packard announced they had developed a new higher-speed PCI bus that they gave to Intel for consideration. The PCIx bus, as it is called now, is reported to run at about twice the speed of the current PCI platform (which runs at 66 MHz under PCI 2.1 specifications), up to around 133 MHz. More notably, it is supposed to transfer data between the peripherals and the CPU at the rate of about 1 GB per second, or a lot faster than PCI's current 132 MB per second.

As of this writing, no firm proposal from the PCI special interest group had been made available, detailing complete specifications. But CPU chipmaker Intel has already indicated PCI itself should get a break in bandwidth problems in 1999, when they expect to release the 450NX chipset with their 64-bit wide 66 MHz bus coupled with multisegmented PCI support. Intel hopes this will help curb some of the logjam being experienced with PCI as folks move to it for device support and away from ISA.

AGP

Accelerated Graphics Port, or AGP, was first introduced in Intel's LX chipset (and is only supported currently in Socket 7 or Slot -1-type motherboards) as an alternative method for connecting video display and performance hardware to your PC without tying up a precious PCI or (oh so slow) ISA slot. AGP isn't a bus of its own so much as an extension of the PCI bus design. What it provides is a direct connection between system memory and the graphics subsystem, which aids in graphical performance both realistically and aesthetically (through the ability to better appreciate a truer 3D graphics experience).

Intel defines AGP as a "high-performance component level interconnect targeted at 3D graphical display applications and based on a set of performance extensions to PCI."

A lot of hype arrived well in advance of AGP's debut, making speed and performance sound phenomenal over what we had been using to date. Some of it made sense, too. Certainly that AGP video plugged in right on the motherboard itself close to the central processing unit would be preferable over an old ISA video adapter for speed, particularly in relationship to today's high graphical demand gaming.

While PCI 3D video cards were in abundance, the working demands of 3D applications against PCI 3D devices threatened to completely overwhelm the PCI bus, which was already stretching to accommodate newer PCI devices replacing older ISA bus expansion devices. As you recall from Chapter 2, ISA is scheduled for execution, so migration from ISA to PCI and beyond becomes more imperative.

Intel developed AGP to answer two fairly large problems with PCI 3D video implementation: the need for support and storage of z-buffer information and the requirement for more memory available to handle texture mapping (as much as possible preferred). Z-buffers are where information is stored about the depth of a scene shown on a 3D screen. In PCI design, z-buffers and texture mapping data were stored in the same area of memory.

Developers of 3D applications either had to restrict the depth of characteristics stored in z-buffers and texture mapping or risk a conflict when the two might get scrambled in the same memory or moving along the tight PCI data bus. The answer, they felt, was in better system memory resources. But how? Limitations were in place for how speedily information could transfer across the PCI bus, which in turn limited the graphics subsystem (the video adapter attached to the PCI bus) and the system memory resources. A known problem with PCI is that any data stored in system memory is not physically contiguous, and may therefore be less reliable. It hampers speed, too.

Such limitations made it virtually impossible to program for real-time graphics and expect delivery to match what was programmed. So designers were faced with either adding some type of memory resources that might prove costly, especially if tied to the slower PCI bus, or coming up with a solution independent of the PCI bus' limitations. Hence, AGP was born.

Yet AGP's arrival met with mixed reviews. Many found the boosts over PCI video boards not striking enough, while others marveled at what they considered noticeably higher data transfers over standard-issue PCI video adapters. Gamers, who awaited the AGP to see what it would do for the 3D gaming experience, were not happy that there was little performance boost seen at all in DOS.

One key advantage with AGP is the rise in bus speed. Most older bus technology sends just 1 bit of data per wire, per clock cycle. AGP can move 2 bits of data per clock cycle. Also, AGP operated in either x2 or x4 mode can multiply the bus speed in corresponding multiples. For example, standard AGP operates at 66 MHz, while x2 mode operates at 66 MHz x 2, and x4 mode operates at 66 MHz x 4.

Unlike PCI, the AGP port only allows two things to access it: the graphics set and the chipset. So it has less interference and less traffic on the wire, which can enhance its speed. Also unlike PCI, pipeline operations are fully supported, as is Direct Memory Execute, which helps in the texturing process in 3D applications, such as games.

Another big plus over PCI is that AGP was specifically designed to allow the graphics subsystem (video adapter) to retrieve data quickly and seamlessly from system memory, despite how poorly organized this data may be stored there. This makes real-time graphics more feasible.

Correspondingly, the bus bandwidth jumps from 266.6 MB per second under standard AGP, through to 533.3 in x2 mode to top off at 1066.6 MB per second in x4 mode (remember, original ISA offered just 8.3 MB/s and VESA local bus and standard PCI only 133.3 MB/s).

Universal Serial Bus (USB)

Universal serial bus is another form of PC interconnect, but it is unique from PCI because the devices attaching to a USB connection are plugged into external ports on the outside of the PC (usually at the back, but more front-mounted USB ports may be visible soon). There is no peeling off the case or trying to wedge a device into place. This makes hardware installations and removals simple for everyone concerned.

What is truly novel is that USB theoretically will connect up to 127 different devices, and no matter how many devices are hooked up through USB (whether 1 or 100), only one single interrupt (IRQ) is needed to service all these devices. This represents considerably more connections, at less cost to vital system resources, than we have seen before. Because it's an extension of the Plug and Play ease of installation design, USB devices very rarely require special software to help install them to your system.

USB devices are also generally cheaper to manufacture, because they don't require the power cords necessary to run more standard connection peripherals like printers. The device instead receives its power from the USB port itself. This does raise problems with plugging in multiple USB devices: There may not be enough power from the port to run all of the devices attached once you take advantage of the multiple connection technology. The solution is a powered hub you can add to the USB port to help sustain power demands. How soon you move from the port itself to the hub depends on how many devices are connected, what type they are, and what level of energy they consume.

With all of these pluses, many in the computing industry are left wondering why people are not embracing the USB solution more enthusiastically, considering it can help pricing, allows multiple devices while using just one IRQ, and connects easily. The single-most likely reason is overall support. USB-capable hardware actually predated an operating system written to support its use. So did motherboards to support it, which Intel began introducing with the HX and VX PCIset in mid 1996. Microsoft first included USB support for Windows 95 in a special supplement to its "b" or Service Release 2 (calling it OSR 2.1) in early mid 1997, though fuller support for more types of USB devices was not seen until the release of Windows 98 in June 1998.

Even those who were awaiting USB technology and hurried to get the components needed to add it to their PC systems were often disappointed in the choice of devices on the market. Until recently, there hasn't been an embarrassment of riches, nor did those available push forth features designed to take advantage of USB's bandwidth, which is 3 to 5 times faster than parallel ports, some 20 to 40 times faster than standard serial ports, but nowhere near as fast as the speediest grade SCSI of today.

Continuing today, there are fewer than the estimated 250 USB products that were expected to be on the market by the time this book was being finished. Most of these are cameras, keyboards, computer mice, printers, and scanners. Modems plus telephony products, as well as MPEG-2 video-based devices such as data gloves are also beginning to appear. In fact, USB speakers are being introduced that will plug right in and play sound without requiring a sound card/adapter, but you will still need to have a sound card to play audio CDs through your CD-ROM drive, as well as to hear sounds in DOS-based games.

Those looking for DOS-side support may be frustrated. Not all USB devices will function in DOS, partly because of a failing of the device and drivers itself, and partly because the motherboard's BIOS may not properly support this operation. Lots of people, for example, found USB keyboards failing to work in DOS and no dates for support from their BIOS suppliers. Even if the BIOS and device worked fine, however, there is ever-dwindling interest in creating device drivers for the DOS arena.

But the tide may be turning. One factor is the lowered prices on portable laptop/notebook PC technology, where USB ports have been implemented for a while to help serve a mobile market with a need to be wired to peripherals to support a miniature remote office setup. For example, I use my notebook as a sort of portable photo lab in conjunction with my digital camera. Once the digital camera's flash memory fills up with images (much like a roll of film), I simply connect the camera to the PC, offload the digital images to the camera's management software through the USB port, and go back to taking photographs. It's reasonably fast, very easy, and saves a bundle in film processing fees (even if I spend a lot in batteries to feed the camera).

An associate with a small office equipped with one USB scanner and four USB-equipped PCs avoids the hassle of setting up the scanner on a network by simply moving the USB scanner back and forth between PCs. If the second PC needs it, he detaches it readily from the back of the first PC and simply plugs it into the second, where it's ready to go without an installation process and without powering down.

Industry reporting groups, like Dataquest, forecast that some 50 million USB devices will have been sold by the end of this year (1999), and see USB as an steadily growing market. When Apple released its new iMac computer in late summer of 1998, it provided USB as the primary connection for peripheral devices. Also, older machines can be "refitted" to USB capability by obtaining a USB converter kit (average cost is $50 to $100). Note that you also need a USB device itself and the proper version of an operating system that supports it to have the USB device work. To see if your system is USB-ready, download and run USBREADY.EXE, a program to test USB capability available for free by visiting the USB Implementers Forum at *http://www.usb.org*.

If USB has a single-largest flaw, it is that the technology won't tolerate high-throughput devices, such as broadcast video quality, top-speed mass storage devices, and revamped consumer electronics such as digital camcorders or digital video cassette recorders. Instead, the high-throughput bases are covered by FireWire/IEEE1394.

NOTE At the time of this book's printing, a further development called USB 2 is on some drawing boards.

FireWire/IEEE1394

By definition, FireWire, also known as IEEE 1394 or (these days) just 1394, meets the criteria to be considered a true, full Plug and Play interconnect device. According to specifications, FireWire is a high-speed serial bus-style data pipe capable of moving up to 400 MB per second, which is more than 33 times faster than the specifications for its slower workmate, USB. It also only connects about half (63) the number of devices that USB is capable of allowing, but it's aimed at far more powerful hardware than USB, like implementation for professional-quality, high-resolution video streams.

Besides speed and multiplicity of devices, FireWire boasts one other important ability: It can be connected and disconnected on the fly without a need for powering down, installing, then rebooting to configure. Take a video device like a high-end digital format camera or a high-throughput mass storage device and move it between the various PCs in your office or home, without a lot of fuss or downtime. Couple that with FireWire's higher bandwidth and its scaleable nature, and you finally achieve hardware speed, ease, and versatility a full generation away from where we have been.

Perhaps more interesting is the promise of FireWire as *the* way to hook digital consumer electronics appliances or equipment like television, stereo, VHS, and telephony products to your PC. Traditionally, consumer electronics existed on a separate tier from personal computers, separate because they were each based on widely divergent technologies and formats. Today, connections for FireWire capability are already beginning to appear on various consumer electronics products, and this is expected to markedly increase in the coming year. In the very near future, Intel says we shall be shooting video on our 1394-wired digital camcorders, then passing it along to our 1394-ready Pentium II PCs for editing, with none of the typical reduction in picture quality.

Only a small handful of FireWire-ready devices exist currently, and these are mostly in the area of video, which fits considering the high price-tag. A few motherboard manufacturers have also released the first system boards containing FireWire technology.

Yet the promise of FireWire remains just a promise for the time-being. By the end of this year (1999), more FireWire devices are expected to be available on the market, but even Windows NT 5.0 only supports it on a limited basis. Like any type of connection, the hardware won't be able to do what it is designed to do unless it is used in conjunction with an operating system programmed to properly support it.

Plus, as you may recall, Microsoft and Intel's PC99 Specifications only just gave the ISA bus its execution date, while not promoting USB and FireWire technology as aggressively as some expected. The specifications nudge, rather than shove, FireWire into the design consciousness. Also, some news reports have indicated PC manufacturers want Intel to pull back the throttle on aggressive FireWire promotion as an interconnect platform. This may be at least in part because of the higher price of 1394 technology at a time when total cost of ownership (TCO) is still a major consideration in the computing industry.

Finally, FireWire is intended to complement, not replace, USB. While the former will be used for high-speed, high-performance devices like professional video, mass storage devices, and as an interface for integrating consumer electronics onto the home or office PC, the latter will take care of lower-demand hardware such as keyboards, mice, and low-end Webcams.

For more information about FireWire, visit its official information Web site at *http://www.firewire.com*.

Device Bay

This one, unlike USB and FireWire, is still in the talking-about stages, but it represents something of the brave new world we are perhaps heading into with PCs of the next millennium. It didn't rate even cursory mention in the PC99 specs from Microsoft and Intel, in fact.

If reading is believing, Device Bay may be the threshold of a high-end, elegant, more complete Plug and Play realm. It takes the easy attach-and-use basis of USB and FireWire and goes further, while still incorporating these interconnects into the design. Almost all peripherals in use in PCs today—with some exceptions—will be able to attach through Device Bay, USB, and FireWire.

Device Bay basically involves moving what we traditionally add within a PC—such as hard disks, CD-ROM drives, modems, and network cards—and pushes them out into externally mounted bays where the user can readily add and remove them as needs and demands change. It would also support completely external access to peripherals like DVD drives, high-capacity removable media drives like ZIP and Jaz, audio devices such as effects processors and multichannel decoders, satellite TV decoders, Smart Card readers, and more on the design board.

In fact, eventual design could lead to leaving just the motherboard proper with CPU, RAM, and video adapter in place within a modified case format. These components are currently excluded because of bandwidth considerations.

Virtually everything else you may add would go into these conveniently accessible bays, which require minimal technical acumen. In fact, according to Microsoft, Intel, and Compaq, the supporters of this technology, hardware installations will become as easy as inserting and ejecting a videotape from a VCR. Push the device into place, and it installs and is automatically configured. Push a button and the device ejects into your waiting hand. All of this is accomplished without removing your PC from the work it may be doing at the time, for there is no need to power down. No screwdrivers would be needed. The plan is that PCs running chipsets that support Device Bay, which is also a PnP-capable operating system, would be able to automatically handle the plug-in and make it available for use.

Part of that would be possible because Device Bay is seen as a deterministic hardware model, meaning here that a Device Bay-capable PC would map devices to specific bays. This helps the system know what it should find residing in a bay that is suddenly occupied. But it would allow you to share a hard disk, a DVD drive, or a network card between other computers also using this technology. If one device fails, you can have another installed in moments.

Consumer electronics are pictured as allowing for Device Bay technology as well, allowing you to add components easily to audio/visual setups, for example. Beyond that, says the literature, envision using the same recordable DVD drive to back up your hard disk that you use to record a television program, all done from the PC desktop.

The downside, as perhaps you have realized, is cost. To make the hardware this conveniently accessible (and pass aesthetics tests) as well as readily usable is costlier than the design we currently use.

At this point in time, while Microsoft and Intel both say they plan future versions of their operating systems and chipsets (respectively) to support Device Bay, Microsoft recently said it has no plans to include it in any planned operating system upgrade at this time, and it's not on most lists for inclusion into Windows NT 5.0.

Because of the computing industry's very nature, a few years' delay in developing a new design standard can mean its death. So we have yet to see whether Device Bay represents only a promise of making our physical side of computing a great deal easier, or whether this idea will be replaced in popular use by a whole other design standard we haven't heard about yet.

For more information, check out the Device Bay information site located at *http://www.device-bay.org/*.

CHAPTER 8

A Deeper Look at the Windows Registry: Important Tips to Work with, Modify, and Rescue

This chapter includes the following topics:

◀ What the Registry is

◀ What you find in the Registry

◀ How changes to your system and its configuration affect the Registry

◀ How to back up and restore the Registry

◀ How to make successful modifications to the Registry

First, I need to say that one chapter on the Windows Registry—found in Microsoft Windows 95, Windows 98, and NT 4.0, but not quite the same in Windows 3.1x—simply cannot do this subject proper justice. Most books solely concentrating on this component have a difficult time telling you all that you may need to know, since the Registry is both large and fairly complex.

The closest parallel in 16-bit Windows 3.1x is the series of text-format .INI files that help make up its operating base. A much more rudimentary version of the Registry is indeed included in 16-bit Windows, but it's very limited in the data it stores—mostly file associations. Of course, 32-bit Windows (95/98 and NT) also offer .INI files. These are still included, according to Microsoft, to help 32-bit operating systems handle 16-bit programs you may still run from it. But the Registry serves as an important integrated step beyond them, pulling together what Windows needs to know to operate properly all within one unified base of information. Also, the Registry entries can accept binary data (which is how most hardware component data is stored), not just the simple text strings found in many .INI files.

Virtually every aspect of your Windows work sessions on your PC refers back to information contained in this Registry, so its health and well-being is mandatory. Various things can begin to mar and even fully damage the Registry, such as deleting an application without properly uninstalling it, improper editing of the Registry itself by the user, and incompatible programs that leave confusing or disruptive entries in the Registry. The result can range from a lot of extant entries that lead to Registry girth to annoying dialog box error messages to far worse.

As I guide you through a better understanding of the Windows Registry, it is important that you appreciate both the critical nature of it and how dangerous careless modifications to it can be. If there is one part of Windows you shouldn't tweak without some adequate information, it is the Registry.

What the Windows Registry Is

Simply put, the Windows Registry is a centralized database that stores information specific to your PC configuration and what you add and run in Windows itself. When you first install Windows, the Registry collects all the information it can on the hardware and software installed on your machine, including specific settings. It then stores this in a hierarchical format that in turn can be referenced by other parts of your Windows operating system. Each time you add or remove either hardware or software, Windows automatically updates the Registry. There are exceptions to this; for example, you must use the Add/Remove Programs or Add/Remove Hardware wizards found in Windows Control Panel, and only 32-bit programs can be installed and uninstalled using these. When installed applications or other software need to check on the status of something, say, the presence of a specific, installed printer, the Registry informs them appropriately.

The actual size of the Registry is dependent on several things, including the hard disk space available, the number of additions you have made to your operating system, and whether it has been cleaned.

Cleaning the Registry is something I will touch on only briefly here, because there are not a lot of good products readily available that perform this function aggressively, effectively, and without risk. For a better-tuned Registry, one wants an aggressive cleaner to ferret out and remove defunct or unnecessary entries (this is the cleaner's job); safety concerns causes one to want to err on the side of leaving some junk if the cost is losing everything and needing to start again.

On a regular basis, I use Microsoft's RegClean, which is a free download from their support download site at *http://www.microsoft.com/ msdownload*. RegClean is one product for which you *want* to read the accompanying documentation, to make sure it's compatible with your version of Windows and with any special extras you may have added on. Get it from Microsoft or another reputable source to ensure you are getting the most recent version. The results I see are not dramatic post RegClean's use, but I do notice a slight pickup in overall Windows speed, and it sometimes aids in removing some recalcitrant entries that are no longer useful to include.

NOTE Make certain the RegClean you download is rated to work with *your* version of the Microsoft Windows operating system and for your version of Internet Explorer, if you're using it, making note of any service pack releases you may have installed. Some versions of RegClean have had problems either with certain service pack installs or IE version upgrades, so read the fine print and the README file before proceeding.

Another option is to manually remove or revise entries to the Registry itself, which I'll go over shortly. One thing you need to be aware of, especially since this book's focus is on hardware resolution: The vast majority of common hardware conflicts won't be resolved through tweaks to the Registry. I discuss the Registry here because it's central to your operating system, not because it is a vital tool in overcoming tricky IRQs.

What the Registry Contains

Two files make up the core of the Windows 95/98 Registry: SYSTEM.DAT and USER.DAT. These files are located in your Windows System directory. Specifically, SYSTEM.DAT stores specific hardware and PC settings, such as those found in Device Manager in Control Panel, while USER.DAT maintains user-specific data. In NT 3.51 and 4.0, the core files are named WIN.DAT and System.DAT, but you want to backup everything really in the \SystemRoot\System 32\CONFIG directory that is Registry oriented, located in the personal profiles directory.

One very useful feature Microsoft built into 32-bit Windows is that the operating system automatically backs up, as a safety precaution, the last working configuration used to launch Windows. Check your C:\Windows\System directory. Do you see the .CAB files located there? Those are the backed up Registry files, stored in compressed cabinet, or .CAB, format. You will also find current backup versions of Registry data stored as SYSTEM.DA0 and USER.DA0.

Stored here are memory configuration settings, as well as specific information related to the hardware and software you have installed, combined with specific settings for default operating values (fonts, display, file associations, and more). As mentioned, each time you install something using the Add/Remove wizards in the Windows Control Panel, the Registry is updated appropriately to reflect this information. The same is true when you install a new Plug and Play hardware device. Once it is properly in place, the very next time you boot your PC and load Windows, the operating system should recognize the presence of new hardware and adjust itself—and the Registry—accordingly.

In fact, virtually every option available in the Windows Control Panel helps you by automatically editing the Registry to reflect any changes you make to options within Control Panel (see Figure 8.1). Depending on your version of Windows, these change options include but are not limited to the following:

◄ *Accessibility Options.* Contains setting to make the graphical user interface easier to use for persons with some physical limitations.

◄ *Add New Hardware.* Allows you to manually install Windows support for new hardware you have added.

◄ *Add/Remove Programs.* Used for installing 32-bit applications.

◄ *Date/Time.* Permits adjustments to the operating system clock/calendar.

◄ *Display.* Allows you to alter resolution, font, and desktop appearance, as well as turn the screensaver on and off and perform routine customizations regarding the physical appearance of the desktop environment.

◄ *Fonts.* Enables you to add additional fonts to Windows, as well as edit/modify some options.

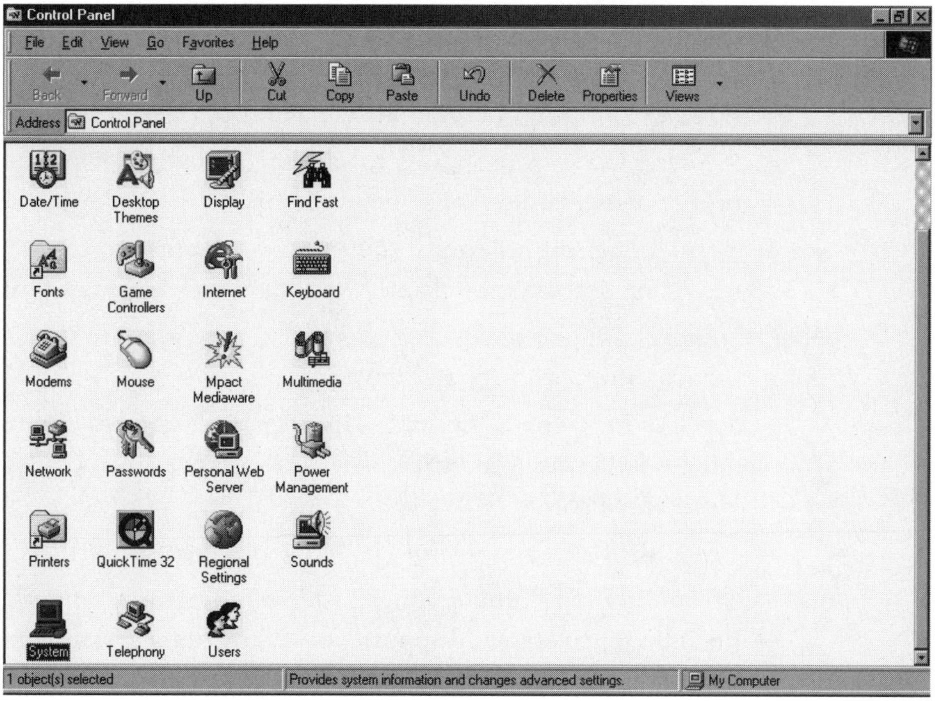

Figure 8.1 Windows 95 Control Panel.

◀ *Internet.* Gives you options for making modifications to your Internet connections; if Microsoft Internet Explorer Web browser is installed, its properties will be available here.

◀ *Game Controllers.* Provides information or lets you add game control devices.

◀ *Keyboard.* Lets you choose between speed, supported language, and exact keyboard type.

◀ *Mail (& Fax).* Provides configuration options for (Internet) mail and optional fax features (the latter is not available in Windows NT 4.0).

◀ *Modems.* Offers settings and change functions for any modems installed to your system.

◀ *Mouse.* Lets you set pointing device properties.

◀ *Multimedia.* Changes settings for multimedia devices such as CD music, MIDI, audio and video, adjusting sound and other performance variables.

◁ *Networks*. Allows you to modify network appropriate information.

◁ *Passwords*. Lets you alter user and administrator passwords.

◁ *Power*. Configures power management options.

◁ *Printers*. Gives you options for adding, deleting, or modifying the profile of any printers installed to your PC.

◁ *Regional Settings*. Permits you to make changes to certain operating system information display options based on geographic region.

◁ *Sounds*. Assigns designated sound files to Windows event like a Critical Stop, Startup, and more.

◁ *System*. Lets you view and adjust critical settings for hardware devices in Device Manager, check Performance, and copy or rename Hardware Profiles.

◁ *Users*. Provides options for changing specific user settings.

◁ *32-bit ODBC*. Permits you to add, remove, or configure options (including drivers and support) for ODBC data system administrator functions (as in databases, for example).

Differences between Windows 95 and 98 Registries

As I mentioned, Windows 95 and 98 both save copies of your Registry to try to help if a problem develops—and yes, that problem can sometimes be hardware-related, or at least hardware driver-related. But there are a few important differences in how Windows 95 and 98 handle this work.

One big difference is that Microsoft got smarter about how people tend to respond to problems in Windows. Windows 95 backs up a copy of the Registry every time it is loaded, which should work well. But a majority of Windows users tend to reboot when they experience a serious situation in Windows, which means that when Windows reloads, it backs up the copy of the Registry that may have already been corrupted or badly changed by the problem the user encountered during the previous session. Restore *that* backup then, and you're effectively guaranteeing continuing problems.

Windows 98 appears to have smartened up as a result. First, you can make changes to how the Registry scanning utility, ScanReg, operates by editing the SCANREG.INI file (ScanReg is discussed later in this chapter).

Options include changing the number of backups ScanReg will make, as well as what files it backs up besides the two Registry files themselves.

Beyond that, it makes not just the single backup at relaunch; it now makes five separate copies (though never more than one copy a day unless you force it to do so). These are stored as compressed cabinet, or .CAB, files labeled rb000.cab, rb001.cab, rb002.cab, respectively, in the SYSBCKUP folder or subdirectory in the main Windows directory. You should be able to replace your current Registry with any one of these.

In Windows 98, you can get your system to use a saved copy of the Registry on launch by:

1. After booting your PC, during the POST, press and hold down your Control key until the Boot Menu loads.

2. Choose Command Prompt Only, which takes you into a DOS session

3. Type:

```
Scanreg /restore
```

To run a DOS-based version of the Registry scanner and restore a copy of the available backups that will be provided to you in a list (with dates) run Scanreg from the DOS command line with any of its associated switches:

```
Scanreg.exe [/backup][/restore]["/comment=(text("][/fix]]
```

NOTE What you won't find on Windows 98 release CDs is a copy of Emergency Recovery Utility, or ERU, which was found in Windows 95. While this utility was part of the Windows 98 beta, it was excluded from the released product. Windows 98 users, however, can use ERU if they need to make an emergency boot diskette that contains a working copy of the Registry (and thus information about their system). Look for ERU on the Windows 95 CD in the Tools\Misc\ERU folder, copy these to a designated, appropriate spot on your PC's hard disk, and run ERU to make the emergency diskette.

Hardware Assignments Listed in the Windows Registry

Provided here is a list of hardware assignments (and other key functions) for which Windows Registry shows an entry you may be able to adjust. While this list is the one for Windows NT 4.0, most also apply to Windows 95 and 98.

◄ Summaries of entries in the Select, Control, and Services subkeys in HKEY_LOCAL_MACHINE\SYSTEM\CurrentControlSet

◄ Network adapter cards, drivers, and bindings

◄ Device drivers, with entries for disk, serial, and parallel port devices; keyboard and mouse devices; SCSI miniport devices; and video display adapter devices

◄ Services, with entries for the Alerter, AppleTalk and Macfile, DLC, Eventlog, NetBEUI (NBF) transport, Netlogon, Replicator, Server, NWLink, TCP/IP, UPS, and Workstation services

◄ Mail and Schedule+

◄ User preferences

◄ Fonts and printing

◄ Windows NT subsystems

For those familiar with the Windows 95/98 version of Control Panel, Windows NT's own offers just a few additions as well as some organizational differences.

Specifically, more hardware gets its own icon and assignment information in Control Panel. Examples include PC Card (PCMCIA), SCSI adapters, Tape Devices, Telephony, and anything you may specifically add, like a special video adapter with its own controlling package (Matrox installed MGA Display in my Windows NT 4.0 Control Panel, for instance) or a digitizing tablet. This can also vary somewhat depending on which Service Packs, if any, you may have installed to your Windows NT 4.0 setup.

There is no Add/Remove Hardware wizard, but most hardware icons/ entries become far more detailed for setup and configuration than under a Windows 9x environment. There is also a Dial-Up Monitor with more information than its Windows 9x counterpart.

Under the Services icon, you can add and remove specific services under NT, including EventLog, video display control, Remote Access services, Plug and Play, and more.

The System icon also leads to more levels of information (and some of System's information under Windows 95/98 moves to the details provided under the hardware-specific icons in Windows NT 4.0), covering general, performance, environment, startup/shutdown specifics, hardware and user profiles.

Editing the Registry

REGDEDIT.EXE is the primary Registry editor packed with Windows95 and Windows 98, while REGEDT32.EXE is designed and provided to work with Microsoft Windows NT (though RegEdit is also included). These utilities are indeed usable for this purpose, but most people seem to grow frustrated with them fairly quickly—they're a bit clunky and less than intuitive to use. Or perhaps Microsoft was reminding you editing the Registry is not *supposed* to imply a good time.<grin>

Probably the best recommendation for a public domain, freeware, or shareware alternative to REGEDIT or REGEDT32.EXE should come from friends and work associates. I have briefly tried several over the last 3 years, and I invariably end up returning to REGEDIT because it's there and I normally don't make a lot of modifications past one-line removals and additions.

One word of caution, however: There are utilities out there that bill themselves as Registry tweakers, which automatically adjust settings for user profile, modem transmission speed, as well as a host of other "quick fixes." MTU Speed Pro is one of these that I have enjoyed success with for speeding up Internet chat or other-based file transfers. But I would never recommend just trying out any of these you find unless you perform a backup first. I would also suggest asking around—perhaps using some of the resources cited later in Appendix B of this book—to see what experience others have had with a particular tweak. This is one situation where sloppy programming on someone else's part could really hurt. It is also a situation ripe for those who want to incorporate a virus or other harmful function into a file you apply.

Again, I need to stress that such editing is not for the squeamish, the overtired, or the sloppy. It is also not recommended for those who have not properly backed up their Registry files (see "Safeguarding a Working Copy of the Registry and Restoring It" later in this chapter), as well as those who simply don't know and don't care to learn what is involved, since entries can appear cryptic. After all, there is pressure here: You *must* edit properly or face the consequences. Syntax and spelling *do* count! Making wrong changes can result in a variety of problems, ranging from odd error messages to Windows itself failing to load.

Why am I nagging? Because online, I see too many people who succumbed to the allure of a neat tweak without backing up and without doing a bit of study ahead of time to know what they should do and how it should be done. Once the Registry is screwed—if you will kindly excuse the expression—it's screwed. Doing a simple reinstall will not remove corruptions and rebuild the Registry, so when a serious mistake is made, you may wind up moving all the way to formatting the disk and starting over again (see Chapter 9, "Starting from Scratch"). And this is simply unnecessary if you follow basic precautions.

TIP If you have a messed up Registry (or other problems), installing a fresh copy of either that operating system alone or upgrading to a newer version—say Windows 95 to Windows 98—won't provide the cure. The only result will be that you build a fresh house atop a very rocky foundation. The Registry is too integral to Windows' proper operation to allow a damaged Registry situation to continue, *if* you are able to load Windows at all. If you cannot successfully restore a previously saved Registry, you may need to start from scratch.

Likely to prevent the uninitiated from using it, Microsoft hides the Registry editor from easy view. There is no item listing it in the Windows Start menu, nor an icon on the desktop. However, you can always add it by finding REGEDIT.EXE in Windows Explorer and right-clicking with your mouse to drag it to your desktop for future use. As a side note, I would not advise doing this on a PC others have access to, because it would seem an invitation to disaster. Besides, you can foul it up enough yourself if you don't exercise care in using it.

Remember, Registry changes are recognized by the operating system *only after a reboot* of the computer, just like changes to the older configuration files, like CONFIG.SYS and AUTOEXEC.BAT.

NOTE REGEDIT.EXE is *not* included on the floppy disk version of the Windows 95 operating system release. You can download a copy from Microsoft by looking at *http://www .microsoft.com/msdownload*, if needed.

To run the Registry editor:

1. From the Windows Start menu, select Run and then type "regedit" (without quotation marks; also, the .exe is not necessary).

2. Once the Registry editor loads, as shown in Figure 8.2, you will see a double-paned window from which you view the hierarchical list-

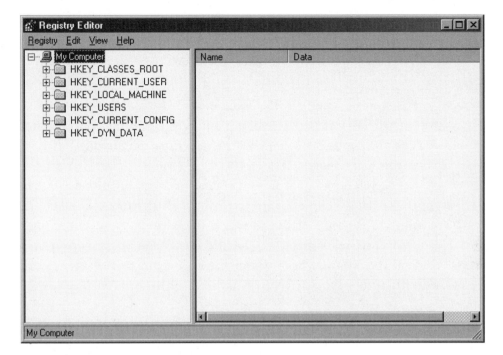

Figure 8.2 Screenshot of RegEdit.

ing. It displays the contents of the Registry itself in six subtrees. The left pane lists Registry keys; the right shows the *value entries* associated with the correlating keys on the left. These value entries are limited to 64 KB in size and comprised of three parts:

- Data type, which appears as an icon
- Name of the value
- The value itself

You can double-click on any Registry key folder icon to display the listing for that key.

or

Pull down the Edit menu from the menubar, click Find, and perform a search on a phrase or text string you wish to locate. If you need to see if there are multiple occurrences of this same phrase or text string, simply press the F3 key to move from the first occurrence to the second, and so on.

3. Once you are satisfied with your changes, if any, choose Save and exit. Registry changes are immediate; you do not have to reboot your PC unless specifically instructed by a dialog window to do so.

Please note, however: If you cannot find what you are looking for, do *not* guess. Exit the Registry editor and get additional information before you try to edit again. Several Registry edits are provided as part of the Microsoft Knowledge Base.

Let me elaborate just briefly on the subtrees mentioned above to help you familiarize yourself with the information you will encounter when viewing the Registry. Each individual Registry key may contain both value entries as well as subkeys as specific identifiers, as shown in Figure 8.3. Each of the subtrees bears the name of a main or root key, which starts with the text "Hkey_". Six keys branch out beneath each subtree:

◄ *Hkey_Local_Machine.* Specifies machine-type information, including what hardware and software is installed and how it is configured to work with Windows

◄ *Hkey_Current_Config.* Looks back to a branch or subset beneath Hkey_Local_Machine called Config, which details hardware configuration data

◄ *Hkey_Dyn_Data.* Ties back to the Hkey_Local_Machine branch, which lists dynamic data or status information for different devices

◄ *Hkey_Classes_Root.* Points back to the Hkey_Local_Machine branch responsible for documenting certain software settings you have assigned (which include shortcuts, OLE, etc.)

◄ *Hkey_Users.* The record of the specific user information stored within Windows, with settings for both all users as well as user-delineated specifics such as desktop look-and-feel and application preferences

◄ *Hkey_Current_User.* Points back to a subkey of Hkey_Users for information specific to a particular user with a profile on the PC (most of us just have one if we have not utilized the user assignment options under Windows, which allow you to specify settings depending on which user is logged into the PC)

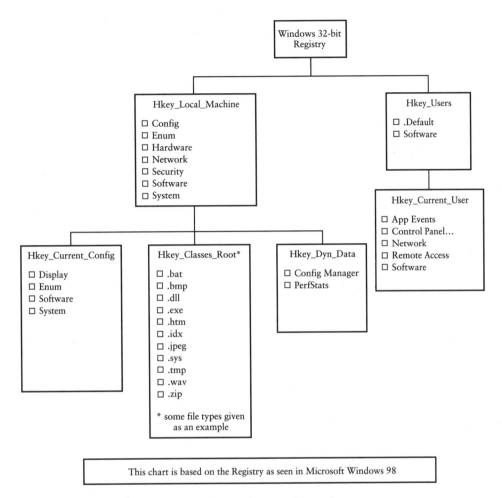

Figure 8.3 Subtrees (sections) of the Windows 32-bit Registry.

An Example of a Common Registry Adjustment

Have you ever wondered how you change the default search engine Microsoft Internet Explorer 4.0 or 4.01 uses when you click on the Search icon? To do so, you need to load RegEdit or other editing utility and modify the page value under the Registry key listed below:

```
HKEY_CURRENT_USER\Software\Microsoft\Internet Explorer\Main
```

The default search points to Microsoft's own portal search engine located at *http://home.microsoft.com/search/lobby/search.asp*. You need to change this to the *exact* Web search engine address you choose to use. Only providing part of the URL will cause problems.

Safeguarding a Working Copy of the Registry and Restoring It

One good feature about the Registry is that it permits you to import a previous Registry, export a working copy, or help recreate the Registry. These functions can be done either through the Registry editor itself normally or, in a pinch, through the real-mode version located on the Windows 95 or Windows 98 emergency Startup Disk (you can also use ScanReg for this in Windows 98).

Locate the Import and Export options on the Registry editor menu. Minimal help is provided for them in the online Help section available from the Windows Start menu, but more help can be found in the Microsoft Knowledge Base at *http://support.microsoft.com/support*.

If you find yourself with a badly damaged Registry, you may choose, or be forced, to use the emergency startup disk, which as I said contains a real-mode version of RegEdit that can be invoked from the command prompt using various switches. For example:

```
Regedit [/L:system] [/R:user] filenm1.reg, filenm1a.reg
```

Here:

/L:system should point to the location of your SYSTEM.DAT file

/R:user should point to the location of your USER.DAT file

filenm1.reg, filenm1a.reg should give the name of one or more .REG files to import into the Registry; if just one, omit the comma and second filename

or

```
Regedit [/L:system][/R:user] /e filenm2.reg [regkey]
```

Here:

RegKey gives you the option of starting a Registry key from which you may export a portion of the Registry, if you have any special need to do that.

Just typing:

```
Regedit /e
```

used alone exports the entire Registry

or

```
Regedit [/L:system] [/R:user] /c filenm3.reg
```

Here:

-/c filenm3.reg specifies the exact .REG file to use as a replacement for currently used and possibly damaged Registry files. However, you need to be completely certain that the filename specified (in this case, filenm3.reg) is a complete, viable copy of the Registry. If it isn't, you may encounter worse problems than you did before you tried the salvage maneuver.

There is also a utility called *cfgback,* published with the Windows 95 and Windows 98 Resource Kits, that also permits you to back up the data contained in the Registry files.

For those using Windows 98, this upgrade adds a new Windows Registry checker utility named ScanReg (see illustration below). The protected-mode version of this is ScanRegW. When you run Windows 98 setup, one of ScanReg's jobs is to check the existing Registry for problems and try to correct them before it proceeds with the upgrade process. Additionally, ScanReg automatically scans the Windows 98 Registry for empty data blocks and defunct or invalid entries. If a problem is detected, it automatically loads the last good backup you have of the core files. If none exists, it nobly attempts to make repairs.

You can customize settings for how ScanReg operates by editing the SCANREG.INI file with any text editor, including Windows' own SysEdit. Configuration options include where to store the backup files, whether to run the program at all, the number of backups to retain before overwriting, and whether to include other system file backups in the backup set. Note, however, that it will not remove entries for files that are referenced but no longer exist on the system. It also needs extended memory supported in order to run properly and may require up to 580K of available conventional memory to run at all.

For DOS-philes—and in this Windows world, I still count myself as one—you can back up the Registry files in Windows 95 and 98 easily from DOS by performing the following operation:

Make a copy of your Registry by typing the following command at an MS-DOS prompt:

```
CD\<windows folder>

ATTRIB -R -A -S -H System.dat COPY System.dat SYSTEM.PSS ATTRIB +R
+A +S +H System.dat
```

where <windows folder> is the name of your Windows folder.

Of note, you may find that later, when you attempt to determine a Registry key value by double-clicking on a file with a .REG extension that contains Registry entries, Windows itself may thwart your efforts by adding your entry as a new value rather than amending the current value appropriately. This is caused when the Registry key value in the source .REG file does not perfectly match the Registry entry itself. You need to double- and triple-check the accuracy of the entry, remove any trailing spaces, typos, or additional letters added, and make the changes necessary so they match perfectly.

Common Registry Problems (Plus Hardware Issues You *Can* Correct)

First, we need to talk about the errors that Windows may report with the Registry itself. When first loading Windows, you may receive a message telling you that there was a problem accessing the Registry, then prompting you to restore a working copy and restart your PC; or you might receive one telling you that Windows did not have enough memory to load the Registry. These are most likely to occur if the Registry is damaged or otherwise inaccessible for Windows.

If you choose to use the Restore from Backup and Restart option, you may find yourself reading the very same error message the next time you boot. While it is possible to ignore these sometimes and proceed, doing so may result in data loss or further damage. Thus, they are not recommended.

A better option is to restore a previously saved viable copy of the Registry, but if it has been any period of time since you last saved a copy, changes you have made since will not be reflected in the backed up version. You may want to try this instead:

1. Restart the computer. When you see the "Starting Windows 95" message, press the F8 key, then choose Safe Mode Command Prompt Only from the Startup menu.

2. Type the following line to export the Registry:

```
regedit /l:<path1> /e <path2>system.txt
```

where <path1> is the path to the System.dat file and <path2> is the path to the destination file. For example, if Windows 95 is installed in the Windows folder on drive C, type the following line:

```
regedit /l:c:\windows\system.dat /e c:\system.txt
```

3. Type the following lines, pressing Enter after each line:

```
cd\windows
attrib -s -h -r system.dat
```

4. Type the following line to rename the current Registry file:

```
ren system.dat system.old
```

5. Type the following line to import the System.dat portion of the Registry:

```
regedit /l: <path1> /c <path2>system.txt
```

where <path1> is the path to the System.dat file and <path2> is the path containing the file to import. For example, if Windows 95 is installed in the Windows folder on drive C and you want to import the System.txt file from the root folder of drive C, type:

```
regedit /l:c:\windows\system.dat /c c:\system.txt
```

6. Restart Windows 95 normally.

Other Problems

UNINSTALLING DOESN'T ALWAYS MEAN THINGS DISAPPEAR FROM THE REGISTRY

As mentioned in Chapter 6, the integration of Windows requires that programs and hardware support files (including drivers) be uninstalled properly instead of simply deleted in Windows 95, Windows 98, and Windows NT 4.0. Yet even when you make changes in the proper places, by using the Add/Remove Programs and modifying settings or deleting drivers in Device Manager, the Registry may retain information about them, which may either confuse Windows or lead it to produce annoying error messages, if not worse.

There are a number of third-party uninstaller/cleanup programs, including Quarterdeck's CleanSweep, Vertisoft's Remove-It, and Uninstaller, as well as a handful of shareware programs, that help uninstall programs a bit more aggressively than Windows itself. But these programs usually also try to search out and remove stray .DLLs, parts of applications, and other orphaned files they believe your system no longer uses. Definitely, as time passes, we all get bits and pieces left over. Some uninstallation routines are very clean and tidily remove every core and particle of themselves; others leave gaping wounds when you remove them.

But I have some problems with their use. One is that you need to have these programs installed early on, before you install any applications you may want to uninstall later, for them to work properly. Second, they can help point out duplicates and stray files, but these programs are really not smart enough to do a superb cleanup job. The more aggressive they are, the more risk your data may operate under—for instance, if they make a bad decision about what to remove and something that should stay ends up being removed. There are some fail-safes built in, but mistakes happen, and you can wind up with an application that fails to load on a PC that suddenly doesn't do Windows.

Perhaps the most common errors to occur related to hardware as it applies to the Registry is the Registry's habit of retaining information about older equipment. When it does this, Windows may not always recognize and configure a new device to work with it.

One example of this sometimes occurs with various Microsoft pointing devices (the Microsoft Plug and Play serial mouse, the IntelliMouse, and the Playball trackball unit) when you are trying to install them as a replacement pointing device in Windows 95 and Windows 98. According to Microsoft, the problem is more likely if the device you are replacing is a Microsoft, Microsoft-compatible, or Logitech pointer. Using the Add Hardware wizard in Control Panel does nothing to resolve this situation if it arises.

I'll walk you through the workaround suggested by the Microsoft Knowledge Base, because I think it gives you a good idea of the few Registry-based hardware dilemmas you may face:

1. You need to remove the following Registry keys:

   ```
   Hkey_Local_Machine\System\CurrentControlSet\Services\Class\
   Mouse\<nnnn>
   ```

   where <nnnn> is an incremental four-digit number starting at 0000.

2. Remove the following Registry keys, if they exist:

```
Hkey_Local_Machine\Enum\Root\Mouse\<nnnn>
```

where <nnnn> in an incremental four-digit number starting at 0000.

3. Remove all Registry keys under the following Registry key, if they exist:

```
Hkey_Local_Machine\Enum\Serenum
```

4. Remove the following Registry key, if it exists:

```
Hkey_Local_Machine\Software\Logitech\Mouseware
```

5. Use the right mouse button to click My Computer, and then click Properties on the menu that appears.

6. Click the Device Manager tab.

7. Click each serial pointing device, and then click Remove.

8. Click OK.

9. Restart Windows 95 or Windows 98.

When you restart Windows, the attached pointing device will be detected and the appropriate drivers will be installed.

Another such pain arose for me recently when I had to reinstall a Hewlett-Packard (HP) DeskJet 660 Cse printer. I was chagrined to discover that each and every time I booted Windows, it found the new printer again, as if Windows had no idea this printer was already installed. But this turns out to be a known issue with Plug and Play printers, including my model (the 660), the HP 4L, the Epson Color Stylus IIs, and the Canon Bubble Jet BJC-4000.

The culprit in this case is a likely corrupted entry for this value:

```
Hkey_Local_Machine\Enum\Lptenum
```

The solution is to remove this Registry key. Then when you boot Windows next, the printer should be redetected (again), properly installed, but you should not see the message reappear in subsequent sessions.

Now let's turn to a common problem for those using a PCI-IDE hard drive controller that permits serialization between the two IDE channels. If you have this, you may have noticed that Device Manager marks both the primary and secondary IDE channels with a yellow exclamation sign. You may have also seen that 32-bit file system access and 32-bit virtual memory are not available. You may be forced into MS-DOS Compatibility Mode as a result. This goes unresolved by removing and then readding the hard drive controller.

According to Microsoft Knowledge Base, this situation is caused when the protected-mode driver for your hard drive controller is not initialized the last time your PC booted. This writes a NOIDE entry to the Registry, which Windows takes as a command not to try to initialize this protected-mode driver during subsequent boots.

To fix this, locate and remove the following entry from the Registry:

```
HKEY_LOCAL_MACHINE\SYSTEM\CURRENTCONTROLSET\SERVICES\VXD\IOS
```

Windows 98 users only should navigate to the Tools\Mtsutils directory located on your Windows installation CD, right-click the NOIDE.INF file, then select Install. This should remove the NOIDE entry, if it exists, with the problem resolved on the next boot.

Two possible scenarios appear to be responsible for this failure to initialize the protected-mode driver. One is when a supported drive is present on the primary IDE controller, while the drive on the secondary IDE controller—a CD-ROM drive is a likely suspect—requires a real-mode driver to operate fully. When serialization is required, a conflict results between the primary using protected-mode and the secondary using real-mode. When push comes to shove, both drives are forced into real-mode status.

It also reportedly can occur when the driver for the IDE controller is purposely removed and then reinstalled from Device Manager, or the protected-mode driver is purposely disabled and then enabled again, *if* this happens on a PCI controller not designed for dynamic disabling and enabling.

In Windows NT 4.0, Dr. Watson, the diagnostic/troubleshooting utility, is enabled by default. For many, this is good news because NT often can benefit from the kind of scrutiny that helps NT system administrators detect performance issues. But for those who want to turn it off, try this amendment to the Registry:

1. From the Start button, choose Run, and type in then type "regedit" (without quotation marks; also, the .exe is not necessary).

2. Search for and locate the following entry in the Registry:

   ```
   HKEY_LOCAL_MACHINE\Software\Microsoft\Windows
   NT\CurrentVersion\AeDebug
   ```

3. Select the AEDEBUG key to highlight it, then click on the Export Registry file from the Registry menu.

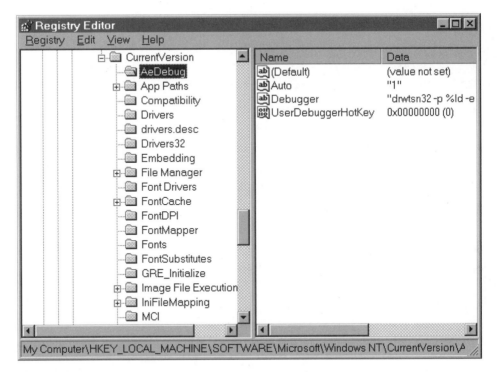

Figure 8.4   NT RegEdit edit of HKEY_LOCAL_MACHINE.

4. Choose a location and name for the saved Registry file, then choose Save.

5. Finally, delete the AEDEBUG key

This method allows you to restore the saved copy of the Registry if you find removing the Dr. Watson option was not a good choice for you. But you can also reinvoke it by typing this line from the Run option on the Start menu:

```
Drwtsn32 -I
```

Then choose the Registry file created above.

NT also packs with a command line Registry manipulation utility called Reg.exe.

Other Registry Utilities

Following are a few other Registry utilities you might find useful. Keep in mind that before you try any of these out for the first time, you should back up your current Registry (Fig. 8.5).

RegMon

The free Windows 95 utility works as it sounds, to provide a monitor. It reports all accesses to the Registry while telling you the process that accessed it. It also provides information on any API calls used and the Registry keys employed from that API, as well as the value and parameters of each of these calls. I recommend it as a tool for becoming savvy about the processes that go on invisibly—as you work—between Windows and the Registry. You may also use it as a tool for troubleshooting a particularly difficult Windows error or application issue.

Setmeup98

This shareware utility allows you to view and configure both hidden and advanced options within Windows without requiring you edit or tweak the Registry yourself.

TweakUI

This is a suite of tweaks and quick fixes available from Microsoft separately from Windows and developed by their Power Shell team as part of the Windows PowerToys collection. While it's marvelous for Registry tweaks that would be hard for you to perform yourself with only intermediate knowledge of the Registry, it doesn't make serious adjustments useful to overcoming hardware conflicts. Use it to achieve certain desktop changes and customizations.

Be sure to use the version of PowerToys and its tweakui specific to your version of Windows. Windows 95 users can download a copy from Microsoft at *http://www.microsoft.com/windows/downloads/default.asp? CustArea=pers&Site=family&Product=&Category=Power+Toys+%26+ Kernel+Toys&x=9&y=20;* Windows 98 users will find their copy tucked away in the Tools folder on the Windows 98 install CD. This is another situation in which it will truly pay you to read the README.TXT file that accompanies the utility so you can understand what it is and does.

One final note about Windows Registry:

> I've said it before, but let me reiterate: Registry editing is serious business. Don't do it casually, don't do it without backing it up, don't it with less information than you need, and don't do it unless you are prepared to deal with any problems that may arise. Registry tweaking is analogous to

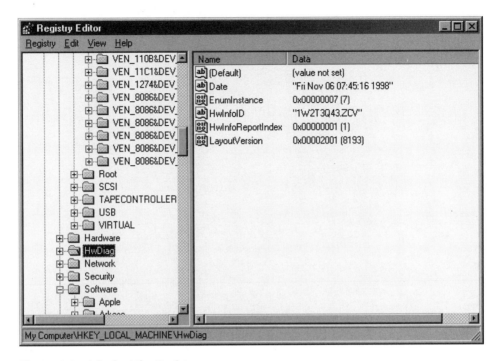

Figure 8.5   A look at the Registry.

surgery. There are minor procedures, there are major ones—and both can result in the grave discomfort and sometimes even the death of the patient if precautions and protocols are not followed.

I don't want you to be scared away from ever touching your Registry. I just want you to know how important it is to read and develop a better understanding of the Registry so you can perform surgery with some precision and good results. The Microsoft Knowledge Base, several Windows and PC user magazines, and many books cover this matter with specifics and detail, and I recommend you use them to build your base of information.

CHAPTER 9

Operating Systems: How-Tos of Starting Over from a Disaster

Topics covered in this chapter include:

◀ The Dos and Don'ts of starting over

◀ What you need handy when you do start fresh

◀ Special setup considerations by operating system

◀ Importance of backing up once you are fully operational

There comes a time when Windows can be probed and patched no more. At least, it becomes no longer practical to mend or build on top of a rocky foundation. This is particularly true of Windows 95 and Windows 98, and to some degree, Windows NT. Since Windows 3.1 doesn't use the Registry indexing approach, it is easier to simply expand a fresh copy of a corrupted file and continue on with business. As a general rule, the more complex the operating system, the less it enjoys being simply patched when there is a serious problem like an errant Registry, mismatched drivers or files, or worse.

Making the Decision to Start Anew

Before you go off and reformat, let's talk for a minute about good and bad reasons to start fresh. Too often, people reformat and reinstall for the wrong reasons. I happened to inventory the lame reasons I have heard for doing it within just a 10-day period, and they include:

◀ To do a routine modem installation (there are easier ways, and I can't think of one situation I've encountered in my work in the last 10 years that required this as part of a routine modem addition).

◀ To improve the PC's video output (wouldn't trying a new driver be a great deal easier?).

◀ To install DOS support for hardware to run a game (this could be added with the hardware's DOS install routines, usually on a floppy or CD packed with the device or found on the manufacturer's Web site; or you can just get the drivers and add them to the CONFIG.SYS and AUTOEXEC.BAT, if necessary, using any text editor).

◀ To remove Microsoft Office 95 routinely (here, the person wasn't looking for a fresh start, but thought that removing a large application required reformatting and reinstalling).

◀ To free up disk space (well, you won't have the old clutter after a reformatting, certainly).

These are rather silly, uninformed examples of why people start fresh, but since they are ones I hear daily, I think they are worth noting. The point is a good many people do this for the wrong reasons when something less drastic will fix whatever issue they have. If Windows never had the proper settings or drivers to start with, and you haven't successfully resolved these problems and noted what steps you took to fix them, how will installing a fresh copy or formatting help? It may, but the odds of it being worthwhile are slim to none. All you're doing is starting from scratch and making yourself go through the old issues again.

Also, you may have resolved some initial problems over time and find those problems back. You probably won't recall everything you did before to fix these problems. In this situation, of course, a backup could work wonders.

Personally, I don't think reformatting and starting fresh occasionally is a bad idea at all. Most of us tend to be moderately to very disorganized in our PC work, and a surprising amount of clutter can amass. A fresh system tends to run faster, because you haven't weighted it down yet with all the things we tend to add when we're using our PC daily for months or years.

But starting fresh is an elaborate, time-consuming prospect. If you don't have any programs, software, or data/text files you care about losing, the process is easier. FDISKing, if you do that, will wipe a disk of data, so too will formatting (both discussed more in the "Hard Drives" section in Chapter 10). Most of us have things stored on our hard disks we would not care to lose. Yet many of us are not doing regular backups to protect the loss of those files.

With these caveats in mind, following are some good reasons to start fresh:

◀ After working with a beta program or application that has left your system unstable

◀ Overall operating system instability that you cannot isolate and resolve, after investigating the Windows Registry, hardware, and hardware conflict issues, and tracking back to the last thing you installed or changed before the system became unstable

◀ Slower and slower Windows performance despite regular defragmentation with DEFRAG or other compatible hard disk optimization programs, and other regular maintenance

◀ When having severe problems with an application that creates many hooks into the operating system so that it shakes the operating system when it does not work properly (Windows 95 and Internet Explorer 4.0 is one example; also service releases and updates)

◀ When a virus or other calamity renders Windows completely incapacitated

What If Your Boot Disk Doesn't Work?

But what happens if you find you cannot boot your PC from a boot or recovery disk in your floppy disk drive? One of several different issues may be to blame, including:

NOTE Your system may be set to bypass the floppy drive on boot, jumping instead right to the hard drive. Look in CMOS settings (usually in the Advanced screen) and make sure your computer is set to boot from the correct floppy drive letter. See Figure 9.1. Remember to save any necessary change.

The boot disk itself may be bad. Hopefully, you have a spare (and if you don't, you will of course make spares immediately after this crisis passes). If

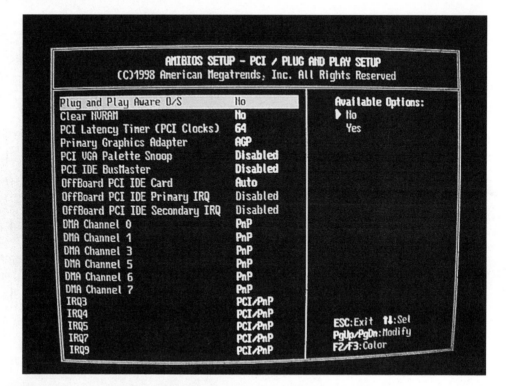

Figure 9.1 CMOS - Plug and Play setup

not, use another PC in your home or office to make one, or ask a responsible friend or associate to create one for you. Remember that you need to include any drivers or additional files required, such as a DOS driver for the CD-ROM drive if you're reformatting and reloading Windows.

There may be something wrong with the hardware itself. The first thing to check is that the 34-pin floppy cable is seated properly at both ends. It could also indicate a bad floppy drive controller or sometimes just a floppy drive with a high accumulation of dust within the mechanism that prevents the boot disk from being read.

Why DELTREE May Not Be the Best Option

If you have been using Windows for any period of time, you likely saw someone recommend that the best way to do a complete kill-and-clean (wiping out Windows to install it all fresh) was by using the DELTREE command. DELTREE has its place as a tool, because it does indeed make sure lingering corrupt files or files—including all the folders or subdirectories under the Windows directory—that may not be overwritten during a problem with the installation/setup are gone, gone, gone.

But DELTREE was a tool designed when Windows was a much smaller entity. Using it to delete the massive Windows versions of today can take longer than even performing a format or using FDISK. The time necessary to reinstall Windows is the same either way, and it's required whether you use DELTREE or FDISK/FORMAT (again, mentioned more in "Hard Drives" in Chapter 10).

Reinstalling vs. Reformatting

WINDOWS 3.1X REINSTALLATION

If you're not deleting or formatting to achieve a completely fresh start, you can reinstall Windows so that it retains many if not all of your existing settings (Program Manager configuration, INI files, desktop options, and more). To do this properly, you need to install Windows to a new directory and *not* the existing Windows directory, where C:\WINDOWS may be the existing Windows and C:\NEWWIN the new setup. You then need to rename certain key settings files to different names, such as the .GRP files, which maintain your different Program Manager groups. It is also necessary to rename all your .INI files, the REG.DAT (which maintains Registry information), and your .FOT files (fonts).

You do this by going to the DOS command line (quit to DOS rather than double-clicking on the MS-DOS icon on your Windows desktop), and then typing:

```
Rename c:\newwin\*.grp *.grn

Rename c:\newwin\reg.dat reg.dan

Rename c:\newwin\*.ini *.foo

Rename c:\newwin\system\*.fot .foo
```

What this accomplishes is to rename the new installation's key information files to names other than ones Windows can recognize and use

(Windows can't run SYSTEM.INN, for example—it needs an .INI extension). This prepares the new installation to be copied into the existing Windows directory to freshen possibly corrupted or nonworking Windows situation, while not copying new, default settings, which would remove all the customization you have done.

Next, you need to modify the file attributions of any and all files in the existing Windows directory and its C:\Windows\system subdirectory. Again, you do this from DOS by typing:

Attrib -s -h c:\windows*.* /s

Attrib -r c:\windows*.* /s

Attrib -s -h c:\windows\system*.* /s

Attrib -r c:\windows\system*.* /s

Xcopy c:\newwin c:\windows /s

Xcopy c:\newwin\system c:\windows\system /s

where

> Attrib is attrib.exe, which allows you to modify file attributions, such as hiding or unhiding a file or making it read-only or making a read-only file into a normal file. The latter is what we're doing here.
>
> where -s removes the files' designation as system files
>
> where -h removes the files' hidden status, rendering them visible in File Manager without specifying to Show Hidden Files or from DOS
>
> where -r removes their read-only status, meaning the existing files in Windows—*except for* the old settings for customization—can now be overwritten by the fresh Windows files being copied from the new directory

When you next type WIN to load Windows, it should load with freshened necessary files but retained personal settings.

Remember, if you have your existing Windows set up in a directory named other than Windows, or you rename the temporary new directory something other than NEWWIN, make the appropriate changes in the commands run to reflect these naming differences.

Using the EXPAND Command

Remember, if you only have one file you can identify as corrupted, or know you need a fresh copy of it to troubleshoot a problem, use the EXPAND command. If you're using DOS 5.0 or later, type:

```
EXPAND /?
```

at the DOS command prompt to get a listing of switches and options for using this command to decompress files off your master Windows 3.1x diskettes. Files on your Windows master diskettes are kept there in a compressed format to squeeze more files onto the diskettes, allowing fewer diskettes for installation. EXPAND allows you to do just that: expand them and change their filename appropriately, into your existing Windows directory.

First, you need to locate the diskette on which the file you need to expand is located. Say for example you need a fresh copy of SWAPFILE.EXE. On the master diskettes, in compressed format, you can find this file as SWAP-FILE.EX_. To properly expand this file into your existing Windows directory overwrite or replace the SWAPFILE.EXE already present, do this:

1. Make certain the proper Windows installation diskette containing this file is located in the floppy drive of your PC.

2. At the DOS command prompt, type:

```
EXPAND A:\SWAPFILE.EX_ C:\WINDOWS\SWAPFILE.EXE
```

This file is expanded and copied from the master Windows diskette and renamed to its appropriate uncompressed filename in your Windows directory.

Here's a good second example, I think, in case you don't realize that unless you have MOUSE.COM or MOUSE.SYS already loading in your AUTOEXEC.BAT or CONFIG.SYS (respectively), it doesn't expand a mouse driver off the Windows installation diskettes. Once you are assured Windows is running properly again, you can use the DELTREE command from DOS to remove the directory in which you installed the temporary new Windows setup.

NOTE If you suspect that it is indeed your Windows-configuring .INI files causing the problems for which you want to do a fresh install, this method of retaining the .INI and other customization files is obviously not for you. It will overwrite all the detail files, support files, and executables for Windows while retaining all the files that included information on your customization choices. You can either omit .INI from the list of files provided to retain by renaming or start completely fresh. DELTREE might be your best option here.

Need Just a New WIN.INI or SYSTEM.INI for Windows 3.1?

Many times, either because your WIN.INI or SYSTEM.INI file is corrupted, damaged, or simply clogged with entries that you suspect may be causing errors, you need to replace this to see if you can get by the problem.

Replacing Windows 3.1 WIN.INI

To do this, have your master Windows 3.1 installation diskette set handy, then:

1. Rename the existing WIN.INI in your C:\WINDOWS directory to WIN.WAS by typing at the DOS command prompt:

   ```
   RENAME WIN.INI WIN.WAS
   ```

2. A fresh WIN.INI can be found in the compressed WIN.SR_ file on Disk 1 (Disk 2 or 3, respectively, for Windows for Workgroups 3.1 or 3.11) of the master Windows 3.1 diskettes and copied/decompressed to your Windows directory by typing, at the DOS command prompt:

   ```
   EXPAND A:\WIN.SR_ C:\WINDOWS.INI
   ```

3. Using any text editor, including Windows Notepad or DOS EDIT, open WIN.INI.

4. Add this line to the [windows] section of WIN.INI:

   ```
   COOLSWITCH=1
   ```

5. Add (or modify, if existing) this line to the same section:

   ```
   DOCUMENTS=TXT
   ```

6. Remove this line:

   ```
   SetupWin=1
   ```

7. Save your changes and load Windows, as you would normally.

However, if after you do this, you note that the fonts appear to be overly large and distorted, Microsoft recommends the following steps to correct them:

1. Reinstall your printer driver by choosing the Printers icon from Control Panel.

2. Select the printer from the list of installed printers, and click the Install button. When complete, click on Close.

3. Next, double-click the Fonts icon in Windows 3.1 Control Panel, click OK.

4. From the directories list, locate and choose the Windows System or C:\WINDOWS\SYSTEM directory (which is where your TrueType font files are stored for use).

5. Click on the Select All button, click OK, then click Close.

6. Quit Windows and restart

Remember to use your former WIN.INI file, renamed WIN.WAS in this example, to troubleshoot your current WIN.INI file and to reference and copy any particular lines you think you may need for operation.

Replacing Windows 3.1 SYSTEM.INI

This allows you to copy and construct a fresh SYSTEM.INI that knows what hardware you have connected overall but loads no third-party drivers, which may interfere or cause an error (great tool for troubleshooting).

1. Rename your existing SYSTEM.INI in your Windows directory to something else, like SYSTEM.WAS

2. Copy and expand the copy from your Windows 3.1x master diskettes (Disk 1 of the 3.5" diskettes or Disk 2 of the 5.25" diskettes) by typing:

    ```
    EXPAND A:\SYSTEM.SR_ C:\WINDOWS\SYSTEM.INI
    ```

3. From DOS, move to the Windows directory by typing:

    ```
    CD \WINDOWS
    ```

4. To launch Windows setup so you can configure for your hardware, type:

    ```
    SETUP
    ```

5. Select your hardware as prompted from the Setup program, approve the changes, and quit Setup.

6. Using any text editor, including DOS EDIT, open the fresh SYSTEM.INI file and make the following changes:

a. In the [Boot] section, change the SHELL= line to read:

```
SHELL=PROGMAN.EXE
```

b. Remove or disable the line TASKMAN.EXE=

c. In the [386Enh] section, add these lines:

```
32BitDiskAccess=<Boolean>
device=*int13
device=*wdctrl
```

Note that <Boolean> here should be substituted with the word ON if you wish to turn on 32-bit disk access or with OFF if you want to shut off 32-bit disk access in Windows.

7. Save your changes and then restart Windows.

Windows 95/98 Reinstallation

If you haven't reformatted and you're installing something like Windows 98 over the top of Windows 95 or an existing Windows 98 installation, it's not a bad idea to check for existing hard disk problems or issues before you run Setup. While it's true that ScanDisk runs as part of Windows Setup, it does nothing more than scan for problems. If it finds any, it does not fix them—it prompts you to exit and run a thorough ScanDisk yourself.

Very important to remember is that the vast majority of people have their Windows 95 and Windows 98 install packages on CD-ROM and not floppy diskettes, so you *need* to have the CD-ROM drive operational. This means that you need to have the driver for the CD-ROM and the file MSCDEX.EXE available. These should be on the boot disk. For information on how to make sure you have them and how to have them properly installed on your boot disk, refer to the section "Boot or System Disks" in Chapter 3.

TIP For Windows 98 users: If you're installing Windows 98 for the first time—or you have freshly formatted your current hard disk or replaced it with a new one and you're adding back Windows 98—you may be able to make a Windows 98 startup disk even if Windows 98 fails during Setup. To do this, at the DOS command prompt, change directories to the Windows Command directory by typing:

```
CD \Windows\Command
```

And then run the BOOTDISK.BAT file located there by typing at the DOS prompt:

```
BOOTBAT
```

> **NOTE** *Never* leave software running in the background when you try to rerun Windows Setup or do anything like an operating system upgrade. Among the programs to disable include virus checkers, crash prevention tools, Windows management helper interfaces such as First Aid, and, yes, any games or system monitors you have running. Check your Startup Menu and then double-check what tasks are running by pressing Control-Alt-Delete. Anything you know you can safely stop from running should be halted by using the End Task button.

SPECIAL NOTES ABOUT UNINSTALLING WINDOWS95B/C AND WINDOWS 98

Like all recent Microsoft operating systems, both Windows 95B/C and Windows 98 allow you to uninstall them if you choose to do so. That is, it allows you to uninstall them *if* you have retained the backed up previous operating system files on your hard disk that your current version of Windows created during the original installation process.

But these versions present a special problem with uninstalling because they support the use of FAT32 drive use. Both allow you to run a conversion utility that changes your typical FAT16 drives into ones using smaller clusters and, thus, less disk space gets wasted—returning more for your use. Since earlier versions of Windows, as well as Windows NT 4.0 (NT 5.0 is expected to read FAT32 and does in beta), can't read FAT32 drives, uninstalling these versions once you have converted to FAT32 means you have to reformat and start over. (Did I just hear a groan?)

Other conditions prevent uninstalling. These include:

◅ Missing winundo.dat, winundo.ini, and winlfn.ini files (required for uninstallation)

◅ A system that has been upgraded to Windows 95B or later while using DriveSpace disk compression

◅ Data corruption, such as may occur with a boot sector virus

◅ After using a third-party hard disk partitioning utility, such as PowerQuest's Partition Magic (if the partitioning was performed *following* the original installation of Windows)

◅ Missing unstal.exe file (some programs remove this to prevent Windows 98's uninstallation following these programs' installation); check your Windows\Command folder

NOTE If you have a problem shutting down Windows during the uninstallation procedure, try rebooting your PC and at the boot menu, select Command Prompt Only and run UNSTAL.EXE from the DOS command line.

To uninstall Windows 98, for example, if you have none of the above-listed conditions:

1. Choose Start|Settings|Control Panel.
2. Double-click the Add/Remove Programs icon.
3. On the Install/Uninstall tab, click Uninstall Windows 98, and then click Add/Remove.

NOTE If you have one file or one set of files you simply need to replace in your existing Windows setup, you can use the EXTRACT command to extract files from the compressed *cabinet* format in which they reside on your Windows 95 or 98 CD. For a complete list of switches and options when using the EXTRACT command, at the DOS command line, type:

```
EXTRACT /?
```

TIP If you have the hard disk space, and many of us today with larger hard disks do, you may want to copy all of your installation and .CAB files for Windows 95 or 98 from the CD into a separate directory on your machine. This way, you can install directly from the hard disk during times if you need to reinstall or just extract some files from a .CAB when you have not done a format or FDISK operation. It's faster to install from your hard drive than from the CD.

NT AND HARDWARE AT SETUP

As we already discussed in Chapter 6, NT during its Setup will not install all the device drivers you will need for hardware connected to your PC. Most notably, these include drivers for your pointing device (mouse or trackball), video adapter, hard disk, and network interface card (NIC), if present. It also won't load a driver for your sound card, most likely, and may give few options for adding a printer or scanner.

Here is how these devices can be added: When NT's text-based part of Setup is initiated, you can specify (by responding with the letter S) that you need to install various drivers not packed with Windows NT itself. You will, of course, need the floppy disk or CD containing the appropriate drivers for the specific hardware you need to add. NT Setup then looks for a file labeled OEMSETUP.INF and extracts information from it, then displays a list of drivers contained within that file.

Once text-based Setup is complete, Windows NT 4.0 then reboots back into the graphical Setup portion, where it performs a system search for a video adapter and/or a network card, then loads the appropriate device driver(s). When installation of NT is finished, you are then able to add devices not picked up during NT's Setup, such as your sound card. To do this:

1. Choose Start|Settings|Control Panel.
2. Locate the icon representing the device category you want to install—for example, modems or printers, or choose Multimedia for a sound card.
3. Double-click the appropriate icon.
4. Choose the Device tab from the menu.
5. Install as prompted, providing the necessary drivers.

You can check IRQ conflicts from the Device tab once something is installed, but NT also provides a utility called the Windows NT Diagnostics program, which rapidly analyzes and reports problems of a system resource or general hardware conflict nature to you, which you can then correct.

Windows NT 4.0 and Reinstallation

Unlike other versions of Windows, Windows NT won't let you simply reinstall a fresh copy of itself over an existing version. This is because the setup check function in NT 4.0 is trained to look only for versions of NT earlier than 4.0; if it finds 4.0 already residing on your drive in the default location for NT 4.0, it simply won't install. You will likely see one of the following error messages displayed:

◀ Setup could not find a previous version of Windows NT installed on your computer. To continue, Setup will need to verify that you qualify to use this upgrade product. Please insert your Windows NT Workstation CD- ROM from Windows NT 3.1, 3.5, or 3.51, into your CD-ROM drive.

◀ Setup could not find a previous version of Windows NT installed on your computer. To continue, Setup will need to verify that you qualify to use this upgrade product. Please insert your Windows

NT Server CD-ROM from Windows NT 3.1, 3.5, or 3.51, into your CD-ROM drive.

◀ No previous version of Windows NT could be found on your computer. Setup is unable to verify that you qualify to use this upgrade product. Press F3 to exit.

What you can do is install Windows NT 4.0 to a different folder or use the full version of Windows NT 4.0 Workstation or Server to install, rather than use, the upgrade version (if that's what you tried). Also, don't try moving or copying your existing Windows NT 4.0 installation to another drive or hard disk. It's not supported and likely won't work. Operating systems beg to be installed to have everything work properly anyway. You don't want your operating system "taped" in.

On reinstalling Windows NT 4.0 to an existing installation, please realize that your settings, profiles, and files will not exist on the new installation (meaning you chose to reinstall and not upgrade). This is because installation removes all user/administrator-defined settings and Registry entries, because the installation process assumes there is no previous installation and nothing to carry over to the new installation from an old one. Also, anything in the Profiles folder under NT, for example, is lost as well because new profiles and their related files are written. According to Microsoft Knowledge Base, the Profiles folder (C:\WINNT\PROFILES \username—where username is the name of the account you use to log into Windows NT) may include the following folders:

◀ Application Data
◀ Desktop
◀ Favorites
◀ NetHood
◀ Personal
◀ PrintHood
◀ Recent
◀ SendTo
◀ StartMenu
◀ Templates

To preserve these settings, profiles, and files, you need to use the upgrade option, or face manually resetting everything.

STOP errors

If you're installing Windows NT 4.0 again over an existing installation, you need to know what service packs for NT you may have installed since you first installed NT. This is because the application of service packs (particularly SP2) prior to a reinstall of NT can send NT into a flurry of STOP errors when trying to load NT, such as:

```
STOP: 0x0000001E (0xC0000005, 0xFF1BBD79, 0x00000000, 0x00000038)
KMODE_EXCEPTION_NOT_HANDLED Address ff1bbd79 has base at ff1ae000 -
tcpip.sys.
```

or

```
STOP 0x00000050 (0xFF10c004, 0x00000000, 0x00000000, 0x00000000)
PAGE_FAULT_IN_NONPAGED_AREA
```

If this occurs, you need to try to restore NT to a bootable state and remove the offending service packs (which you can reapply later, as needed or desired). To accomplish this, Microsoft recommends the following steps:

1. If the partition is formatted as NTFS, install Windows NT to a different directory so the files on the partition are accessible.

2. If the partition is formatted as FAT, boot instead to MS-DOS.

3. Change directories to the Service Pack 2 uninstall directory:

   ```
   (%WinRoot%\$NtServicePackUninstall$)
   ```

   or

   ```
   ($NTSER~1 or similar name if under DOS)
   ```

4. Copy all the *.sys files in the uninstall directory to the %WinRoot%\System32\Drivers of the original Windows NT directory.

5. Copy Win32k.sys from the uninstall directory to %WinRoot%\System32.

6. Copy all other files to %WinRoot%\System32.

7. The system should now be starting correctly. Other errors may be encountered at this point, but the system should start.

8. Start the Service Pack 2 update program, but select to uninstall the service pack. This should bring your system back to a PRE-SP2 configuration.

If the service pack was not the source of your original problem, Microsoft suggests you reapply the service pack, but choose *not* to make an uninstall directory in order to preserve your original Windows NT system files already contained in the previous uninstall directory.

Again, as noted earlier, you may avoid a lot of this hassle if you try *not* to install NT 4.0 again over an existing version, because it leads to system confusion, mismatches, and errors that can render NT nonfunctioning.

NOTE You cannot install Windows 95 or 98 over an existing version of Windows NT 4.0. It will not work.

CHAPTER 10

Performing and Achieving
Successful Upgrades

In this chapter are included the following topics:

◄ Basics of a successful upgrade/new install

◄ Adding manufacturer drivers

◄ Multidisplay (extended desktop) setup in Windows 98

◄ NT-specific issues with hardware installs

◄ Disabling onboard sound and video for replacement by fully featured adapters

◄ Installing various devices

◄ Installing operating systems from a hardware perspective

The worst installs and upgrades, or the ones you remember the longest because they were the most treacherous, are the ones you are not prepared to make. Yes, adequate preparation beforehand has been a recurrent theme in this book. So, too, has been providing you with the information you need to identify and assign resources, how to troubleshoot problems as they occur, and how to know what you want to add will work for you on your setup.

Which brings us to the point of planning those upgrades and achieving them with the highest probability of success. Certain things are constants throughout almost all installs. These include drivers, because most devices need drivers in which to work. Windows packs with a standard list of drivers for popular devices, but it may not always support your particular make and model. The driver also may have been updated since your device was packaged for shipment, and it may be the later driver you need just to get operational. If you need the device to work while in DOS as well as within Windows, you need to add drivers to the DOS configuration files (CONFIG.SYS is usually the holder of all drivers, but the DOS-based mouse and CD-ROM utility MSCDEX load in AUTOEXEC.BAT). Sometimes all you will need to do is update a driver for a device already installed (and we cover that here as well).

In fact, let's create a checklist of things you definitely need to have on hand before you begin a device installation:

◁ The device itself; if applicable, this device should be kept in its anti-static bag until you are ready to work with it (meaning prepare and install, not look at and then lay aside for 2 hours while you tinker—I could tell you a very disgusting story about what my cat and her dyspeptic stomach once did to a brand new Matrox video board I removed from the antistatic bag before I was ready, but I'll spare you).

◁ Documentation for the device, which you have read.

◁ Drivers and/or driver installation programs for both Windows and DOS, if applicable.

◁ The assurance from documentation, packaging, or from the manufacturer's Web site that the product is rated to work with your version of Windows.

◁ Clean work area with enough room to comfortably remove the PC's cover, if necessary.

◁ Tools including a grounding strap, if used, a screwdriver, plus any accessories needed like cables or interface cards.

◁ Boot or system disk for your specific operating system version.

◁ Recent backup of your system, already done.

◁ Your Configuration Worksheet, discussed in Chapter 4; a copy for your use resides in Appendix D—this will point out available system resources.

◁ Patience and a 100-count bottle of your favorite headache remedy (optional, perhaps).

Always remember post-installation to check your hardware resources, usually done through Control Panel in Windows, to make sure you know what resources the new device has been assigned. Use this to update your Configuration Worksheet for that PC, but also use the information to adjust the resources, if necessary, working around other device assignments based on information you have learned in this book and from other sources.

ADDING HARDWARE IN WINDOWS 3.1

Of all mentioned, Windows 3.1 is probably the least fussy for new installations, but also perhaps the least elegant and efficient. You can readily use a different driver other than the one indicated for a particular device. This is useful when you know your driver won't work with the operating system and the device in question, but it also means you can install the wrong driver . . . potentially even install the wrong device, and Windows 3.1 won't stop you. Windows 95/98 and certainly Windows NT 4.0 make that a good deal harder to do.

But Windows 3.1, as mentioned, is not Plug and Play-compatible, so it won't "know" your hardware additions in the same way as Windows 95/98, nor will it so cleanly step you through an installation as they do. In many cases, however, all that is required is to physically install the hardware in question, and then copy a new or updated .DRV (driver) file to the WINDOWS\SYSTEM directory. Yet most hardware devices pack with a set of files, including a .DLL or dynamic link library and an OEMSETUP.INF, which provides an editable DOS configuration file listing default settings for that device, in addition to the actual driver file. These are typically installed by running a Setup or Install routine found on a floppy or CD-ROM provided with the piece of hardware. Additionally, you will find Add options on some of the device icons in Control Panel, such as Printers.

NOTE Make sure the device you are trying to add has Windows 3.1 or DOS drivers (you need one of each, except for things like your mouse, where Windows packs one of its own and you just need to supply a working mouse driver for DOS). You won't be able to use a later driver, written for Windows 95 or 98, for example, to get this to work.

ADDING HARDWARE IN WINDOWS 95/98

For those devices not automatically detected on boot and load after installing a new device, you can use the Add New Hardware wizard in Windows Control Panel in Windows 95/98, which will walk you through the installation and prompt you to provide the appropriate driver, if needed.

ADDING HARDWARE IN WINDOWS NT 4.0

As I've already indicated, Windows NT 4.0 is pretty fussy about hardware. It has to be, since it's a more powerful operating system expected to do more. Since more demands are placed on a system running NT 4.0, more demands are made upon the hardware attached to an NT 4.0 system. This is logical, but it's also a pain because not everything you can run under Windows 95 or 98 will happily work when installed in Windows NT instead.

If you are currently running another version of Windows and decide to make the move to NT, do read and digest Microsoft's NT Hardware Compatibility List (HCL). This tells you exactly what devices are and aren't supported in an NT environment. Often, you can make a piece of hardware work that is not on the HCL, but you have to prepare for an uphill battle sometimes. You will also find it nearly impossible to get support from either Microsoft or your hardware vendor if you choose to use a non-NT-certified product under NT. If you choose to go the road of using non-NT-specific hardware, you may want to check out the NT and hardware newsgroups on the Internet backbone to get help from fellow users who have been down that road before.

You should also be sure you have the drivers you need, in case Windows does not list either your device or the exact model of your device (better to have the right one than kludge along with the wrong one). Also have drivers for DOS mode operation, if needed, available at the time of installation.

Drivers

Sometimes, you won't need to install a whole new device but simply install a new driver for a device. These directions will guide you through installing manufacturer-supplied hardware drivers:

1. Choose Start|Settings|Control Panel, then double-click on the Add New Hardware icon to launch the Add Hardware wizard.

2. Windows 95: Click Next, then choose No, then choose Next

   Windows 98: Click Next, then Next, then Next once more, which brings you to a scan for Plug and Play devices.

   If Windows 98 can't find the device, choose No, This Device Isn't in the List," then click Next. Then choose No, I Want to Select this Hardware from a List. Then click Next again.

   If Windows 98 does find the device in its search, select instead, Yes, the Device is on the List, and select the device from the list. Then click Next. Finally, click Finish. In this situation, it's unnecessary for you to provide a manufacturer-supplied driver, because it was included in Windows 98's hardware list.

3. Click on the type of hardware whose driver you need to install, then click Next.

4. Click the Have Disk button.

5. Provide the path for the device driver you need to install (from CD-ROM, hard disk, or floppy), then click OK

   or

   Click Browse to locate the device driver you want to install.

NOTE You must provide the path for Windows to locate this device's OEMSETUP.INF file, provided from the manufacturer.

6. Make sure the appropriate .INF file is displayed in the dialog box. Click OK.

7. Choose the correct driver. Click OK.

8. Click Finish to finalize the driver's installation

NOTE If your new hardware installed is Plug and Play-compatible, you will need to click Next, then click Finish above.

BIOS (Flash)

Until the last few years, upgrading the programmable part of a motherboard—the part that allows you to configure and store settings read at boot—was nothing short of horrendous. You were lucky if all you had to do was order a chip to replace. Today, however, many motherboards allow you to flash or update your BIOS by downloading and applying it according to directions. This can add much-needed functionality and settings to your BIOS, but it also packs with some caveats, including:

◁ Not all motherboards are flash-upgradeable; of those that are, not all will permit you to return them to their prior state before the upgrade if there is a problem. You need to research this thoroughly through your manufacturer's support section either online or by telephone before you do this.

◁ Don't simply locate *a* BIOS upgrade and decide to apply it; verify that it is the upgrade offered for *your* motherboard make and model, and that it updates the specific BIOS already in place.

◁ This is another time when reading the documentation accompanying the product—in this case, the flash upgrade—is not optional; doing so may be the only way you can preserve current settings.

◁ As a means of more fail-safe backup, jot down critical BIOS settings before you perform the upgrade to help you reset a faulty setting as needed later.

◁ Flash upgrades must be done start to finish. Don't perform them when there is any danger that power may be lost due to storm or other conditions; this may affect your supply of uninterrupted electrical service.

◁ Since your BIOS is likely to be made by one company and your PC (or at least the motherboard) by another, consult both before you attempt an upgrade to note special considerations.

It's important to know what motherboard you need to upgrade the BIOS on, and that information may not always be readily available (the date and sometimes revision number of the BIOS you are using should show on the screen during bootup). There are ways to tell, and many motherboard and BIOS manufacturers provide tips for identification on their Web sites. Try the following steps for identifying the BIOS in use by your motherboard, offered by American Megatrends Inc. (AMI):

1. Shut down your PC, and pull the power plug.

2. Next, either unplug your keyboard altogether or hold one key down (which jams the keyboard buffer).

3. Power-up your PC, and wait as it stalls through bootup because of the missing keyboard or jammed buffer.

4. In the left-hand corner of your screen, you should be able to read a long string of letters that identify your BIOS (and called the BIOS identification string). For example:

```
51-0102-zz5123-00111111-101094-AMIS123-P
```

If the BOLD number is:

1, 2, 8, or a letter - it is a NON-AMI Taiwanese motherboard

3, 4, or 5 - it is a TRUE AMI motherboard

50 or 6 - it is a NON-AMI US made motherboard

9 - it is a Evaluation BIOS for a Taiwanese manufacturer

If an AMI board, contact AMI or visit their Web site at *http://www.amibios.com*; if not, check the identification number against other BIOS manufacturers, such as Award.

Motherboard

Let me take a moment here to explain the complexity of a motherboard upgrade. The reason I'm doing this is because I see so many who think it's either completely impossible and shouldn't be done, or they think it's a no-brainer. In reality, it's neither impossible nor is it something you should attempt without proper information and guidance.

Swapping out a motherboard is no small operation, because many connections must be made to the replacement motherboard and each must be right. Guesswork is not encouraged. Plugging the wrong connection in the wrong spot may not only result in failure of whatever that connection does, it can potentially blow out the motherboard's delicate electronics itself, perhaps taking with it anything currently attached to that motherboard.

Shopping for and selecting a motherboard is no walk in the park, either. There are many types of boards out there, with many varying chipsets, and each one has its own set of features and limitations. Asus and Abit motherboards are popular favorites, as are Tyan, Soyo, Intel, AOpen, and Gigabyte. These are but a few of the many manufacturers.

When making the decision to upgrade or change out your motherboard, you have to consider what you need in the new one. Motherboards based on the BX chipset—based on 100-MHz clock speed and full support for AGP, USB, and more—are where we are at right now, and anything less leads you to a quicker upgrade. Combine a BX motherboard with a Celeron (this is a lower-cost Intel Pentium II processor; original ones had no L2 cache, while new ones have 128 KB L2 cache) that you carefully overclock, and you may achieve something close to a full Pentium II's speed for well below the going price of a PII-capable motherboard and PII CPU.

If you experience instability—ranging from the minor to the obscene—following a motherboard installation, it is critical that you recheck your installation. Look at the cables and connections, check for broken pins and motherboard mountings, which could produce a short, assure that power connections are complete, and carefully examine the seating of RAM and add-ons cards. Use a light to check for fractures in the motherboard itself, which can be caused by rough installation.

Give particular attention to the metal standoffs that mount the motherboard in place on the chassis. If any of these standoffs are coming into contact with the actual printed traces seen along the printed circuit board that comprises your motherboard, electrical shorting may result. Some recommend using insulator/protectors, like a nonconductive washer, between the motherboard and the metal standoffs to prevent interaction. Don't hope things will be ok if forced into place.

You can try booting your system from a boot diskette. If stability improves, the problem may not be your new motherboard, but an improperly installed—or failing—hard disk or hard disk controller. If the instabilities remain, however, even if diagnostics don't state a problem conclusively, you may need to replace the motherboard yet again. Never run a system for long using a motherboard you think is damaged or unreliable. A motherboard is too important, and a failure with it can be catastrophic.

Video

Adding a new video adapter can be lots of fun, but sometimes, the trick is all in the driver:

1. First, power-down, unplug PC, unplug monitor, open case, and ground.

2. Once inside the case, locate the video card you want to replace. If you don't know which one that is, find where your monitor plugs into the back of the PC. The video card should be attached to this assembly, within the case in its expansion slot.

NOTE Separate instructions follow on issues related to replacing on-board video (a video adapter built into the motherboard) with a free-standing video card

3. Loosen the screw holding the board in place, and gently pull the card from its slot. You may need to rock the board gently to help dislodge it, but take care not to be rough. Such mishandling may not only damage the video card itself, but the motherboard as well.

4. After thoroughly reading the documentation that accompanies it for specific installation steps as well as configuration information, remove the new video card from its antistatic bag and mount it in its slot. Exercise care to seat it properly so you won't need to come back inside the case to check your work. The rule of thumb is *do not force* the device into place; you should feel it fit into place properly. The pins on the card should line up neatly with the depressions in the slot. When they do, simply push the card into place. Make certain one end isn't jutting out because a perfect, even connection is necessary.

TIP Be very careful of all the cables and wires inside your PC when you are doing this sort of work inside the case. Snapping wires or snipping cables is not good for the PC, and some of the printed circuit boards we work with in installing PC hardware can be very sharp (with artifacts from manufacturing making some of it nearly as sharp as jagged glass). Keep the cables and wired pushed gently but firmly out of the way of your (albeit tiny) work area. Consider a drive tray that allows you to tuck the cables around a slide-out tray for accessing hard drives, etc.

5. Once the card is seated securely in its expansion slot, screw it into position.

6. Once you are certain everything is back in proper place, you can return the cover, and plug both the PC and monitor back in again, and turn the PC back on. Windows 95, Windows 98 and Windows NT 4.0 should notice the new video adapter and arrange accordingly.

PROBLEMS INSTALLING NEW VIDEO ADAPTERS ON PCS WITH ONBOARD VIDEO

Some PC manufacturers, particularly those with cheap clones of the type you can buy in many discount department stores, save money and space by including the video adapter as part of the motherboard, instead of as a separate plug-in card. While they can work fine, they can be touchy to replace with a better-grade, separate video adapter.

Of the PCs with onboard video, some are designed to detect a new video card replacing its onboard video. These will automatically disable the onboard video and help set up the new video adapter almost seamlessly. Others, however, require your intervention in disabling the old video setup. You do this by entering CMOS, locating then disabling any settings provided for the onboard video, then saving the changes. You may want to delete the driver for your current video adapter using Device Manager. You then shut down the PC and prepare to install the new video adapter, as detailed above.

While you have the cover off your machine, take a moment to recheck the documentation for your motherboard. This is to cover the chance that the motherboard also has a hardware switch or jumper located on it, which also must be disabled to completely disable the onboard video. Once you've checked that, go ahead and install the new video adapter. Windows should be able to find the new installation and try to install the proper driver for it accordingly (have the disk or CD-ROM handy if the video adapter isn't on the list of supported devices).

NOTE Some motherboards may require a BIOS upgrade to allow the disabling of onboard video, while some motherboards prevent such disabling altogether. It is important that you check with your PC manufacturer before you try replacing a video adapter in a PC equipped with onboard video.

LARGER RESOLUTIONS AND WINDOWS 98

Let's take a side trip and discuss monitors, displays, and a known problem with Windows 98. We are seeing this happen more often because larger monitors with higher resolution are becoming far more affordable.

When you go into Windows 98's Control Panel and double-click on Display to try to increase the screen area, you may find yourself unable to properly select (or select at all) a higher resolution. Microsoft says this is caused by the monitor's Extended Identification Data, or EDID, which in this case stores incorrect information about itself. This erroneous information is passed along to your PC and Windows 98, which has no way to determine that you are actually using a different monitor, capable of the higher resolution.

The suggested workaround involves disabling Windows from automatically detecting PnP monitors, which should force yours to be detected more accurately. To try this:

1. Choose Start|Settings|Control Panel, then double-click on the Display icon.

2. Select the Settings tab, then click on the Advanced button.

3. Select the Monitor tab, then click on the Automatically Detect PnP Monitors checkbox to clear it. Click Apply

4. Click Change, then Next. Then click on Display A List of All Devices in a Specific Location (which allows you to pick the driver from its location on your hard disk, CD-ROM, or floppy drive) Click Next.

5. Click on Show All Hardware, and follow the instructions provided there to complete the installation of your correct monitor and driver combination

WINDOWS 95 AND 98 IRQ CONFLICTS WITH PCI VIDEO ADAPTERS

Here we come up against an almost newly classic conflict. For the most part, 32-bit Windows display/video drivers do not reference an interrupt request (IRQ), but PCI video adapters do demand an IRQ be assigned to help ensure backward compatibility on the system. ISA and VESA local bus (VLB) video adapters don't do this.

The problem crops up when you install a PCI video adapter that is specifically configured to use one identified IRQ, because Windows may blithely assign the video adapter an IRQ that is already in use. You may see error messages, video instability, or lockups as a result, or the issue may be limited to a conflict message in Device Manager, under the device in question.

Now, as I already told you, PCI does support (albeit carefully) the sharing of PCI IRQs. However, Windows won't let a PCI device share an IRQ with a non-PCI device (an ISA sound card or an IDE controller, for instance). This is in part because Windows doesn't configure PCI devices for implementation—the PC's BIOS does that during POST. Windows just believes whatever BIOS reports to it about the state and status of PCI devices attached to it.

The solution is to go into Device Manager, determine what device is trying the share the IRQ with your video adapter, and assign that device a new IRQ setting.

3D VIDEO AND IRQS

Most regular video cards use an address space rather than an IRQ when configuring for installation to your system. However, today's popular 3D video cards—in high demand because of their added graphical gaming capability—do indeed require an IRQ. (PCI cards use them too, as mentioned in the previous section.) This is needed to cover what is considered the critical timing necessary for processing advanced 3D functions like rendering and MPEG playback.

While it is still possible to use a 3D card without assigning it an available IRQ, you will lose the enhanced features just mentioned. Since a 3D card minus these options may largely cancel out your reasons for having one, reevaluate your interrupt list to try to make an IRQ available.

However, it is far from uncommon to see some erratic system behavior, odd error messages, or even occasional lockups following a new 3D video card installation. Sometimes, this is because the 3D card's BIOS is out-of-date and requires a flash upgrade to stabilize its operation. Both older BIOSes and the nonstandard design of some of the cheaper 3D accelerators have been blamed for incompatibilities with specific types or makes of motherboards and CPUs. Check the 3D card manufacturer's Web site for specifications and compatibility warnings.

Alternatively, the problem may lie in a classic hardware interrupt conflict. When you installed the new 3D card, you assigned, or it grabbed, an interrupt already in use by another piece of hardware. The errors and oddities encountered may be very erratic in frequency. This can be explained by the possibility that the other hardware addition using the same interrupt is not always engaged at the same time as the serious 3D components of your 3D accelerator. When just one or the other is on, your PC may behave fine. When both try to work simultaneously, the conflict surfaces and you see the bad behavior. To investigate this, go back to Device Manager and check for identified conflicts. To be sure, check the properties settings of the 3D card against other hardware. Adjust as needed.

TIP If you're installing a 3D card for the first time, and you know your PC has been prone to run at a warmer range as a general rule, watch the temperature for a few days post-3D addition. Some of these cards run very hot and could theoretically drive a poorly cooled PC into the red zone. Read Chapter 12 to learn more about PC cooling techniques.

TIP When installing PCI cards/adapters, remember to double-check that the PCI's gold-stamped bus connector is appropriately seated in the 32-bit bus expansion slot.

USING ADDITIONAL MONITORS/VIDEO CARDS IN WINDOWS 98

One often-cited addition to Windows 98 is that it will support multiple monitors. But for each additional monitor you want to run, you also need to add another video card (up to 9 are supported, numbered 0 to 8).

There are some rules you must live by with this. One is that the adapters used must be of PCI or AGP type, particularly for the primary adapter (the first adapter with the first monitor in the chain). They don't all have to be identical, and you can configure them using different resolutions and color depth, depending both on your needs and what the hardware itself supports. But ISA and EISA won't work for this arrangement. Also check documentation on a video adapter because a few PCI and AGP devices won't work properly in a multiple-monitor situation.

To tell if your video adapter's chipset supports multi-display, do this:

1. Choose Start|Settings|Control Panel, then double-click on the Display icon.

2. Choose the Settings tab, then click on the button marked Advanced, as shown in Figure 10.1.

3. Compare the adapter type listed here with the drivers for adapters Microsoft indicates are supported for multi-display support in Windows 98:

ATI Mach 64 GX (GX, GXD, VT)ATIM64.drv
ATI Graphics Pro Turbo PCI
ATI Graphics Xpression

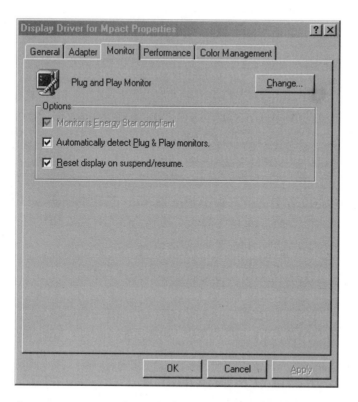

Figure 10.1 Control Panel/Display Settings Tab/Advanced/ Monitor.

ATI WinTurbo
ATI Rage I, II, & II+ATI_M64.drv
ATI All-In-Wonder
ATI 3D Xpression+ PC2TV
ATI 3D Xpression
ATI 3D Xpression+
ATI Rage Pro (AGP & PCI)ATIR3.drv
ATI Xpert@Work, 4 & 8 MB
ATI Xpert@Play, 4 & 8 MB
ATI All-In-Wonder Pro
S3 765 (Trio64V+)S3MM.drv
S3 Trio64V2(DX/GX)S3MM.drv
Diamond Stealth 64 Video 2001
STB PowerGraph 64V+

STB MVP 64

Miro TwinHead 22SD

Hercules Terminator 64/Video

Number Nine 9FX Reality 332 (S3 ViRGE)

Number Nine 9FX Reality 334 (S3 ViRGE GX/2)

Number Nine 9FX Reality 772 (S3 ViRGE VX)

California Graphics V2/DX

Videologic GraphicsStar 410

Cirrus 5436CIRRUSMM.drv

Cirrus Alpine

Cirrus 5446CIRRUSMM.drv

STB Nitro 64V

S3 ViRGE S3V.drv

(ViRGE (325)

ViRGE VX (988)

ViRGE DX (385)

ViRGE GX (385))

Diamond Stealth 3D 2000

Diamond Stealth 3D 3000

Diamond Stealth 3D 2000 Pro

Number Nine 9FX Reality 332

STB Nitro 3D

STB Powergraph 3D

STB Velocity 3D

STB MVP/64

STB MVP/64 3D

STB WorkStation (2 & 4 output)

Miro Crystal VR4000

ET6000ET6000.drv

Hercules Dynamite 128/Video

STB Lightspeed 128

Compaq Armada S3MM.drv

Trident 9685/9680/9682TRID_PCI.DRV /9385/9382/9385

Jaton Video-57P

If your adapter type is not on the list, don't panic yet. Check your manufacturer's Web site to see if a more recent driver has been released for your adapter that will allow you to use it in multidisplay support. If it hasn't, ask when it will. You want to be sure to have the correct driver for your card; this means either asking the manufacturer to identify a very similar adapter's driver you can use temporarily or buying another adapter altogether which is supported.

TIP If the Extend My Windows Desktop option is grayed out so you can't click on it, go to Control Panel and double-click on the Display icon. Choose the Settings tab and click on the Second Monitor icon. This should make the Extend My Windows Desktop option available to you.

Be aware that if you mix and match PCI and AGP adapters in the same machine, your system will automatically see the PCI adapter as the primary adapter. Why? Because the PCI bus is enumerated first, which means it is seen and identified first. This is a function of your BIOS and not something you can readily tweak in Windows 98 itself. For you to force the AGP adapter to be enumerated first and thus recognized as the primary adapter in a multidisplay arrangement, you either need:

◁ A PCI adapter capable of disabling VGA functionality at the hardware level (check with your PCI adapter's manufacturer to see if yours fits this); or

◁ A BIOS that supports the enumeration of AGP before PCI (check with your motherboard manufacturer or BIOS creator to see if your BIOS meets this or if an update is available that you can apply)

You will also find that not all programs work well on an extended desktop, multidisplay arrangement. These tend to fall into some general categories, such as remote-control programs such as PC Anywhere, programs that use Adobe Type Manager (supporting ATM fonts), and both drivers and software designed to either alter the display driver or modify the GDI.EXE file.

Finally, you must enable multidisplay support, since it normally isn't set to be on automatically. If you don't, Windows may not be able to detect the presence of the additional adapters/video cards.

If you want to enable multidisplay support, install the adapters as indicated earlier in this section. Then:

1. From Windows, install the video adapter (and monitor driver, if necessary).

2. If prompted (you may not be), restart Windows.

3. Choose Start|Settings|Control Panel, then double-click on the Display icon.

4. Select the Settings tab.

A Display box pops up, as shown in Figure 10.2. Here, select the adapter you want to install for use, then click on the checkbox next to Extend My Windows Desktop onto this Monitor to enable multidisplay support. Click OK.

TIP You can test how well your multidisplay setup works in Windows 98 by opening something like MS Paint. Open the program, but keep it out of Full Screen mode. If you can drag the program icon for this properly from one monitor to the next, you're in business.

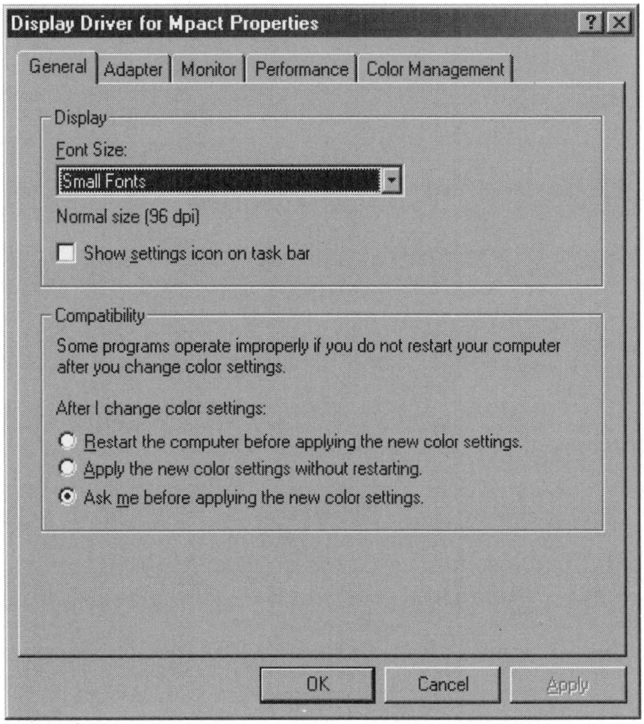

Figure 10.2   Control Panel/Display/Settings/Advanced.

Should you need to disable multidisplay support for any reason—say, to test the primary adapter during a troubleshooting scenario or to remove the capability entirely, you reverse the above process:

1. Choose Start|Settings|Control Panel, then double-click on the Display icon.

2. Choose the Settings tab, then click on the icon showing the second monitor.

3. Clear the Extend My Windows Desktop onto this Monitor option by clicking on it (make sure the check is removed from the checkbox). Click OK to finish.

If you install an additional adapter and monitor and find that you're not getting any graphic output on the second display, you need to check certain details. This includes making certain that the second video adapter is showing as installed in Device Manager and under Display, that the proper driver was installed for this adapter, and that the Extend My Desktop option is enabled. Also check physical connections, like the monitor being plugged in and turned on.

RAM

A problem with RAM—either dying old memory or freshly installed but untested new—is often evidenced by recurrent fatal exception errors in almost all versions of Microsoft Windows (regular and NT). These errors are jokingly if not lovingly referred to as BSoD or Blue Screen of Death, a nickname referring to the bright blue lockup screen you encounter (see Chapter 5 on troubleshooting). If you have just installed RAM and immediately begin experiencing these errors when you boot into Windows, shut down and recheck your installation. The new RAM could be defective, it could be of the wrong type for your motherboard, or you did not seat it properly when you installed it.

Very occasionally, I have witnessed systems develop problems when a tower or desktop case was simply moved; the result being that poorly seated RAM became further unseated during the move. Reseating it should clear this problem. However, RAM is very sensitive. Mishandling or improper installation can irrevocably damage it, requiring replacement.

One of my senior assistants in Microsoft/MSN ComputingCentral offers this tried-and-true method for determining if frequent Windows errors are RAM-based:

Try disabling the L2 external CPU cache and take the PC for a test run. If the problems go away, consider the RAM a suspect. It could also be that the BIOS settings for the memory are wrong. Double-check these in CMOS.

Sound Cards

INSTALLING SOUND CARDS IN WINDOWS 95/98

The more elaborate a sound adapter/PC sound system is, the more elaborate the installation process can be. You definitely want to consult any accompanying documentation for specifics on connections, information on installation utilities (many pack a configuration program), and any preinstallation tips that might be offered. And since these configuration utilities are likely to make changes to both Windows .INI files and DOS's CONFIG.SYS and/or AUTOEXEC.BAT, it's smart to make copies of these files before you start the installation process. After you've done this, follow these steps:

1. If you have another sound card installed that you are replacing with the new adapter, delete the driver from Device Manager. Then shut down Windows, power off the PC, and disconnect it from its power source (wall outlet, surge protector, or other).

2. Using a (usually Phillips head) screwdriver (if necessary, some of the newer cases have pull out drawers that allow you to access most if not all of the internals of the case through a simple slide-out tray), remove the PC's cover, and properly ground yourself, as discussed in Chapter 3.

3. Locate either the sound card you are going to replace and remove it, or locate the available slot you wish to place the new sound card into. Then install it in much the same way as we detailed in the earlier section on video cards, being careful to follow any special instructions from the manufacturer. In particular, you need to make certain the CD-ROM connection to the sound card is made, and that the board is properly seated in its slot and then screwed into place. Once it is, you

can hook up the speakers, microphone, or other external sound-input devices into the appropriate jacks located in the sound card's interface in the back of the PC (see sound card's documentation for details).

When you boot 32-bit Windows, it should see the card and try to install, but don't forget to run any configuration utilities that packed with the card. Once installed, if the volume is muted or very low, check the audio settings by clicking on the speaker icon in Windows SYSTRAY. Make certain none of the appropriate options are muted. Also double-check options under the Multimedia icon in Windows Control Panel.

If you upgrade or change your sound card, you may find that you no longer have volume control options. This can also happen after a reinstall of Windows. What happens is that the factors that determine whether you have sound tools such as volume control may be a function of the sound card itself and must be detected by Windows and recognized to work as they were designed to work. If your computer has an ISA PnP device that doesn't get switched on in the PC's BIOS, the device isn't seen by Windows until *after* Windows has evaluated what you have plugged in and what controls the device should be assigned. The result is that Windows may not know that your sound card is capable of being adjusted with these tools, and you may be locked out of them.

To get around this, you basically have to install the controls manually. To do this if Windows is also being installed:

1. Select the Custom Setup option.
2. When prompted to select the components you want to install, choose Volume Control in the section labeled Multimedia.

If Windows is already installed, here's how you manually add the Volume Control option:

1. Choose Start|Settings|Control Panel, then double-click on the Add/ Remove Programs icon.
2. Select the Windows Setup tab, choose Multimedia, then click on the Details option.
3. Click on the Volume Control checkbox to select it for addition. Click OK, then click OK once more.

Sound Card-Induced Lockups

While we often tend to think of video cards and RAM causing lockups, sound cards can cause them too—and probably far more often than we think. Evidence of a sound card-induced problem is apt to be less dramatic than that of other types of hardware crises. And because sound cards tend to want to use specific system resources (not just any IRQ and address range will do), it becomes more likely you could inadvertently create a conflict between a sound card and another device. Beyond that, they're fussy, because sound cards are actually complex multifunction devices and require resources not just for overall sound but for MIDI and drive interface as well.

If you begin to experience lockups you have reason to believe may be rooted with the sound card itself, just disabling the driver won't work. Your system will only find it anew on reboot, and then it will reinstall the driver. First, check Device Manager to try to spot a conflict going on with the system resources in use by another device. Do so with care because this is the most likely culprit.

If you absolutely can find no conflict in Device Manager, pop the hood on your PC and pull the sound card out. Notice any physical settings on the card and compare it against any documentation you have for it. Do they match?

If this checks out, try installing the sound card in a different slot, if one is available. If this doesn't work, pull the card again and leave it out until you can test it on another machine (which should produce the same results on a defective card) or just replace the card.

SCSI Adapters and Sound Cards

Two devices that can rather easily come into conflict are SCSI controller/ adapters and sound cards, because they often seem to grab the same I/0 range in which to set up shop. You might get an error report, for example, that your controller is working at 300 to 330h, right along with your sound card. This should be verified by a conflict reported in Device Manager as well.

Although you might think it's easier to adjust the sound card, this device generally requires residency on this address range to help make sure it's compatible with MIDI use, while the SCSI controller can live elsewhere more easily. So first change the SCSI controller's assignment to a different address range not in use, make certain any changes are reflected in Device Manager, then reboot, if prompted to do so. This should resolve the current situation (and create a new one, if you mistakenly move the SCSI controller into something else's address range).

Disabling Onboard Sound to Replace with a Sound Card

If you read the section earlier on disabling onboard video, understand that you run into a similar situation with removing sound that is provided through chips on the motherboard to replace with a separate sound card (mostly found with cheap clones). First of all, you want to check CMOS to see if, under Advanced PnP options, it gives you the option of turning off onboard sound. You also need to check the documentation for your motherboard or from your PC manufacturer (this information is on the Web; for example, for Packard-Bell PC clones using a modem/sound card combo) to see if it details specifically how to disable sound.

Once you have done this, you need to remove support for this onboard sound by removing its drivers in Device Manager. To do this:

1. Choose Start|Settings|Control Panel, then double-click on the System icon.
2. Choose the Device Manager tab, then click on the + sign in front of Sound, Video and Game Controllers, which expands to a listing of the various devices installed under this category.
3. Locate the driver for your onboard sound system (check PC manufacturer information if you're unsure which).
4. Choose Properties, then click on the Original Configuration box to clear it.
5. Repeat for any additional components of your onboard sound listed here.
6. Save changes.
7. Using a text editor (Windows Notepad works), remove, or REM out, the line for the DOS-based onboard sound driver from your CONFIG.SYS file, if applicable.
8. Save changes.

INSTALLING SOUND CARDS IN WINDOWS 95/98

If you're planning to install Windows NT 4.0 on a system with a sound card or plan to install a sound card to Windows NT 4.0, you need to know that NT, by default, does not detect or install them. You need to install them into the NT manually by doing the following:

1. Choose Start|Settings|Control Panel, then double-click the Multimedia icon.

2. On the Devices tab, click Add. See Figure 10.3.

3. Click the appropriate driver for your sound card, and then click OK.

Installing SoundBlaster Drivers to NT 4.0

To install support for Plug and Play-capable Creative Labs SoundBlaster sound cards under NT 4.0, you must install the Pnpisa.sys driver to enumerate the settings for the sound card, and then install the drivers available on the Windows NT CD-ROM. To do so, use the steps listed below.

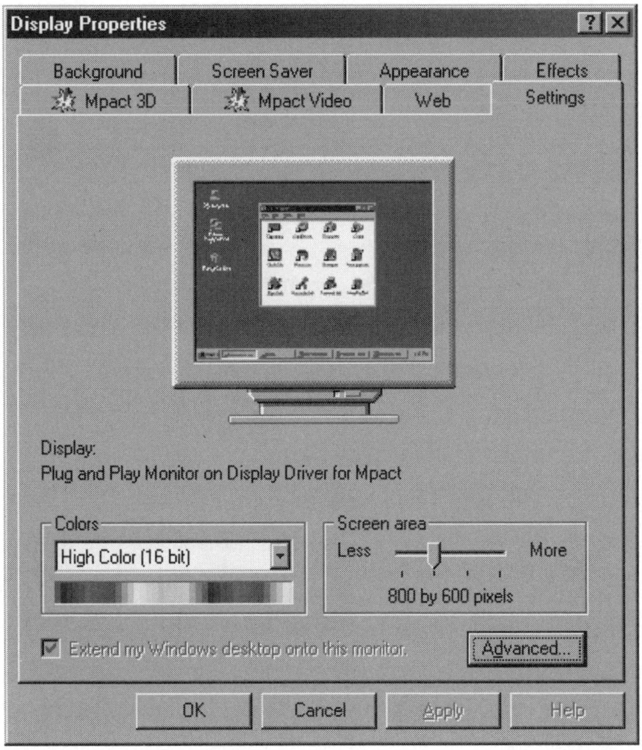

Figure 10.3 Control Panel/Display/Settings toward multiple monitors.

NOTE You must have administrative privileges to complete these steps. Also, you may want to install the updated drivers available directly from Creative Labs instead of the drivers included with Windows NT 4.0. If you choose to install drivers available from Creative Labs and you installed Windows NT 4.0 Service Pack 3, run the DEVPRE utility available with Service Pack 3 to install the Creative Labs drivers. Remove any previous sound drivers, if present (see Step 2 below). If you downloaded Service Pack 3, place the self-extracting Nt4sp3_i.exe file in a temporary folder and extract the files. To extract the files, type "nt4sp3_i.exe /x" (without quotation marks) at a command prompt. To run the DEVPRE utility, type "devpre devupd.inf" (without quotation marks) at a command prompt in the temporary folder. Type the path to the Creative Lab drivers when you are prompted.

Now, to install SoundBlaster drivers:

1. Install Windows NT 4.0 Service Pack 3 if it is not already installed. You can download the service pack from the following Microsoft Web site:

   http://support.microsoft.com/support/downloads/

   For more information about the availability of Windows NT 4.0 service packs, see the following article in the Microsoft Knowledge Base:

   ARTICLE-ID: Q152734

   TITLE : How to Obtain the Latest Windows NT 4.0 Service Pack To install Service Pack 3, open the folder containing the self-extracting executable file, double-click the Nt4sp3_i.exe file, and then click Yes when you are prompted to install Service Pack 3.

2. If any sound drivers are installed, remove them. To do so, follow these steps:

   a. Choose Start|Settings|Control Panel.

   b. Double-click the Multimedia icon, then on the Devices tab, double-click Audio Devices. Click the audio device listed, if any device is present, and then click Remove. Note that this step also removes any corresponding Musical Instrument Device Interface (MIDI), sound mixer, and line device drivers.

   c. If more than one sound driver is listed, repeat Step b for each audio device.

   d. Restart your computer.

3. Place the Windows NT 4.0 CD-ROM in your CD-ROM drive, open the Drvlib\Pnpisa\x86 folder on the CD-ROM, right-click the Pnpisa.inf file, and then click Install. Restart your computer when you are prompted. Note that you may not see the Pnpisa.inf file if Windows NT Explorer is set to hide extensions for known file types. To see the file, click Options on the View menu, click the Show All Files checkbox to select it, click the Hide Extensions for Known File Types checkbox to clear it, and then click OK. Now complete Step 3.

4. When the New Hardware Found message appears and you are prompted how to install a driver, click Driver from Disk Provided by Hardware Manufacturer in the Select Device box.

   If you choose to install the sound drivers provided by Microsoft, type the following path, and then click OK:

   `drvlib\audio\sbpnp\x86`

   If you choose to use the drivers provided by Creative Labs, type the path to the Creative Labs driver files.

NOTE See the note at the beginning of this section about installing Creative Labs drivers with Windows NT 4.0 Service Pack 3.

5. If you are prompted for a driver for the Creative Labs 3D Stereo Enhancement Technology device, click Windows NT Default Driver, and then click OK.

6. If you are prompted for a driver for the IDE CD-ROM (ATAPI 1.2) /Standard IDE/ESDI Hard Disk Controller device, click Do Not Install a Driver (Windows NT Will Not Prompt You Again).

7. If you are prompted for a driver for the Microsoft Joystick Port Enabler device, click Windows NT Default Driver, and then click OK.

NOTE If this choice is not available, click Driver from Disk Provided by Hardware Manufacturer, and then type the following path to the Windows NT 4.0 Joystick Port Enabler driver:

   `<cdrom>:\drvlib\audio\sbpnp\i386`

   where <cdrom> is the drive letter for the CD-ROM drive.

8. Restart the computer.

If you have problems installing a SoundBlaster device, please contact Creative Labs.

Modems

INSTALLING A MODEM IN WINDOWS 95/98

Adding an internal modem to your PC is very much like installing a sound card or video adapter, as previously detailed. Follow those instructions and you can get the card in place, but note any markings on the interface panel of the card, as it projects against the back of the PC. These are usually marked LINE IN to accommodate a phone line from your house phone line into the modem, and LINE OUT, where you can optionally attach a physical desk phone for use when you are not online. These appear immediately above or below modular phone jacks (RJ-11).

Don't underestimate how many modems are returned as defective because the incoming line was plugged into the outgoing line jack and vice versa. Also don't underestimate how many are returned because of a conflict with the mouse for the same IRQ, which usually isn't a tough one to resolve.

External modems are easier both to install and remove, because they don't plug into a slot on the motherboard but freely stand outside of the PC and pack their own power supply. They attach to one of the existing COM ports on the back of the PC via an RS-232 cable and connectors (internal modems provide their own). Externals are more expensive, because of the power supply. USB modems are external.

If there's one sage piece of advice to offer you in modem shopping, it's try to avoid purchasing a WinModem. For one, WinModems only work in Windows. Granted, not a lot of us do DOS-based communications anymore, but some do. A bigger reason is that they can be harder to manage. A WinModem is basically a regular modem stripped of some of its hardware components to reduce the cost of manufacturing. To make up for the reduction in hardware used, a WinModem depends more heavily on the PC's processor to take over some of the work typically done by the modem itself.

To keep prices low, many PC manufacturers—not just budget clone producers but heavyweights like Dell—now include WinModems as the default modem installed on their PC. The general consensus is that they'll become even more popularly used during these final years before we hopefully move to faster communications standards. After all, why pour a lot of money into a specific leg of this technology that has reached its practical limits over normal phone lines? But if you are offered the option, pay the $20 or so price difference and get a full-fledged modem when purchasing a new PC. It's still a bargain compared to replacing the WinModem with a standard modem later on.

Wherever possible, use standard system resource assignments for the modem and COM port, as shown in Table 10.1.

To install a new modem in Windows 95 and 98, follow these steps:

1. In Control Panel, double-click the Modems icon.

2. If this is to be the first modem installed in the computer, the Install New Modem Wizard starts automatically. If not, click Add.

3. If you want Windows to detect your modem, click Next. If not, click the Don't Detect My Modem . . . checkbox to select it, and then click Next.

4. If you chose to have Windows detect your modem, Windows queries the serial ports on your computer looking for a modem. If Windows detects an incorrect modem, click Change and select the appropriate manufacturer and model. Click Next, and then continue with Step 7.

5. If you chose to select your modem manually, click the appropriate manufacturer and model, and then click Next.

6. Click the appropriate communications port, and then click Next.

7. Click Finish.

TIP WinModems also tend to get "lost" after awhile, and need their drivers properly reinstalled.

TABLE 10.1   Modem and COM Port System Resource Assignments

Serial Assignment	COM Port Number	I/O Address	IRQ Number
1	COM 1	3F8h	IRQ 4
2	COM 2	2F8h	IRQ 3
3	COM 3	3E8h	IRQ 4
4	COM 4	2E8h	IRQ 3

INSTALLING A MODEM IN WINDOWS NT

Again, as with other hardware, you will get your best results with a modem designed and supported for use in Windows NT 4.0. If your new modem is on the NT Hardware Compatibility List (HCL), you should be able to get it working with NT with only minor tweaking, at most. If your modem isn't on the support list, check the manufacturer's Web site or call them to see if they can provide a driver (the file ends in .inf) that is known to work under NT.

Though it's not entirely impossible to use a Windows 95 or 98 modem driver for NT—some work decently and some just won't. Even if a Windows 95/98 driver can be coaxed into working, you'll likely do better with the NT-specific version. You may do all right using the "standard modem" option as well, but not all special features of your modem may be available to you without the specific driver for it.

However, if you need to use a non-NT driver, use the Modems icon in Control Panel to allow yourself to add the modem under NT. But specify Don't Detect My Modem when prompted, then click on the Have Disk option and provide the location of your modem's .INF driver. While the wizard for adding new hardware should start automatically if NT detects the new modem, you may need to manually go into Setup if it does not.

Once NT installs the modem, be smart and double-check what resources have been assigned. Here, you want to look for other hardware device conflicts, before you try using your new modem in dial-up networking.

Verifying COM Port(s) in NT 4.0

If you're having a COM port-related issue involving your modem and Windows NT 4.0, the best solution is to perform a verification of your COM port(s). To do this, double-click on the Ports icon in Control Panel, as shown in Figure 10.4 (you can do this in Windows 95/98 through Device Manager) and ascertain whether the COM port you believe your modem resides upon is listed. If it's not, you won't be using it to dial anyone until you get it recognized for use. (And if no COM ports are listed, is your mouse working?)

Other things to examine include the following:

◀ Check Device Manager for system resource conflicts—remember, for example, that setting a mouse up on COM 1 and a modem on COM 3 will result in a conflict, and that using IRQ5 for your

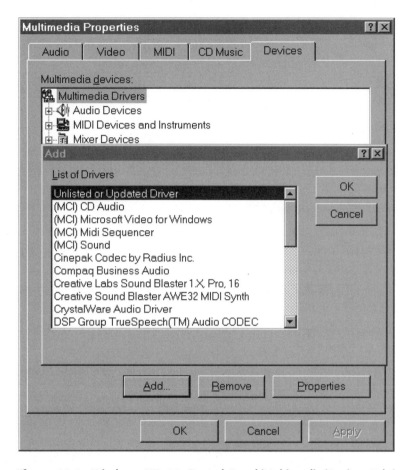

Figure 10.4 Windows NT 4.0 Control Panel/Multimedia/Devices Tab/
Click Add.

modem may cause it to war with your sound card, which really
wants IRQ5, given its choice. A base I/O address conflict should
also be suspected.

◄ Consider reinstalling the modem driver and any associated control
software for it—remember to remove the old driver first to limit
chance of failure.

◄ Check physical jumpers on the modem card itself, making sure any
settings match the documentation and the resources assigned under
NT itself.

◄ Check CMOS to ensure the COM port in question is not disabled,
and not somehow assigned to something else.

◁ Try the modem temporarily on another COM port—if it works there, the modem is not defective, but it may be configured for the wrong COM port or the COM port itself may be bad (try a different slot, too, if you have a like one available for internals).

◁ Check the System log with the Event Viewer for details of I/O or IRQ conflicts.

TIP HyperTerminal, available in Windows 3.1, Windows 95/98, and Windows NT 4.0, can provide an excellent testing tool for troubleshooting modem problems. If using it under Windows NT 4.0, however, make sure Remote Access Server is not running at the time (if it is, disable). Here's how you test under Windows 95/98 and NT 4.0:

1. Choose Start|Programs|Accessories|HyperTerminal, and then click the Hyper-Terminal icon.

2. When the New Connection wizard is displayed, click Cancel.

3. On the File menu, click Properties, and then click the modem you want to test to select it in the Connect Using list.

4. Click Configure, verify that your modem is set to use the correct port, and then click OK.

5. Type "AT" (without quotation marks) in the HyperTerminal window, and then press Enter.

6. If AT is displayed in the HyperTerminal window as you type it and OK is displayed after you press Enter, HyperTerminal recognizes the modem properly. If AT is not displayed as you type it or if OK is not displayed after you press Enter, review the previous steps in this article to verify that your modem is installed properly in Windows NT.

7. Verify that your modem can dial out using HyperTerminal. On the File menu, click New Connection, and then follow the instructions on your screen, as seen in Figure 10.6 on page 242.

8. Click Dial. If the modem's speaker is enabled, you should hear a dial tone and the sound of the modem dialing the phone number.

TIP Can you only see the port speed (usually 115 Kbps) when you use your modem to connect to something like your Internet Service Provider (ISP)? If so, try adding "AT&F1" (minus quotations) to your modem initialization (modem init) string, which should make it properly report actual connection speed. If "AT&F1" doesn't work, try "AT&F" instead.

By the way, if you notice sudden and seemingly inexplicable lockups or hangs on your system whenever you disconnect the modem from online status, the odds are that you are using an internal modem on COM2. First,

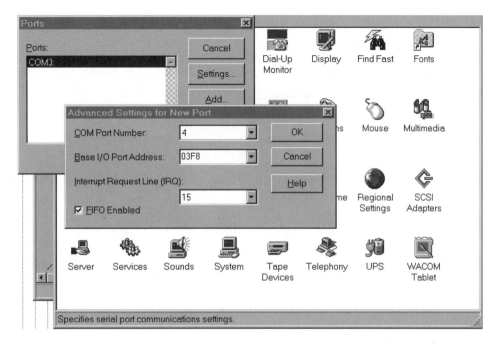

Figure 10.5 NT 4.0 Control Panel/Ports.

try reinstalling the modem's driver (you may want to remove the current one before). If you do have an internal modem using COM2, locate and disable the motherboard's own COM2 (remember, an internal modem adds another COM port to your PC). Check your motherboard documentation for details on how to do this.

Printers

INSTALLING A PRINTER IN WINDOWS 3.1

Go to the Printers icon in Control Panel, select Install or Install Unlisted or Updated Printer option available in the List of Printers dialog box window but check the printer's documentation first for any special instructions.

INSTALLING A PRINTER IN 32-BIT WINDOWS (95/98 AND NT 4.0)

To install a new printer, follow these steps:

1. Choose Start|Settings|Printers.
2. Double-click the Add Printer icon, then click Next. (See Figure 10.6.)

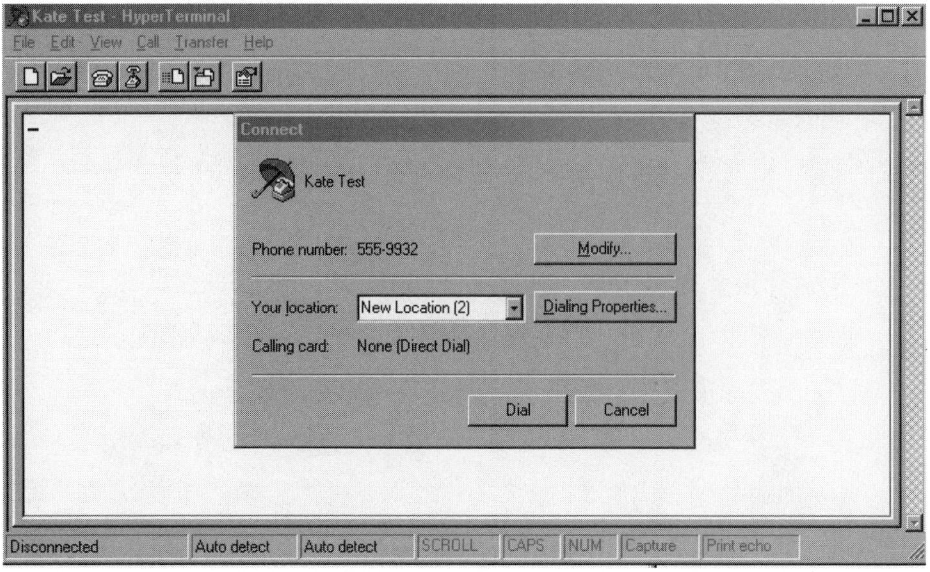

Figure 10.6 Screenshot of HyperTerminal.

3. Click Local Printer or Network Printer as appropriate, and then click Next.

4. If you click Network Printer, you are prompted for the network path for the printer. If you do not know the correct path, click Browse or check with your network administrator. Click either Yes or No in the Do You print from MS-DOS-Based Programs? area, and then click Next.

5. Click the appropriate manufacturer and model for your printer, and then click Next.

6. If you chose to install a local printer, click the correct port and then click Next.

7. Type a name for the printer (or accept the default name), and then click either Yes or No in the Do You Want Your Windows-Based programs to Use This Printer as the Default Printer? area. Click Next.

8. To print a test page, click Yes. Click Finish.

PRINTERS AND PLUG AND PLAY

Watch how you install a new PnP printer using 32-bit Windows' Add New Hardware Wizard. If you use this option (instead of double-clicking on the Printer icon in Control Panel) and end up assigning the printer as an

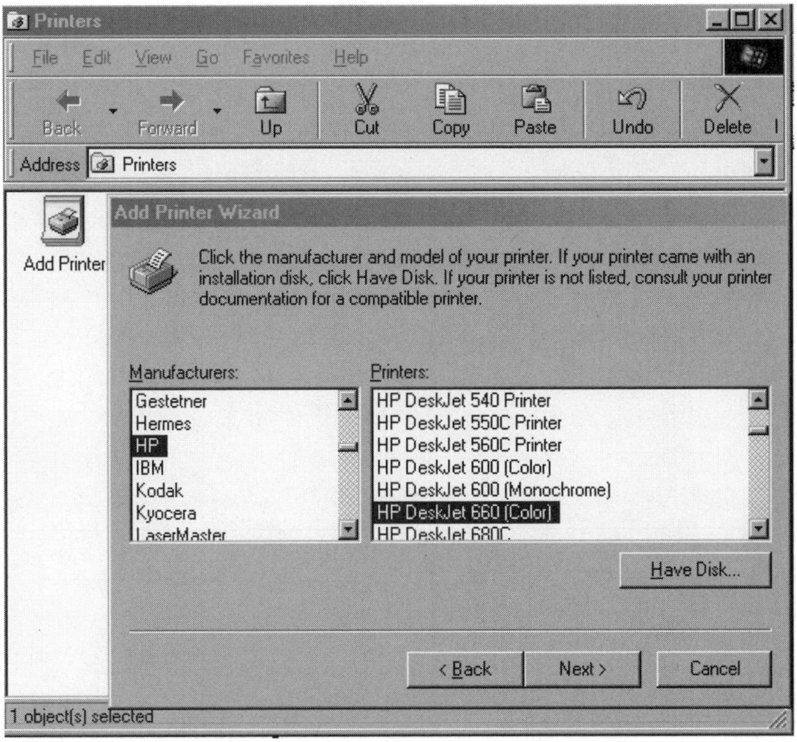

Figure 10.7   Add Printer wizard.

unknown device during setup, no proper driver is installed for it. Device Manager likely will list it as an unknown device, too. This means the printer runs a strong chance of not operating properly. (Remember, too, Windows categorizes any device as an "unknown device" if it does not have a specific driver for it to establish an identity.)

Either change the driver to the correct manufacturer's driver for this product or delete this "unknown device" entry and use the Printer icon in Control Panel to reinstall the printer, providing the correct location of the manufacturer's printer driver (if it's not listed in the driver list).

Hard Drives

NOTE In addition to this information, please consult "Hard Drives" in Chapter 11 for information on specifics, such as handling hard disks over 8 GB in size, more commonly found on today's new PCs.

Hard drive installation is one of the more involved types of hardware upgrades you are likely to do, because they require not only physical hooking up of the drive into an internal drive bay (located under the cover) in the PC itself, but proper prepping. This means preparing the disk to receive an operating system, or at least formatting for operation under an operating system and assigning any partitions necessary or desired. Partitioning, by the way, is a process by which you divide a physical drive into two or more logical disks. Say, for instance, you buy a new 6 GB drive and wish to dual boot between Windows 98 and Windows NT 4.0. You would partition the drive into two sections, perhaps of equal size, making two logical drives (with two differing drive letters) of 3 GB each from one physical drive of 6 GB.

You need a primary DOS partition from which you can boot, but you can have additional ones as well. And you can't just plug in a new disk and have it work; in fact, it's not recommended that you try to move a hard disk from one computer to another without proper prepping.

You also need to have a boot or system disk to do this effectively, and it needs to contain FDISK (or PowerQuest's Partition Magic) for partitioning the drive and FORMAT for formatting the drives. Please review the instructions for boot or system disk creation and additional files needed for you to work found in Chapter 3. (If I haven't suggested a full system backup lately, consider yourself reminded. Doing one before a hard disk installation is an excellent time.)

NOTE Most PC motherboard-onboard IDE controllers can accommodate two IDE drives each; both can be hard drives or one can be a hard drive with a CD-ROM drive attached to it, for example. In this situation, the first drive on an IDE controller is referred to as the master, and the second drive hooked to the first, is referred to as the slave drive.

PHYSICAL INSTALLATION

If you are simply replacing one hard drive for another, all you need to do is note the way the first one is connected to your system before you disconnect and connect the new drive the exact same way. For others, however, you first need to pull the cover, ground yourself properly, and then do a quick check under the cover to see where you want to place the new drive. Considerations include the following:

◄ If it's going in as the primary hard drive, you want it on the first IDE controller and you want to make sure the drive jumpers are set to Cable Select or CS.

◄ If the drive is going in as the first drive with another drive attached to it, it also must go on the first IDE controller; the first drive's jumpers must be set to Master, or M, and the second drive's jumpers to Slave or S; and the second drive must be cabled properly off the first drive (both need a power connection from the power supply).

◄ If you are slaving one hard drive to another, pick the appropriate drive as the Master—make it the larger, faster one; if there is a marked difference in drive speeds, you may want to assign the larger, faster one to the first IDE controller and the smaller, slower one to the secondary IDE controller (but adjust jumpers accordingly).

◄ If you assign a drive for the first time to the secondary IDE controller, make certain support for the secondary IDE controller is turned on or enabled in the BIOS, or any drives on this controller will not be recognized because the controller they reside upon will not be.

Once the PC is disconnected, the cover is off, and you are properly grounded, adjust other drives as necessary, and then (assuming a single-drive installation):

1. Install the new hard disk into its bay per the documentation accompanying the drive itself (and set jumper appropriately).

2. Attach one end of the wide ribbon cable to the appropriate input on the back of the hard drive, and attach the other to the PC's IDE controller; double-check that the connection is secure (if a secondary drive is attached, then a second wide ribbon cable is used to connect the secondary drive to the first drive).

NOTE One side of the wide ribbon cable has a red line running its length; be sure this red line runs along the same side corresponding to Pin 1 on the drive connection; reversing the cable can provide anything from strange errors to outright failure.

3. Attach the power connector firmly to the back of the drive (and to the secondary drive as well, if applicable).

4. Once satisfied that all connections are proper and secure, you can loosely screw the drive into place (enough to hold it, not enough to be difficult if you have to remove the drive again to check a jumper or connection), but keep the cover off until you are sure the drive is operational.

5. Reattach power and boot the PC, immediately jumping to CMOS. Look for a section entitled something like "IDE drive auto-detection," and follow the prompts to try to autodetect the drive, which it should do. (Older BIOSes may require you to provide all the technical information on the drive itself. This information usually accompanies the new drive. If not, check the manufacturer's Web site.)

6. Save your changes, then exit CMOS and allow the PC to finish booting.

7. At a DOS command prompt, type FDISK (this should be on your system boot disk if you cannot reach a hard disk with an operating system in place that provides it), then follow the prompts to create a primary DOS partition and any additional partitions you want on the drive. (FDISKing loses all information on the drive being partitioned; use Partition Magic by PowerQuest if you want to try to retain data.)

8. When partitioning is complete, you need to run FORMAT and provide the proper drive letter(s) needed, such as:

```
FORMAT C: /S
```

If it's a new primary drive, you also need to install the operating system.

SCSI Drives

I touched on the idiosyncrasies of SCSI drives in Chapter 3, but let's go over the differences between a SCSI and IDE drive installation. Physically, they install very much the same, except the drives connect not to the IDE controller, but to a SCSI host adapter, which serves as a sort of base unit from which SCSI devices operate (plugged into and chained out from). At least partly because SCSI allows more devices to be chained off a controller than does IDE, each SCSI device must get its own unique drive ID number (including the adapter). Because this varies by manufacturer, you need to consult your SCSI hardware documentation for specific info on how to assign a device ID to your devices properly. You also need to make sure that the drive is terminated properly, according to the directions provided. Improper drive ID assignment and improper termination are the leading cause for SCSI devices not to work as they should.

Troubleshooting a Drive Upgrade

Use the following as a checklist whenever you are having problems with drive upgrade:

◀ Under Windows 95/98 and Windows NT 4.0, check to make sure that there is no yellow exclamation mark or red warning attached to the hard drive controller and that no conflicts are seen between the controller, which usually takes IRQ 14, and other devices. If there are, resolve them and retry the drive.

◀ Make sure that all connections are secure and properly made (respective of jumpers, etc.).

◀ Make sure that changes have been made to BIOS settings as needed, including enabling the secondary IDE controller if necessary.

◀ If the operating system only sees part of a new drive installed, this problem may relate to incorrect BIOS settings or an outdated BIOS; contact your hard disk or BIOS manufacturer (or both) for details

OK, so what if you get hit with the following problem, which crops up from time to time? You get a PCI drive adapter, install it, and it just won't work. You take it out, pop it into another PC, and find it's now raring to go.

If you paid attention during the troubleshooting practicum in Chapter 5—or you're just possessed of extraordinarily good common sense—you know that if it works in another PC but not yours, the drive adapter is fine. It's something in your PC preventing it from working properly, most likely.

While the majority of PCI systems appear to automatically configure any card mounted in any PCI slot, there remain a lot that require you to manually initialize the settings for the PCI slot and device through CMOS.

As discussed in Chapter 6, modern PC BIOSes allow you to control far more variables related to the working of your PC than ever before. These include elements of PCI function related to how it relates to ISA (trying to assume command over the bus to reduce the hoggish influence of ISA devices), assigning IRQs to specific PCI bus slots on the expansion card, adjusting timing and latency, assigning specific details to the hard disk and controller being used, and far beyond.

In the scenario described above, you should check first to see if the PCI drive adapter is installed into a PCI bus-mastering slot. This is required. You also need to see if the slot it does reside in has been assigned an IRQ already in use by something else, which would create a conflict and perhaps the behavior you are seeing. If it is, you need to change the CMOS setting for this PCI slot to a unique IRQ. Both IRQ9 and IRQ10 are good ones, if available (or can be made available), but IRQ11 will work. An I/O address must also be provided.

Once you resolve this in CMOS, you must go back into Device Manager and change any entries necessary to make the system resources reported in Device Manager exactly match the values

CHAPTER 11

Hardware Dirty Dozen: Working Through 12 Common Conflicts and Problems

Topics covered in this chapter include:

◄ Basics of common hardware installation, including video and sound adapters and printers

◄ Common installation problems

◄ Specific instructions for troubleshooting video difficulties and multiple-monitor setups

◄ Variety of problems related to bad or improperly installed RAM

Now is the time to try to wed what you knew about resolving common hardware problems before and what you may have learned from this book about resource assignment, typical types of hardware conflicts, and how to identify the source of the problems.

Problem #1. IRQs, DMA, and I/O

Remember, not all hardware troubles are resource conflicts. Enough are, however, that there is good reason to check resource assignments whenever you hit a snag with an install or an issue with a feature or function once a device is installed. I've said it before, but it bears repeating: Familiarize yourself with Device Manager and visit it regularly, since what you learn here can help you more readily identify a resource conflict.

One tip-off to a resource conflict—besides a screaming error message in Device Manager—can be a device displaying intermittent malfunction. For instance, you install a new mouse, and it seems to work great most of the time. Yet whenever you use your modem or something else installed to a COM/serial port on your PC, the mouse locks up or just stops functioning. This should tell you another device is using the same IRQ (if not the same COM port) as the mouse, and whenever it's the dominant device, the mouse can't work. The same is true if you share the IRQ and COM port between your mouse and your digitizing tablet, but this shouldn't present a problem, since you are likely to use one or the other, and not both simultaneously.

Yet not all conflicts will behave this way. Devices with conflicts may not work at all until the conflict is resolved. Potentially, you can also have a situation where installing a piece of hardware without the proper configuration could keep the PC from booting at all (this can also be due to poor seating of the hardware itself) or just prevent that device from being seen and enumerated for operation under Windows. You may also boot into Safe Mode only when you did not intend to do so.

Some of the behavior in a conflict can be mystifying, however. Take for instance a phenomenon in Windows 95 and 98 whereby having a device assigned to IRQ12 may leave your PC hanging when you try to shut down Windows using the Restart option. This is most likely to occur with a BIOS that expects to see a PS/2 mouse using IRQ12 and instead, you are using IRQ12 for another device. In this scenario, you may want to try to reserve IRQ12 rather than use it for something other than the PS/2 mouse. You also may want to check with your BIOS provider to see if there is an upgrade available that rectifies this situation.

For those using Windows 95 and 98, it is possible that you may attempt to change the resource properties for a given piece of hardware in Device Manager only to be met with the message, "This resource setting cannot be modified." Unfortunately, when you see it, it means what it says: that you will be unable to change the resources for that particular device or assignment. To get rid of the error message—which still won't mean you can adjust it—check Use Automatic Settings instead.

Since COM port conflicts are probably the most common install problem seen, you should be on the lookout for these whenever you install something to a COM/serial port.

Additionally, you should know that Windows 95 and 98 provide a set of Basic Configurations for your COM ports, meant to help avoid a potential conflict. Besides a default configuration for each COM port that can't be altered, there are additional configurations that allow you to edit IRQ settings and/or I/O ranges.

Microsoft identifies these Basic Configurations in a table in its Knowledge Base Article ID: Q123992. These are shown in Table 11.1.

COM 1 defaults to Basic Configuration 0. The IRQ can be changed by selecting Basic Configuration 1.

COM 2 defaults to Basic Configuration 2. The IRQ can be changed by selecting Basic Configuration 3.

COM 3 defaults to Basic Configuration 4. The IRQ can be changed by selecting Basic Configuration 5.

COM 4 defaults to Basic Configuration 6. The IRQ can be changed by selecting Basic Configuration 7.

Basic Configuration 8 can be used to configure additional COM ports, because it lets you change the IRQ and the I/O address (and it's the only one that does).

You can change to different Basic Configurations by accessing COM ports in Device Manager and altering your configuration there (be sure to click on the Settings Based On option).

TIP If you're still using 8-bit expansion cards for equipment, be aware that 8-bit cards will only use one of the available first eight IRQs (0 to 7), while 16-bit cards should use any available IRQ. Similarly, your 8-bit expansion cards, if they need DMA resources at all, will only use any of the available first four channels (0 to 3), which gets tight (and two of them are taken to start). Consider upgrading when you can.

TABLE 11.1   Basic Configuration Settings for Windows 95/98.

Basic Configuration	IRQ Setting	Editable?	I/O Setting	Editable?
0	4	No	03F8-03FF	No
1	4	Yes	03F8-03FF	No
2	3	No	02F8-02FF	No
3	3	Yes	02F8-02FF	No
4	4	No	03E8-03EF	No
5	4	Yes	03E8-03EF	No
6	3	No	02E8-02EF	No
7	3	Yes	02E8-02EF	No
8	Variable	Yes	Variable	Yes

Problem #2. Inability to Boot or Load Operating System (by Platform)

TROUBLESHOOTING BOOT AND LOAD PROBLEMS IN WINDOWS 3.1

Since Windows 3.x is just a graphical operating environment loaded on top of DOS and not a full operating system by itself (i.e., you don't boot into it), it's not so much of a crisis if you can't boot Windows itself. You should still have DOS to work in, and with DOS, you can DELTREE and reinstall Windows, if need be.

The more serious issue is one in which you can't boot DOS itself. While this can potentially be a device conflict or bad DOS driver or other program trying to load at boot and causing a hang, there may be other concerns. These include a dying hard drive, a computer virus, bad physical connections, or other problems. If the PC boots but then hangs, try booting with a DOS system disk then changing over to the hard drive from the floppy. Consult your CONFIG.SYS and AUTOEXEC.BAT, and consider running stripped-down versions, particularly if you have just installed or changed something and you feel one of these changes is the cause. If you know the specific items added, simply remark those out, save your changes, and try booting again. Should Windows still fail to load, try invoking it in Standard Mode, by typing:

```
WIN /S
```

TROUBLESHOOTING BOOT AND LOAD PROBLEMS IN WINDOWS 95/98

If you have just installed a device or changed your hardware configuration in Windows 98 itself, restore the system to the state it was in just prior to the upgrade, either by pulling the device installed or returning the settings to their previous configuration. Should the problem occur during the Windows 98 install itself, there are several things to consider. One is that if you have DOS or real-mode drivers loading in your DOS configuration files to support hardware in a DOS environment—such as a CD-ROM drive for a DOS game—you may hit a roadblock. Try removing or remarking out these entries in CONFIG.SYS, attempt the Windows 98 installation again, and then re-add the real-mode drivers in CONFIG.SYS once Windows 98 is successfully installed and operating.

WINDOWS NT 4.0

Having a problem with your hardware and possibly even your ability to boot immediately after applying an NT service pack release? Before you try uninstalling the service pack or moving all the way to reformatting and starting fresh, it's possible that what you need is to reinstall hardware drivers, particularly OEM drivers.

TIP **With any upgrade or new operating system install, always check out your equipment manufacturer's Web site prior to doing the installation for tips, tricks, special requirements, or updated drivers. It's very common among all operating system upgrades to have behavioral problems on certain devices (as well as applications) until you update drivers or apply patches.**

Problem #3. Printers

With printers, the behavior they display can tell you a lot about the problem at hand. First, evaluate the obvious. Is it plugged in to a *working* wall outlet? Does it have a power-on indicator, and if so, is it lit? Is the cable attaching it securely mounted to the parallel/printer port? Garbage or random printing often points right to a loose connection; what the PC is sending for print isn't being "heard" properly by the printer and garbage results. Do you have a spare cable you can verify is working that you can swap with the cable in question?

Also, have you powered down and restarted since the problem began? Something in Windows itself could be preventing you from printing, but for just this session. Once you start back up, you may be able to print normally, as if no problem ever existed.

Some printers provide an error code on the display panel of the printer itself. Does yours? If it's reporting something unusual, find your printer manual and check the reading against any list of error codes the documentation may provide. Your answer may lie there, pointing you to a paper jam, an empty ink cartridge, or some other cause with the unit alone (unrelated to your PC and its operation).

Do you have anything else that you sometimes attach to your printer port instead of the printer itself? If so, triple-check that this item is unplugged and otherwise disabled and that the printer is the only device and that it is what is plugged in.

Most printers allow for an easy self-test. Your printer manual should tell you how to run one. If the self-test prints properly, it's reasonably safe to assume that your printer isn't dead.

Once you eliminate all of these, try removing the printer driver in Windows and then re-add it, either manually or by powering down and restarting to see if Windows recognizes the hardware as new and tries to reinstall it. Just moving the PC or printer along a desktop a matter of inches can sometimes "lose" interaction between the PC with Windows and the printer. If resecuring the cable and connections alone doesn't rectify the problem, removing and reinstalling the driver—for whatever reason—should. Also check Device Manager for printer port assignments and resource use. Make sure nothing you added tried to assume control of the resources your printer requires.

While we are discussing printers, it seems like a good time to take a hardware reality check. Let's say you try to outsmart your PC's resources. You want IRQ7 back for something else, so you install your single solitary printer not to LPT1 that uses IRQ7 but to LPT2, which should use IRQ5. Nice try, but no cigar, because if there's just one printer on the system, no matter how many times you install it to LPT2, your system will see it as LPT1, and it will want to use IRQ7.

Problem #4. Scanners

With a scanner, how it interfaces with the PC can be a big determining factor in the type of problems you may have with it. Like printers, most scanners have an LED power light (usually green, sometimes red/orange) that indicates it is getting juice. If the light isn't on, this means it has no power to operate. First, make sure the power connection for it is secure. If it appears to be, check the power source. If it plugs into a wall outlet or surge suppressor, check something else you know is working in the same outlet to make sure it is functioning.

If the light is on but trying to scan seems to accomplish nothing, you need to look at a series of issues, such as the following:

◄ The cable running between scanner and back of PC, if present. If the cable is secure, check for any indication of damage to the cable itself. If possible, try exchanging it for another cable.

◄ If you're using SCSI, don't go cheap on a SCSI cable. Check to be sure the length of the cable falls within the specifications for the type of SCSI (you may need a longer cable, but a longer cable may not work; the signal may effectively die out before it gets to your PC).

Problem #5. Sound

Again, it's critical to eliminate the possibility that an incomplete connection is the cause of the problem, so check these first. If the problem is that you aren't getting sound from your CD-ROMs, look at the connection between the CD and the sound card. There has to be one for the CD-ROM's sound to be played through the sound card and out into the room via your PC speakers. Also check that the sound card itself is properly seated in its expansion slot.

If you aren't seeing error messages on screen, but you simply hear no sound, it's time to check the speakers. Are they connected, and connected appropriately to the connection on the sound card interface? If the speaker jack is not clearly marked, consult the documentation for the sound card or the PC itself (if the sound card came preinstalled with a new PC purchase). If you plug a set of headphones in instead and they work, this may indicate bad speakers. A bad sound card shouldn't provide output to anything, including speakers or headphones. Also check to see what happens if you plug your speakers into the headphones jack on the faceplate of your CD-ROM drive, if you have one.

Bad speakers can sometimes be tough to isolate. A bad sound card may give you messages within Windows itself, while speakers won't. Since they're strictly output devices, they have no way to send a signal back to your system to alert you when they stop working.

You also need to check Windows audio settings for volume (usually accessible through the horn in the SYSTRAY in Windows 95 and 98. Make sure none of the settings have been improperly set to Mute (shown with a checkbox near the bottom of the slide). Then you should check Device Manager for error messages or conflicts preventing the sound card from functioning properly.

If everything else checks out, try swapping speakers out first (since they are generally far cheaper and definitely easier to remove). Finally, if new speakers don't resolve your silence, you'll need to install a new sound card.

Problem #6. Video

TROUBLESHOOTING VIDEO ISSUES IN WINDOWS 3.1

When confronted with video problems and recurrent General Protection Faults (GPFs) and Unrecoverable Application Errors (UAEs) and Unrecoverable Application Errors (UAEs) for which you think video may be a possible culprit, it's important to scale back to basics.

This means you should try returning to the generic VGA driver supplied by Windows itself. To do this, quit Windows, then run the SETUP found in the Windows directory. Should the problem persist, you may also want to try the VGA (3.0) driver listed there.

The possibility exists that something you recently installed doesn't like the age of your video adapter's BIOS. Like motherboards, today's video adapters allow themselves (usually) to be flash-upgradable to accommodate newer needs. Contact your video card manufacturer if you think the age of your video adapter's BIOS may indeed be an issue.

However, you may run up against a wall here; if you're using Windows 3.x on an older machine using an older EGA or VGA video adapter (perhaps original equipment on this more vintage PC), you may find it tough finding a BIOS upgrade. While some older style adapters are still available, the speed at which video has developed (along with processor and motherboard speed), has forced many companies to withdraw support for anything out of significant current use for more than a year or two.

TROUBLESHOOTING VIDEO ISSUES IN WINDOWS 95/98

Windows 95/98 packs a tool for troubleshooting video, permitting you to adjust hardware video acceleration up and down and also adjust the level of demand Windows places on the video card to perform. This slider-bar tool is illustrated in Figure 11.1.

You can see that the slider-bar adjusts to four different settings, ranging from None to Full. To get to this panel:

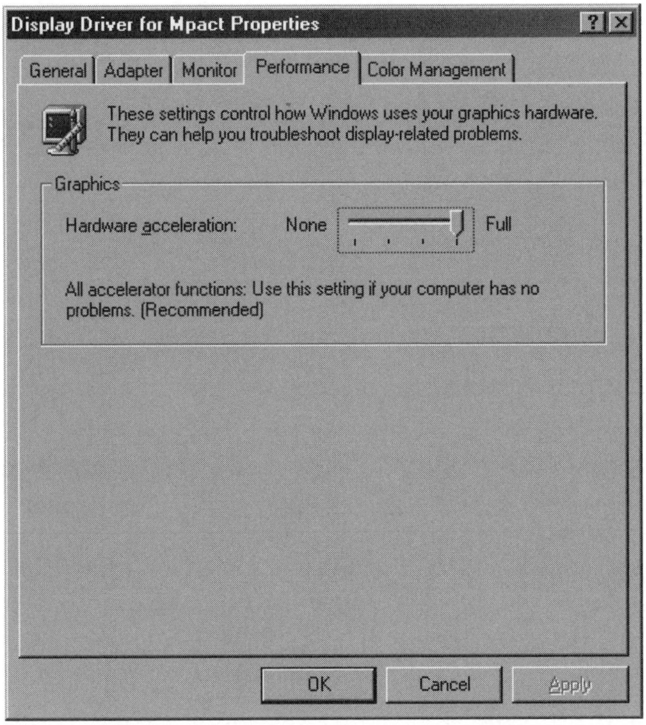

Figure 11.1   HW Video Acceleration Tool in Win98.

1. Choose Start|Settings|Control Panel, then double-click on the System icon.

2. Select the Performance tab, then click on Graphics.

3. You will now see the slider-bar tool screen pictured above, giving you the option of adjusting the slide to one of four settings:

    Full—The default setting, which permits the greatest hardware acceleration for video, as well as the heaviest demand by Windows on the video adapter/card.

    Most—Allows for some moderate acceleration but also affects the way the mouse behaves, so use this option if you experience problems related to the cursor/mouse pointer's performance in the video display.

    Basic—Provides for very basic acceleration only and adds a Safe Mode option to the [Windows] section of the WIN.INI file; it also turns off memory-mapped I/O handling for S3 and S3-

compatible drivers and renders the hardware cursor incapable. Use this setting to troubleshoot issues with random video lock-ups or if you have an S3 or compatible video card.

None—Disables all acceleration, adds a higher Safe Mode setting to the [Windows] section of the WIN.INI file, and disables the hardware cursor and memory-mapped I/O handling, again, for S3 and S3-compatible video cards. Choose None if the Basic setting doesn't resolve random video lockups and/or the presence of an S2 or compatible video adapter.

Microsoft recommends that you first attempt to use this tool on its Full setting (fully to the right), with adjustments made one setting to the left at a time to monitor how each degree of change affects your video performance.

Another plus with Windows 95 and Windows 98 is that if a serious problem occurs related to video, it will happily fall back on a standard default VGA driver, which gives you the best chance of getting your system booted and readable enough to resolve whatever problem is causing it.

If you decide to use Safe Mode to troubleshoot a video problem and note that the problem completely clears when in Safe Mode, the video driver you were using prior to Safe Mode comes under suspicion. For one, you could be using a video driver meant to run with Windows 3.1, which may not give you the best results. To determine what generation (3.1 versus Windows 95 or 98) you are using, try this test:

1. Load a text editor and open file SYSTEM.INI located in the Windows folder.

2. Locate the [boot] section, searching specifically for a line that begins DISPLAY. If this line reads:

    ```
    Display.drv=pnpdrvr.drv
    ```

    you will know it's a Windows 95 or 98 driver. If any other entry is provided instead, the driver is for Windows 3.1 and should be replaced as soon as possible.

Also, related to this, understand that pnpdrvr.drv is simply the default entry for *any* Windows 95 or 98 video driver. The actual video driver you use—obtained from your video card manufacturer—loads not in the SYS-

TEM.INI but from the Windows Registry. Remember to check your video card manufacturer's Web site often to see if an update you need to apply has been made available. Be sure to read carefully any warnings or suggestions offered in the documentation, however. Some patches or driver updates are not recommended for every card owner to apply, usually because of certain other hardware issues or software incompatibilities.

In troubleshooting, you may also find it valuable to verify that you are indeed using valid, appropriate driver files that haven't been corrupted, infected by virus, substituted with something less specific to your video card, or deleted. To verify:

From Windows 95: Load Windows Setup, and as prompted, select the Verify option. Verify forces Windows to check all files installed and replace any that can no longer be located or that are seen as damaged.

From Windows 98: Choose Start|Run, then type "sfc.exe" (without quotation marks) in the Open dialog box. Click OK. This launches the Windows 98 System File Checker utility from which you can verify and replace.

You also must realize that adjusting the monitor type specified in the Display properties in Device Manager will *not* alter your video card's refresh rate output. Special options like that are only going to be found in a utility, again provided by the hardware manufacturer. Such utilities will allow you to adjust features specifically engineered into the manufacturer's video adapters. Check your documentation and any CD-ROMs or floppy diskettes that accompanied your video card purchase.

For working through problems with a multiple-monitor setup new to Windows 98, consult Chapter 10 on Successful Upgrades.

Problem #7. Modems

What if Windows finds your (new) modem, but detects it erroneously as a Standard Modem, or as some other wrong make or model? I just had this experience with a PCI modem in beta test using preliminary-release drivers.

Using the Standard Modem option may not be a total loss, especially if you think the problems you're troubleshooting relate in any way to communications. But it may limit the ability of your modem. It will use the modem's default factory settings (not necessarily a bad thing, if you want to try the default mode again) and render you unable to modify certain settings, like speaker volume and cellular protocols, if applicable.

To work through it, try the following:

1. Choose Start|Settings|Control Panel, then double-click on the Modem icon.

2. From Windows 95, you can highlight the wrong modem choice and choose Remove, then click Add to add a new modem. You can try to let Windows detect the correct one this time, or you can manually select it from the list provided; you need to be aware, however, that choosing the wrong one may interfere with some of your modem's specific features or functionality. Because of this, you must check the documentation for your modem (or your PC itself, if packed as part of a new PC purchase) to try to ascertain which make/model or compatible you should choose.

   or

   From Windows 98, click on the Change button available on the Install New Modem tab to make a different choice. When satisfied, find the first wrongly selected modem drive, highlight it, and click Remove.

NOTE This was mentioned in an earlier chapter, but it bears repeating here. WinModems are increasingly popular add-ins in today's PCs, even when going with a better-name clone, such as Dell or Micron. But their developing presence is because they are cheaper to manufacture, putting some of the traditional workload of the modem onto the processor instead. The result is often seen in an overall slow response, temporary lockup, or slow background Internet file transfers. On anything slower than a Pentium 100 MHz, they can sometimes be almost too painful to use. Even on my PII-450 MHz, a PCI WinModem tended to grab control for seconds at a time and background file transfers seemed to suffer more than their share of slow deaths.

You also may find them a bit more difficult to configure and manipulate in terms of system resources. For this reason, you may want to swap a WinModem with an ISA internal modem or a freestanding external modem on older machines, or choose between an external or a USB modem for more current PCs. If you're lucky, however, you have, or will soon have, access to higher speed forms of communication, such as a cable modem or advanced digital subscriber line (ADSL) modem.

Problem #8. CD-ROM

Situation: You have decided to place your CD-ROM drive not as a slave to a master hard drive on the first IDE controller but as the primary device on the second. But the drive doesn't work.

Resolution: Check the physical connections first. If there is no light and you cannot eject the CD-ROM drive tray, you want to ensure the power connector is secure. If it is and there is still no light, look to see if you have another available power connector and try that. If that still provides no power light, there is a vague possibility the power supply itself could be heading south. You sometimes see a power supply not fail outright, but fail almost on a device-by-device basis.

While you have the cover off, look at the CD-ROM drive's jumpers. If it's the sole component on the second IDE controller, it needs to be jumpered to Cable Select, (CS), and not to Master, (M, which is reserved for the primary drive on an IDE controller), or Slave (S, which is used for the second drive connected to the first or master drive on an IDE controller).

Now let's turn to the issue of the CD-ROM drive's placement on the second IDE controller, because this problem could have an easy solution. Properly shut down and reboot the PC, then go into CMOS. You want to look for a setting for the second IDE controller, and you need to make sure it is enabled. If it is not, your PC has no intelligent way of discerning you have a second IDE controller.

But wait: Are you using a proprietary IDE controller built into some older sound cards instead of an actual IDE controller on your motherboard? If so, try moving the CD-ROM drive onto the actual second IDE controller (and make sure it is enabled in BIOS). The kind of IDE controller built into older SoundBlaster and compatible sound cards is not a great solution and should be avoided, if possible. This was something of a kludge solution on older PCs, which didn't always pack two IDE controllers (and earlier than that, when CD-ROMs were exotic additions needing a connection), but that's a rare occurrence these days. Use the real second IDE controller (and consider replacing the older sound card, perhaps with a PCI version if your PC has a PCI bus).

Problem #9. Network Cards

As we talked about earlier in the book, network cards and sound cards often compete for the same resources, and this is the first thing to check when you have a network card that is not behaving. If you're using an older, 8-bit network card, it's very possible that the network card's failure has to do with IRQ assignment. Since it wants one of the first eight IRQs, of which very few are available, it might not be happy being forced onto another IRQ. Network cards sometimes require some tweaking, and this is doubly true for trying to fit an 8-bit network card in under the first eight IRQs. With 16-bit cards, you have a few more options, but look carefully at the configuration worksheet (Appendix D) we discussed in Chapter 4.

If problems persist, check to make certain your network card is indeed supported by the operating system version you are using, and if possible, try the network card in another PC to ensure it's not a dead card.

WORKING WITH PNP NETWORK CARDS AND 16-BIT DOS/ REAL-MODE DRIVERS

You can hit a definite snag trying to run Plug and Play-capable network cards in real or DOS mode, and the problem is severe enough to mimic a dead card. The situation arises because the 16-bit DOS drivers for the network interface card (NIC) load a bit before 32-bit Windows switches on recognition of PnP devices (remember, it's Windows 95/98 that are PnP-capable, not DOS). Obviously, this only happens when you have to load DOS drivers for DOS-based network protocol and functions.

Microsoft Knowledge Base reports the additional problem that not all 16-bit NIC drivers will recognize PnP devices, particularly network cards of NE2000 PnP or compatible type, and recommends the following:

1. Locate the SoftSet utility that packed with your PnP network card, and run it.
2. From the utility, set the card to non-PnP mode (it can be set back to PnP later if you only need Windows-based drivers).
3. Go to Windows Control Panel, double-click on the Network icon, and select and remove the network card as currently listed.

4. Return to Control Panel, double-click on the Add New Hardware icon to launch the wizard, then follow the directions on the series of screens which take you through detection and installation.

5. Windows 95 and 98 should be able to detect your network card, and you should be able to work with the card.

Problem #10. RAM

A problem with the actual RAM can masquerade itself in many ways and display these symptoms:

◄ Fatal exception errors

◄ Failure of HIMEM.SYS to load either in regular mode or Safe Mode

◄ Random, sometimes inexplicable system lockups

◄ A PC that stops responding or hangs on bootup or very shortly thereafter

◄ Special beeps from the PC on boot (see the section on beep codes at the end of this chapter)

If you have just installed new or additional RAM and you encounter any of these problems, one of three situations is most likely: the RAM itself is bad (and fairly delicate, so even simple mishandling could damage it in transit or if you were too rough in the way you installed it) or the RAM is improperly installed or you installed the wrong RAM just fine.

Double-check how the RAM is seated in its holder. You can also try removing any or all of the new RAM installed to see if the problem clears or swap out each stick of RAM until the situation is resolved. If removing the RAM clears it (and you already know it was the right RAM and seated correctly), the RAM is likely bad. The bad news is that defective RAM will not always be explicitly reported to you by bootup messages or beep errors, by Windows itself, or by utilities that check memory resources. This is because many testing tools do not exactly test the RAM quite the same way Windows itself utilizes it, so the reports may be far less reliable than they should be.

Another way to test for defective memory is to limit the amount of memory Windows can use. To try this, follow this procedure:

1. Load any text editor (including Windows Notepad or WordPad, which is similar to Write in Windows 3.x) or SysEdit.

2. Open SYSTEM.INI (see Figure 11.2).

3. Add this line in the [386Enh] section:

   `MaxPhysPage=<nnn>`

   where <nnn> specifies the amount of memory you want Windows to use. For example, if you want to limit Windows to 16 MB of RAM to test, modify to:

   `MaxPhysPage=FFF`

4. Save changes.

5. Reboot your PC.

A common issue with RAM is parity error messages. Most notable when you are in Windows, these errors are caused by the generation of

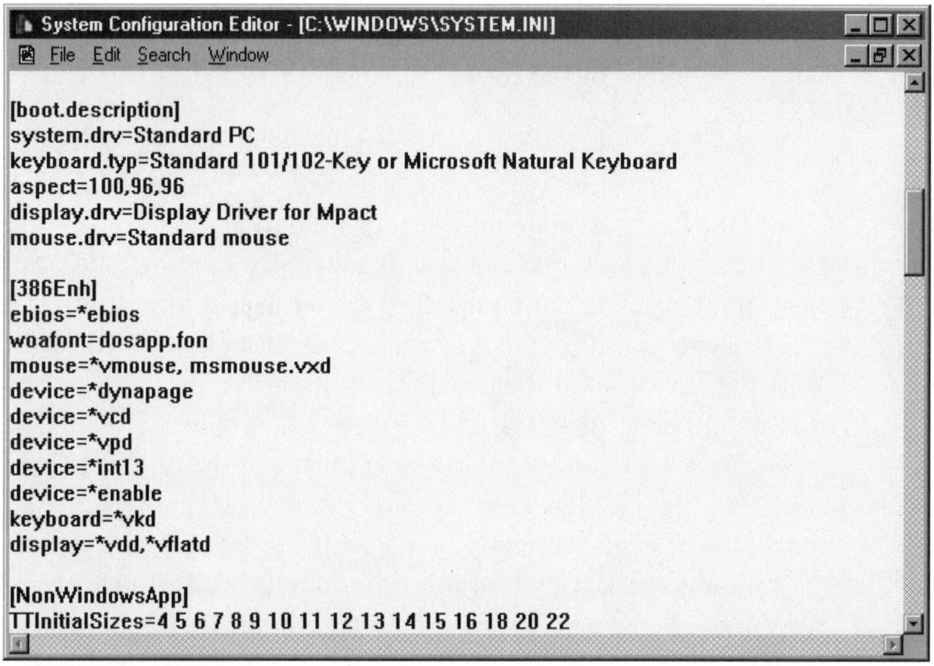

```
System Configuration Editor - [C:\WINDOWS\SYSTEM.INI]
 File  Edit  Search  Window

[boot.description]
system.drv=Standard PC
keyboard.typ=Standard 101/102-Key or Microsoft Natural Keyboard
aspect=100,96,96
display.drv=Display Driver for Mpact
mouse.drv=Standard mouse

[386Enh]
ebios=*ebios
woafont=dosapp.fon
mouse=*vmouse, msmouse.vxd
device=*dynapage
device=*vcd
device=*vpd
device=*int13
device=*enable
keyboard=*vkd
display=*vdd,*vflatd

[NonWindowsApp]
TTInitialSizes=4 5 6 7 8 9 10 11 12 13 14 15 16 18 20 22
```

Figure 11.2   SYSTEM.INI.

nonmiscible interrupts (NMIs). Here's a tip to note: If you have recently experienced strange errors you think may be memory related and you unsuccessfully tried to resolve them through a recent full reinstall of Windows, the problem is likely a parity error. This is because a fresh install of Windows free from corruptions cannot generate NMIs itself, so it's more likely to be the memory doing it.

Mismatched memory speeds can be a contributing factor; this is sometimes aided by incrementing upwards the number of wait states specified in advanced CMOS setup. This acts in turn to slow down the PC to try to synchronize better with the memory. Some motherboards permit the use of different-speed memory, while others balk, so check your motherboard's specs or call the manufacturer. Better still, replace the memory with one of the same speed.

You should check specifications for your motherboard, too, since not all permit the use of parity memory. Adding it when you shouldn't have may lead to the difficulties cited here. Also, know that using nonproprietary RAM on a motherboard that requires proprietary RAM can produce bad results.

But parity errors are not exclusively generated by memory itself; video cards, for example, can lead to them, as can faulty power, including a malfunctioning power supply. If possible, once you have exhausted other options, try swapping out the hardware itself to see if the problem resolves.

TIP How much memory should you have on your PC to operate comfortably, if not extravagantly? On Windows 3.1 systems, 16 MB should be more than enough for the majority of things you need to do; less than 8 can produce a real overall sluggishness and may lead to other problems. On Windows 95/98, 32 MB is the start of the sweet spot, because 16 MB will be too limiting if you need to work with several applications and resources open, as often happens when we use the Internet, for example. Be aware that some motherboard types limit the RAM they will cache to 64 MB, so adding more to these machines either will not help or may actually serve to slow them down. Check your motherboard specs for details. Windows NT 4.0 utilizes memory differently and more effectively, and as a power operating system, should not be limited by too-little RAM. While NT will run on 32 MB, 64 MB is much better for workstations and 128 MB for server configurations.

Also, you need to know that in both Windows 95 and 98, you may discover that the amount of memory reported (in the Performance Tab under System Properties) may differ from the actual amount of RAM you have installed in your PC. A number of things can cause this, including:

◀ CMOS setting may be disabling some of your RAM.

◀ Windows Registry is damaged.

◀ Either a driver or program loading in CONFIG.SYS or AUTOEXEC .BAT is draining a portion of your RAM away; this is a good situation to evaluate using single-stepping.

◀ Virtual device driver (.VxD) being loaded in the SYSTEM.INI is claiming part of your RAM; here, you may want to try replacing your current SYSTEM.INI with a fresh copy.

◀ On EISA machines, HIMEM.SYS is not using all the RAM that is installed.

◀ A protected-mode driver may be causing a memory mismatch; try unchecking the Original Configuration option in Device Manager.

◀ Your SYSTEM.INI has a setting:

```
Maxphyspage=nnnn
```

which is set to a value preventing Windows from using some of the installed memory.

Problem #11. Drives

HARD DRIVES

With hard drives, you need to separate out the previously installed and functioning from the brand-new drive you have added to an existing one or incorporated as a replacement for a previous drive. If an older drive, what kind of error messages are being generated? If they concern MS-DOS Compatibility Mode, refer back to "Troubleshooting MS-DOS Compatibility Mode" in Chapter 5.

Has the hard drive developed a significant noise, perhaps like the scraping of ball-bearings? If so, this is a drive that should be backed up and replaced as soon as possible. It's probably not a matter of *if* a drive exhibiting this behavior will fail, but when. Also, spot-check that the power cable and the ribbon cable are both attached properly to the drive. Use another open power connector and a spare ribbon cable, if you have them, to eliminate bad connections as a factor. If you have recently changed any jumpers or switches related to the hard drive, change them back to old settings to see if this restores the drive to functionality.

When you check CMOS, does your BIOS still see the drive with the same configuration as before the problem developed? If not, what happens when you let CMOS auto-detect the drive again, or you restore the settings for the drive to their default? A dying CMOS battery can, in its final stages, "lose" drives temporarily in CMOS, requiring you to re-find them each time you boot. If CMOS can't detect a drive, however, the drive may be dead. Do try testing it on another machine before you heave it in the waste can. In addition, while in CMOS, turn off any special power-management options that may contribute to a drive's disabling after a period of inactivity to rule this out.

Try booting the system with a boot or system disk, and then check the hard disk in question. If all you are seeing is what appears to be garbage or you can't log into the hard disk from the boot floppy, you may have a dead drive. If you can read the drive, scan it for viruses to make sure one hasn't overwritten the master boot record (the part of the hard disk your system references to boot). Also check it with FDISK or another disk preparation utility to determine that the primary partition is active (active = bootable). Also check for the presence of COMMAND.COM in your root directory on the hard disk, and scan the CONFIG.SYS and AUTOEXEC.BAT files for any clues to why your disk won't boot.

If it's a new drive, has it been formatted and partitioned for use? A new hard drive right out of the box you purchased it in must be prepared for use, which means using FORMAT and FDISK, which are two DOS utilities, or something like PowerQuest's Partition Magic. Check that the drive is connected properly and that it is jumpered appropriately for whether it is the master, the slave, or a standalone drive. A master drive is the primary when more than one drive is cabled together, while the slave is the secondary drive connected to the master. Each of these settings, plus settings for a single drive, are jumpered differently. Check your accompanying documentation for details on setting these jumpers.

Hard Disks in Excess of 8 GB

Windows 3.1: For those wanting to install an over 8-GB hard disk in a system using DOS and Windows 3.1, the suggestion is, don't. Wait until you upgrade your PC and your operating system.

Windows 95/98: For the rest of you, here is a checklist recommended by Robert Proffitt, one of my associates in the Hardware Forum on The Microsoft Network's ComputingCentral:

◄ Make sure the BIOS is updated to include greater than 8-GB support.

◄ Have Windows 95a/b/c, Windows 98, or Windows NT 4.0 (with Service Pack 3 installed and POST SP-3 HOTFIX called Atapi).

◄ Don't plan to dual-boot to DOS, since DOS 6.22 is currently limited to 8 GB, and even with software-based hard disk extenders, the amount of drive beyond 8 GB is not often recognized.

A BIOS dated earlier than November 1997 is definitely not suitable for such a hard disk. Problems will occur either in the machine hanging upon detection of the greater-than-8 GB drive or in reduced capacity.

The following recommendations are from *http://www.maxtor.com/ technology/whitepapers/capbar0.html#solutions*

Phoenix: [*http://www.ptltd.com/*] Version 4 Revision 6 or Version 4 Revision 6 or greater can support capacities greater than 8.4 GB. If the BIOS is revision 5.12, it does not support extended interrupt 13. All Phoenix BIOS are Version 4, so 5.12 is an older release than 6. Phoenix recommends Micro Firmware [*http://www.firmware.com*] (877-629-2467) for BIOS upgrades.

Award: [*http://www.award.com/*] BIOS dated after November 1997 will support drives greater than 8.4 GB. Award recommends Unicore [*http://www.unicore.com/*] (800-800-2467) for BIOS upgrades.

American Megatrends INC., (AMI): [*http://www.megatrends.com/*] BIOS versions with a date of January 1, 1998 or greater support drives greater than 8.4 GB.

The workaround *if* your machine does boot but you have diminished space is to use a software solution to extend the BIOS. However, this is highly discouraged, since many people forget that you can no longer boot a DOS or Win9x diskette to fix up a drive that's been prepared in this manner. Such software has names like EZ-Drive, MaxBlast and others.

Windows NT 4.0: Windows NT requires a slightly different approach to the 8G plus drive. I won't dive too deeply into it here, but NT 4.0 has a 4-G boot partition limit and that will allow you to get NT installed and running. Here's the trick to getting the rest of the drive going. Do not partition anything but the first partition until you have NT 4.0 running. Visit the Microsoft Knowledge Base and search for Article Q183654. It will explain the problem and supply a link to fetch the Post-SP3 Hotfix. Now we install the Hotfix, and after a reboot, we can run Disk Administrator and continue to prepare the HD as we see fit.

FLOPPY DRIVES

Before you decide a floppy drive may be broken or disabled, try more than one floppy in it to test its capacity to read. If the drive is dirty from using dusty floppy diskettes, it may need cleaning.

If that fails, check CMOS. Does it see a floppy drive? Can you detect any settings in your CMOS that disable the use of the floppy (besides the one that states something like, "Seek (floppy) drive at boot," since this just affects the system's way of looking for a boot drive at the time of the PC booting)? Having the floppy drive turned off as part of the boot seek should not affect its ability to read floppy diskettes the rest of the time.

You can also try shutting down and rebooting; perhaps something temporarily disabled the floppy that you clear with a fresh boot. You may also want to try grabbing a good boot or system disk and try booting from that. This technique might help a recalcitrant floppy wake up.

Is your floppy drive's LED display (power light) staying on all the time, even when the drive is not running? This is usually the sign of a reversed cable. Reverse it again, and see if it clears. Also, are you hearing odd noises from the unit? This may be a sign of a mechanism not quite in place or of excessive wear. With the cost of these drives—about $25—it may not pay to spend much time troubleshooting a problem. Consider replacing it and moving on. A bad floppy controller may be the issue, too, as well as the cabling supporting the floppy drive's connection.

But don't forget to check out the resource information available for this drive in Device Manager; perhaps another device is suddenly jockeying for control of a resource the floppy is assigned to use.

TAPE DRIVES

Don't be completely surprised if you can find neither hide nor hair of an installed tape drive unit in Device Manager, even if the unit works fine. The reason is that Plug and Play software won't detect tape drives. This is coupled with the fact that the actual tape drive detection is really a function of the drivers actually packed into the backup software (like the one that packed in your tape drive, if you have one). Because of this, the only tape drives that appear in Device Manager are SCSI tape backup units, if *no* backup software is actually installed on your PC. If a SCSI tape drive does appear, it may be listed under a very generic name or reported as an unknown device.

Beyond that, a lot of backup programs do not provide tape drive detection support, which is another reason you may not see a tape drive listed. But if your backup software really doesn't recognize the drive to work with it, you need to contact whatever company made the backup software for assistance.

Problem #12. DOS-Based Programs

Those of us who used computers during the long-ago days of DOS remember well the worries of having enough conventional memory—a worry far less discussed in a 32-bit Windows world, where an amazing number of folks rarely even drop to DOS to do anything.

Games represent the biggest reason folks continue to use DOS (though I admit I still do a great deal of my regular file management there). But many also continue to use other DOS-based applications (WordPerfect for DOS 5.1 lives on in more than a few PCs) or perform functions more appropriately done in DOS (formatting, FDISKing, using LAPLINK to connect two PCs together for quick file transfers, and such).

Yet errors and problems related to an inadequate amount of conventional memory still occur and can even affect some 32-bit Windows work (particularly those with DOS components). While conventional memory isn't used directly for Windows, it is needed for any DOS-based programs you run from Windows (as well as when dropped to DOS).

Conventional memory is the first 640 KB of the first megabyte of RAM on a PC, and it is in this area that DOS does its work. Here, it loads and runs DOS applications, and manages drivers and terminate-and-stay-resident programs that are not loaded into an area above conventional memory, called "high memory," which makes up the remaining 384 KB of the first MB of RAM.

To load special programs and drivers into high memory means you will have more of the initial 640 KB left available to load and run applications. The closer to the optimum 640 KB you can get, the better. But a failure to load memory manager for DOS and to load such things as drivers "high" means you'll have much less conventional memory available to you. As a result, some programs may not work. In particular, this affects DOS-based games, which tend to be real resource hogs, wanting an almost impossible amount of conventional memory in which to operate.

To check your available conventional memory:

From Windows 3.1: Choose the MS-DOS prompt and from the DOS command prompt, then type:

```
MEM /C /P
```

From Windows 95/98: Go to the Start menu, select MS-DOS prompt from the list of entries available under the Programs menu, and type:

```
MEM /C /P
```

MEM is a DOS-based command that reports DOS-based memory resources, counting your total RAM and specifying what is available and what is used—particularly in the crucial first 640 KB. The /C switch lists memory usage by programs or drivers loaded and taking resources; the /P switch pauses the report after each screen, for easier viewing. See Figure 11.3.

When doing this from my new and as yet untweaked PII-450 MHz, I'm told I have a scant 548 KB of conventional memory left to me, after the things in Table 11.2 load.

What this tells me is that DOS memory management isn't too well configured on this system. For one thing, I'm not using SCSI, so I don't need double-buffering of any drives. TAISATAP and MSCDEX should both be loaded high to give me more room, and they are not, and nothing at all is using the upper memory area.

So I load my CONFIG.SYS, shown in Figure 11.4, into a text editor (SYSEDIT is fine, so too is DOS EDIT or Windows Notepad), and take a look.

My original CONFIG.SYS looks like this:

```
DEVICE=C:\WINDOWS\HIMEM.SYS
```

```
Modules using memory below 1 MB:

Name          Total           Conventional        Upper Memory

SYSTEM       18,304   (18K)    10,608   (10K)       7,696    (8K)
HIMEM         1,120    (1K)     1,120    (1K)           0    (0K)
EMM386        4,320    (4K)     4,320    (4K)           0    (0K)
DBLBUFF       2,976    (3K)     2,976    (3K)           0    (0K)
WIN           3,712    (4K)     3,712    (4K)           0    (0K)
vmm32       110,832  (108K)     1,888    (2K)     108,944  (106K)
COMMAND       7,440    (7K)     7,440    (7K)           0    (0K)
TAISATAP     10,768   (11K)         0    (0K)      10,768   (11K)
IFSHLP        2,864    (3K)         0    (0K)       2,864    (3K)
MSCDEX       28,032   (27K)         0    (0K)      28,032   (27K)
Free        623,040  (608K)   623,040  (608K)          0    (0K)

Memory Summary:

Type of Memory      Total          Used           Free

Conventional       655,360        32,320        623,040
Upper              158,304       158,304              0
Reserved                 0             0              0
Press any key to continue . . . .
```

Figure 11.3 DOS MEM /C /P.

```
DEVICE=C:\WINDOWS\EMM386.EXE NOEMS D=64
DEVICEHIGH=C:\WINDOWS\COMMAND\TAISATAP.SYS /D:MSCD000 /N:1
```

Well, according to this, TAISATAP.SYS (my DOS mode CD-ROM driver) should be loaded high. But wait, where is the necessary:

```
DOS=HIGH,UMB
```

statement?

So I edit my CONFIG.SYS to read like so:

```
DEVICE=C:\WINDOWS\HIMEM.SYS
DEVICE=C:\WINDOWS\EMM386.EXE NOEMS
DOS=HIGH,UMB
DEVICEHIGH=C:\WINDOWS\COMMAND\TAISATAP.SYS /D:MSCD000 /N:1
```

I save my changes, and I know I need to reboot to have these DOS-based configuration files run and memory configured in DOS appropriately. But I also know that MSCDEX.EXE is loading into conventional memory and taking up a nice chunk. So I look at both my AUTOEXEC.BAT (where it may load) and my DOSSTART.BAT (which is where is probably should best load) to see how this CD-ROM utility file is being loaded.

TABLE 11.2 Additional mem info listed

Modules Using Memory below 1 MB

Name	Total	Conventional	Upper Memory
MSDOS	18,288 (18 KB)	18,288 KB (18KB)	0 (0 KB)
HIMEM	1,120 (1 KB)	1,120 (1 KB)	0 (0 KB)
EMM386	4,320 (4 KB)	4,320 (4 KB)	0 (0 KB)
TAISATAP	10,768 (11 KB)	10,768 (11 KB)	0 (0 KB)
DBLBUFF	2,976 (3 KB)	2,976 (3 KB)	0 (0 KB)
IFSHLP	2,864 (3 KB)	2,864 (3 KB)	0 (0 KB)
WIN	3,712 (4 KB)	3,712 (4 KB)	0 (0 KB)
MSCDEX	28,032 (27 KB)	28,032 (27 KB)	0 (0 KB)
VMM32	14,016 (14 KB)	14,016 (14 KB)	0 (0 KB)
COMMAND	7,440 (7 KB)	7,440 (7 KB)	0 (0 KB)
Free	561,616 (548 KB)	561,616 (548 KB)	0 (0 KB)

Memory Summary

Type of Memory	Total	Used	Free
Conventional	655,360	93,744	561,616
Upper	0	0	0
Reserved	0	0	0
Extended (XMS)	65,994,752	417,792	65,576,960
Total Memory	66,650,112	511,536	66,138,576
Total under 1 MB:	655,360	93,744	561,616

Largest Executable Program Size	561,616 (548 KB)
Largest Free Upper Memory Block	0 (0 KB)
MS-DOS is Resident in the High-Memory Area.	

My original AUTOEXEC.BAT looks like this:

```
@ECHO OFF
LH C:\WINDOWS\COMMAND\MSCDEX.EXE /D:MSCD000 /L:E
SET BLASTER=A220 I7 D1 T2
SET SNDSCAPE=C:\WINDOWS
```

Well, according to my AUTOEXEC.BAT, MSCDEX should be loading into high memory (the LH prefacing MSCDEX is an abbreviation for the LOADHIGH command). In fact, LOADHIGH should be used for any TSRs or other programs that must load at boot.So perhaps the earlier fix to the CONFIG.SYS should rectify the memory loading problem once I reboot.

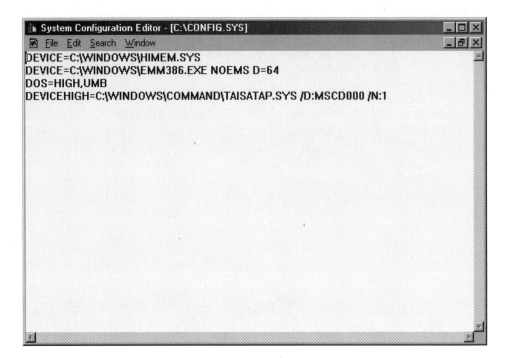

Figure 11.4 CONFIG.SYS in SYSEDIT.

I save any changes, shut down the PC, and reboot. Back in DOS, I type:

```
MEM /C /P
```

again, which now reports I have 608 KB of conventional memory available because all or part of system files, VMM32, the CD-ROM's TAISATAP, IFSHLP, and MSCDEX, are now loading high. With a bit more tweaking, I could probably get it up to around 620 KB which is adequate for most greedy DOS-based games and more than enough for most applications.

ELEMENTS OF A BASIC CONFIG.SYS

HIMEM.SYS

This is your extended memory manager (loads automatically for Windows but must be present in your DOS-based CONFIG.SYS to be run in DOS) for those programs needing extended memory according to the eXtended Memory Specification (XMS).

EMM386.EXE

This is your expanded memory emulator, using extended memory to emulate expanded memory, to hold device drivers and certain other programs (including TSRs) above conventional memory in the upper memory area or UMA (640 to 1024 KB); unless you specifically need EMS memory, use the NOEMS switch with EMM386.EXE as seen in the sample CONFIG.SYS above.

DOS=HIGH,UMB

This loads DOS into high memory, invoking upper memory blocks (UMBs).

DEVICEHIGH=

When specified, this tries to force a device driver into the upper memory area so it doesn't load into the precious conventional memory region.

What device drivers should get loaded high? Your sound card driver and CD-ROM drive, for example, if needed in DOS. Most mouse drivers today end in .EXE or .COM, so these load in the AUTOEXEC.BAT instead. As you know, Windows loads drivers for all of these for operation from within Windows, but you need to load DOS or real-mode drivers for use in DOS itself.

NOTE If you fail to load a DOS or real-mode driver for a hardware device, it will *not* be available for use in DOS. If you have a device failing to load in DOS, the first thing you need to look at is whether you have a valid driver loading properly in CONFIG.SYS and that the driver is present on your hard drive in the location specified in the path in CONFIG.SYS.

REPLACING REAL-MODE DRIVERS WITH PROTECTED-MODE VERSIONS

Windows includes protected-mode drivers for many devices. In addition, many hardware manufacturers provide protected-mode drivers for their devices. To attempt to install a Windows protected-mode driver for a device installed on your computer, follow these steps:

1. In Control Panel, double-click on the Add New Hardware icon.
2. Click Next, verify that Yes (Recommended) is selected, click Next, and then click Next again.

If the Add New Hardware wizard does not detect the device and install a protected-mode driver for it, you can attempt to install a Windows protected-mode driver for the device manually. To do so, follow these steps:

1. In Control Panel, double-click on the Add New Hardware icon.

2. Click Next, click No, and then click Next.

3. Click the type of device for which you are attempting to install a protected-mode driver in the Hardware Types box, and then click Next.

4. Click the manufacturer of the device in the Manufacturers box. If the specific device appears in the Models box, click the device, and

TABLE 11.3   AMI BIOS Beep Codes

# of beeps	What Beep Signifies
1 short	All is well
1 long	System experiencing problems with video; check your video card and monitor (only applies to systems without the video onboard the motherboard).
2 short	Indicates parity error in the first 64 KB of memory or parity RAM found but not supported by your PC. If your video is in working order, you should see an error message. Check SIMMs. If applicable, swap the first and second banks of RAM (since the first is responsible for the first 64 KB).
2 long 1 short	Monitor not connected or found.
3 short	Roughly same as 2 long/1 short.
3 short 1 long	Usually video-related failure.
4 short	Timer 1 failure.
5 short	Usually a motherboard issue with the process reporting an error. Check RAM for seating, just in case it needs replacement.
6 short	Keyboard (8042) controller error. Try another keyboard. If no replacements work, you may need to either replace the controller (possible on some, not on others) or, potentially, change the motherboard.
7 short	CPU/processor problem; may require replacement.
8 short	Video problem; it's either faulty or the PC cannot locate it. Try reseating. If this doesn't work, try the same video card on another PC and if not working there, replace.
9 short	Bad BIOS; the ROM checksum doesn't correlate to the value encoded in the BIOS; replace if possible.
10 short	Serious CMOS error which may require a new motherboard.
11 short	External cache memory is faulty; replace, if possible.

TABLE 11.4 Phoenix BIOS Beep Codes

Series of Beeps	Explanation
1-1-3	Problem with motherboard, unable to read CMOS; motherboard may need replacement.
1-1-4	Problem with BIOS; replace.
1-2-1	Bad timer chip on motherboard; may need motherboard replacement.
1-2-2	Bad motherboard; replace.
1-2-3	Bad motherboard; replace.
1-3-1	Bad motherboard; replace.
1-3-3	Problem with reading first 64K of RAM; motherboard may need replacement.
1-3-4	Bad motherboard; replace.
1-4-1	Bad motherboard; replace.
1-4-2	Some RAM may be bad; check and replace, if necessary.
2-*-*	Two beeps followed by any other beeps may indicate bad RAM; check and replace, if necessary.
3-1-*	Problem with motherboard chips; replace motherboard.
3-2-4	Keyboard controller failure; try a different keyboard - —if that doesn't work, check with your motherboard manufacturer to investigate possibility just the keyboard controller can be replace.
3-3-4	PC can't detect video; try another card.
3-4-*	Bad video card; replace.
4-2-1	Bad chip on motherboard; replace motherboard.
4-2-2	Keyboard problem, try another one - —if that doesn't work, motherboard may need replacement.
4-2-3	Same as 4-2-2.
4-2-4	May indicate a bad add-on card; check each and replace if necessary, but if all cards check out, replacement of motherboard may be necessary.
4-3-1	Bad motherboard; replace.
4-3-2	Bad motherboard; replace.
4-3-3	Bad motherboard; replace.
4-3-4	Bad time/clock; check CMOS battery for failure.
4-4-1	Serial port irregularity. If on motherboard, try jumpering (motherboard could need replacement) and add a separate I/O card or replace the add-on I/O card you have.
4-4-2	Essentially same as 4-4-1.
4-4-3	Bad math coprocessor; disable and/or replace.

then click OK to install the protected-mode driver. If the manufacturer of the device does not appear in the Manufacturers box or the specific device does not appear in the Models box, Windows does not include a protected-mode driver for the device.

To determine if the hardware's manufacturer provides a protected-mode driver for the device, contact the device's manufacturer.

THE BEEPS AS YOU BOOT

Whether you realize it or not, the beep(s) you hear as your PC boots up and implements POST acts a little like Morse code to alert you to the status of your system. For instance, one beep signals one thing, two beeps something else, three beeps reports something entirely different.

Exactly what they report depends entirely on what firm made your BIOS, since the so-called "beep codes" differ depending on whether American Megatrends (AMI), or Award, or Phoenix (and so on) supplied the BIOS for your motherboard. Ascertain which BIOS type you have, and check documentation—or the manufacturer's Web site—for details when you need to diagnose a problem accompanied by the beep(s).

Listed in Tables 11.3 and 11.4 are common beep codes for AMI and Phoenix you can refer to in troubleshooting.

CHAPTER 12

PC Cooling and Power

Included in this chapter are the following topics:

◀ What's involved in PC cooling

◀ How overheating can contribute to hardware problems

◀ The role of the fan, the heat sinks, and good physical space in maintaining internal case temperature

◀ The role and needs of the PC power supply

◀ How home/office wiring and other factors can affect PC performance and hardware

◀ How to keep your system operational during power problems

Why include a chapter discussing both PC cooling as well as PC power issues in a book on hardware conflict resolution? Granted, at first blush, they don't seem to fit. However, PC overheating and electrical improprieties can lead to a number of difficulties—ranging from short-term inconvenience all the way up to eventual permanent damage to the equipment—that can mimic other hardware woes. You can lose precious time and money trying to troubleshoot an error that may completely resolve every time (we hope) your PC is allowed to cool down, for example.

In my experience, PC power setups are rarely suspected of being too underpowered when they are actually causing problems (like all of your PC working except your CD-ROM drive). On the other hand, power supplies are upgraded too frequently under the mistaken belief that a higher-rated power supply will cure problems it will not.

PC Cooling

Let's first take a look at what you need to know about PC cooling to keep your hardware functioning properly. In the heydays of mainframe computers, these massive giants were housed in their own rooms with serious air-conditioning keeping the machines cooled with refrigerated air at a rather constant room temperature and humidity level to ensure their continued performance (and the owner's major investment in them).

Unfortunately, these days, a cool room doesn't always make for a cool PC, because the parts that get hot are contained within a metal casing and individual components can get very hot indeed. Add to this the fact that many of us pack our PCs with more hardware than ever before (scanner cards, modems, extra drives, special adapters), reducing room in the case for air to move. We also tend to buy more of the superfast, hotter-running drives like the Cheetah or Barracuda that can trap heat if not thoughtfully installed.

The rule of thumb to remember is that the more computing power your PC has, the more heat it will generate. What you need to know is that hot components can fail or ultimately wear out much faster than components cooled to reasonable temperatures. Since our PC cases usually feel warm to the touch anyway, not everyone will know when their PC's interior case is running too hot. Background noise may keep you from noticing a fan not running or components starting to groan with heat distress.

How hot is too hot is another question, since different CPUs and other different types of hardware are rated to withstand varying temperatures. While some people start to worry once a PC case's internal temperature climbs to 95 degrees Fahrenheit, others show no concern until it rises to about 110 degrees. Most PC temperature sensors and alarms (discussed later in this chapter) do not sound until a temperature of 120 degrees Fahrenheit has been attained.

Too often, the first indication you are having a problem occurs when hardware begins to fail under the stress, and you develop intermittent keyboard or drive access/write errors, for example, that resolve after you shut down the PC for a bit (effectively letting the unit cool down). However, you can begin to encounter real and permanent failures the longer you run an overheating unit. Plus, a PC should never be allowed to operate for more than a very short period without a working fan, or you may end up with a virtual meltdown.

Special and even mundane circumstances may conspire to make a PC overheat. For instance, overheating is a frequent result of serious over-clocking of a system. Adding a hot new drive to a borderline, packed PC can also drive the temperature into the red without extra precautions taken. But even a lot of office cleaning—where a good deal of dust may be raised and then sucked into the PC through its front vents to be carried out by the fan in the back—may lead to a heat-insulating layer of dust on internal components or clog the fan itself, reducing or eliminating its efficiency.

To understand PC cooling, let's take a quick review of basic principles of thermodynamics, which tells us there are three major ways to cool anything: convection, conduction, and radiation. *Convection* is the transmission of heat into surrounding or moving matter, such as air or water. An example of this is a muffin fan blowing air across a hot CPU chip to reduce surface heat. *Conduction* is the transmission of heat by direct contact between a heat source and something that will draw the heat away. This is commonly called a heat sink and is also known as a heat exchanger. One prime example of this is how your CPU and heat sink work together. *Radiation* simply takes the heat and pushes it out into the "empty space" of whatever medium is ready to receive it, like the air in your PC.

Put simplistically, your CPU or other chips generate heat in the process of working. This heat is transferred by means of conduction to the heat sink, which then radiates the heat out into the air within your PC case. The fan then draws out this heat through the back of the unit (the hot air you feel).

A working fan is quite central to keeping your PC cool, as you can imagine. If you know the difference between an attic room on a hot day and an attic room where an exhaust fan is drawing the hot air out, you can appreciate what I'm talking about. In older PCs, there was really just one fan—the one with the power supply which drew air out of the back of the PC, as shown in Figure 12.1. This one can be checked by placing your hand in the back of the unit, directly in line with the large back vent. If you can feel hot air coming out—the more the better—you have a working fan. If instead you feel very little air movement, the fan may need cleaning or oiling. Replacement may be necessary, and may run you anywhere from $5 to $15 (you can pay a lot more for advanced cooling units, anywhere from

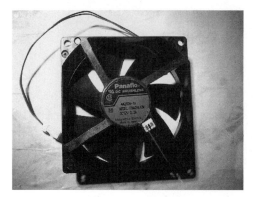

Figure 12.1   Example of a PC fan
(power supply).

$50 to over $100; these may be warranted if more usual forms don't cool
well enough for your setup).

Newer PCs, with their faster CPUs, usually pack with a processor fan
as well, specifically there to draw heat off the hot chip. These fans, shown
in Figure 12.2, are usually powered by a connection to the motherboard or
a tap on a disk drive power connector.

Since this fan resides inside the PC, it's harder to monitor for function-
ality than the power supply fan. So how can you tell if yours is working?
Try this test recommended by PC Power and Cooling, a leading vendor of
PC cooling accessories:

1. Shut down the PC, remove the cover, and after observing proper
    grounding techniques, unplug the processor fan.

2. With the cover still off, boot the PC while you keep one finger on
    the heat sink. A well-mounted heat sink, in operation, should get
    very hot without the fan working to draw the heat off. If it doesn't
    get very hot, the heat sink may not be properly installed.

3. Shut down the PC again, reconnect the CPU fan, then reboot. Once
    the machine has been operating for a bit, the temperature of the
    heat sink should drop considerably, since it now has the fan work-
    ing to draw the heat away. Test this with your finger again. If the
    heat sink remains very hot, something may be wrong, and the CPU
    fan may require replacement. Failure to do so could damage your
    processor.

Figure 12.2   Pentium II CPU cooler.

TIP   **Remember, however, the PC should not run for any period of time without the fan engaged, or you are likely to encounter serious problems.**

Did you know that PC case design can play a big role in PC cooling? A desktop case, for example, can be more prone to overheating because while air usually moves easily past the cards installed, heat can concentrate around packed drive units. The tower design offers a more ideal convection situation, since heat rises and less heat-fussy hardware tends to be located at the top of a tower unit (CD and floppy). A larger tower should provide more airflow through the case than a mini or mid-range tower.

One thing you want to check whenever your PC cover is off is the positioning of the cables. Bunched-up cables "stuck" in the wrong place can impede airflow and drive up the internal temperature of your PC. Errant cables and connectors can also get caught in a fan blade, which is never good. So keep them organized, neat, and out of the way. Just taking this step could add life to some of your more delicate electronic components.

Getting back to cases, some opt to leave their PC case covers off, particularly in hot summer months, to help increase heat dissipation into the room air. How good a practice this is depends on whom you talk to. Many seasoned PC veterans advocate this practice, especially when working in a relatively very clean office environment, while others insist the PC was designed to run with the cover on for maximum efficiency.

Leaving the cover off will definitely move cooler air past hot components, but you may find that your cards and other equipment build up an accumulation of dust and debris much faster than if you leave the case intact. On my primary work PC, which tends to undergo a lot of changes as I tinker, I often leave the cover off for a week or more at a time. To combat dust and other foreign objects, I routinely take out cards and use a can of compressed air to accomplish the same. In several years of operating this way, I haven't run into any serious problems myself.

Now, this brings up something of a small debate in PC-dom: Do you use compressed air or do you gently blow dust off the cards using air from your own mouth. Many do the latter successfully, with no problems. But your mouth is moist, and saliva has a tendency to travel. You don't want moisture—or the remnants of the spinach salad you had for lunch—on your cards, so the safest option is really a can of compressed air, available at any computer store or office supply shop.

But be aware that a coverless PC is also at more risk from prying hands or accidents (tipping over a coffee cup can slosh right into the unit itself) and isn't recommended in an environment where children or pets may be present. If you have other adults working in an office with you, tell them "hands off."

Some software has become available that appears, on demonstration, to reduce the power consumption of Win95 PCs by taking advantage of the kind of CPU idling that Windows NT can employ. Since reducing power consumption can result in a cooler PC, these could help warmer systems, as well as serve to let a laptop last a little longer on its battery. Look for Rain or Waterfall demos to test them for yourself.

For those who want to keep a tighter and more accurate watch on PC temperature, there are temperature gauges available ranging from the very simple to the very fancy, with prices to match. Plus, more of the newest motherboards coming onto the market pack options like chips and sensors for monitoring temperature, fan speeds, and other operating parameters you may need to familiarize yourself with. Some provide audible alarms to notify you when a fan stops turning or the temperature gets dangerously high. If you have one of these newer setups, check your manual for specifics so you won't miss a warning bell.

For those with older systems that tend to run hot, consider getting something like PC Power and Cooling's 110 Alert, which sounds an alarm when the temperature inside the case reaches 110 degrees Fahrenheit ($19 for basic or $32 for one that incorporates both a heat and an rpm alert). It measures just 1 x 1.5 inches and is said to mount easily inside any PC, plugging into a spare drive connector.

PC Power Supply

The job of the power supply is to take the alternating current (AC) coming from your standard electrical outlet and convert it into a usable form of direct current (DC) that your PC needs to power its electronics. There is an added step to this conversion, since your PC needs just a fraction (maybe 10 percent or less) of the voltage available from the outlet. For PCs in North America, the power supplies turning a 110V AC into both 5V and 12V DC.

Now, since the work a power supply performs can produce a fairly decent amount of heat, they pack a feature discussed earlier in the cooling section: a power supply fan that pulls hot air from the case. That heated air is a product not only of the power supply itself, but also the other components within. These components connect to the power supply in one way or another, usually by a plug at the end of a mass of wires extending from the power supply itself. When you apply power to your PC, the power supply is engaged and feeds the many devices attached. These include your CD-ROM drive, hard disk drive (and think of what is needed here to bring one of today's ultrafast drives from dead-still to 5400 or 7200 or even 10,000 revolutions per second in short order), and everything else attached to it.

Considering how integral the power supply is to the function of your PC, you need one that performs its job reliably and one that is rated for the work your PC needs to do. In fact, the rule of thumb is that your power supply should be rated well above the maximum capacity you will ever need to power everything you expect to connect. An underpowered PC can produce a myriad of very strange problems and errors. The hardware profile may show no conflicts, but a CD-ROM drive, for instance, may not power up to operate even with a green LED power display visible.

More 300-watt power supplies are on the market now, but do you need anything that powerful? For most average PC users, 180 watts is quite adequate for today's PCs, which have lower power consumption demands than earlier-generation machines did 5 and more years ago. Of course, the more hardware you add to your machine, the more juice it needs to run everything. Change your standard desktop PC into a server packing five or six hard drives and more than 128 megabytes of RAM, and the 180-watt power supply will be sorely tested. A Pentium II user with a fully loaded PC who is looking at several more additions may want to consider upgrading a 180-watt to a 230- or 250-watt power supply.

If you need to choose a larger or replacement power supply for your computer, there are some basic electrical factors you need to take into consideration:

◀ *Current.* The actual flow of electricity, which is measured in amperes (or amps); abbreviated as (A).

◀ *Frequency.* The rate at which power alternates between positive and negative voltages; measured in hertz (Hz).

◀ *Power.* The product of the voltage multiplied by the current; measured in watts (W).

◀ *Voltage.* The physical force by which electricity is forced through the lines or wires, very much like water being forced along a pipe or house; measured in volts (V).

How do you tell a good power supply from a defective one or one edging toward its demise? A bad power supply would be the likely suspect in a PC that won't turn on. But one that will turn on but has no working fan isn't much better than a dead power supply, so you need to repair (sometimes, they simply need cleaning or a careful application of lubricating oil) or replace the fan or the entire power supply quickly, as mentioned earlier. Remember, the PC's internal components can begin to sustain damage after even just a few minutes without a working fan to draw the hot air away from the delicate electronics and out the back of the PC.

Also, while a working power supply will no doubt feel very warm to the touch, it should not feel super-heated. If it does, this may indicate an inefficient conversion of AC to DC power, which simply wastes energy and generates unnecessarily high levels of heat.

Another signal may be undue sound. Sometimes failing power supplies emit something of a high-pitched whine or the type of straining noise some might more easily attribute to a dying hard drive. The sound may vary depending on the power demands of the PC—audibly protesting more loudly during high demand times while becoming quiet during low power cycles. Check out any abnormal sounds quickly.

With a working power supply fulfilling your power needs, you should be good to go, correct? Here is where you are presented with a real and present danger to your PC that you cannot see: dirty power. Your home or office electrical current is bombarded by both tiny and appreciable fluctuations. Collectively, this is referred to as *noise*.

Yes, lightning, massive power grid problems, and even a car colliding into a light pole are the noise-creating culprits you may readily identify. In truth, however, noise on the signal is almost a constant. Small appliances like a coffeemaker or heavier ones like a vacuum cleaner, a photocopier or big power tools, as well as old or faulty wiring can contribute to noise. So can serious electrical problems along the power line in your neighborhood or even farther away, say, at the electrical plant or one of your community's power substations. The bottom line is that a PC's components really require cleaner power than most of us plug into.

If you are fortunate, a very brief outage will do no more than reboot your PC with no apparent damage done. Yet even if a power spike does not fry your system's motherboard, toast your RAM, or trash your modem, it can still shorten the operating life of much of your hardware, create intermittent and tough-to-diagnose hardware failures, or contribute to a lessening of total system performance.

Here is one fairly common example: You leave your unprotected phone line plugged into the back of your external modem during a close electrical storm. You never lose power or *see* a serious power fluctuation. When you return to your PC to work, everything appears fine and untouched. Then you go to dial out using your modem and it refuses. You verify the modem indeed has power (externals have those nice lights for easy checking) and Windows 95 or 98's Device Manager reports no problem. Refreshing the driver and reseating the modem don't work, even though Windows continues to recognize the modem's existence as if it should work.

The problem is that the external modem was twice at risk: both from its own power supply plugged into your wall outlet and from the unprotected phone line. Yes, I said phone line, because it can bring enough spike over that line to not only damage the modem but ruin the motherboard or other components as well.

This brings us to ways to protect your PC from this dirty power. The first line of defense and the one most frequently employed by PC owners is a surge suppressor, also known as a surge protector, shown in Figure 12.3. Often enough, these are the multiple outlet strips which the PC, the monitor, and other PC-related hardware with an external plug are connected to instead of into the wall outlet directly. Depending on specifications and quality, the prices of such surge protectors vary widely, starting at below $10 and going up to $50 and beyond. Many of these units feature a plug with which you can try to help protect your phone line as well.

You won't necessarily have bad luck with one of the cheap surge protectors available in almost every discount store today. One of my test machines that is plugged into nothing more than a $10 PC Accessories surge protector recently took a serious hit from a brownout that came back with a severe power spike. The surge was powerful enough to kill an unprotected phone answering machine, as well as a cable television decoder box, and to pop a few lightbulbs throughout my home.

The PC in question had just enough time to lower power and start to cycle into reboot when I started to shut it down. It was at that moment the surge struck. I powered down and turned off the surge protector along with my PC.

Once power was stabilized again, I tried turning on the surge protector again to evaluate damage to my PC. Immediately, though, the surge protector began to sputter and spark, finally catching fire. I pulled the surge protector's cord out of the wall. Armed with a spare unit, I plugged the PC and peripherals into it and booted the PC. Running through POST had rarely felt so good. The surge protector had done its job by taking the hit my PC otherwise would have. All of my equipment, save for the toasted surge protector, functioned fine.

Yet surge protectors provide only limited, basic protection; they are better than nothing, but you cannot assume they provide any aggressive form of defense. A poorly designed surge protector may actually create small surges of its own as it tries to redirect power. This can cause problems almost as severe as an electrical hit itself. Also, what voltage surge may trigger the protection may vary widely.

The least-expensive surge protectors tend to depend entirely on metal-oxide varistors, or MOVs, to take any hit that would otherwise be sent into the PC. The function of the MOV is like that of the defensive tackle in a football game. It exists to put a barrier between the supply voltage itself and the protective ground. Once the suppressor detects a surge, the MOV goes after it to redirect it to the electrical ground.

Something like car airbags, a MOV-only surge protector once deployed is no longer functional and needs replacement. Nor does it take a massive

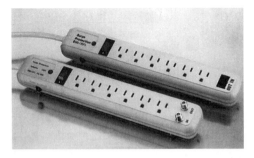

Figure 12.3 Examples of surge protectors.

surge such as the experience I just related. As just one example, a series of smaller power fluxes can knock out the MOV, taking with it the PC's defense against subsequent fluxes. There is no easy or accurate way to test a surge protector for signs of life. The power-strip component of the surge protector may continue to function, and the device's LED power light, if any, may continue to shine, as if the surge protector is operating normally. Better surge protectors use multiple defense technology schemes, combining MOVs with coaxial arrestors, and the slower but more effective pellet arrestors and gas discharge tubes.

Power conditions are another form of protection, bolstering a surge protector's power protection mode with the enhanced isolation (to keep your PC unaffected by the noise on the dirty lines) by means of a transformer. These devices cost more, but at least you know when it's taking a serious power hit: When the transformer is blown, the unit won't power up.

Some of these devices, like the ones sold by manufacturers such as Tripp Lite, even feature an LED readout of the voltage coming in from your outlet to the power conditioner itself. This may help you track problems before they get worse. Those who know their buildings are subject to imperfect wiring or who live in an area with a problematic power feed may prefer something like this.

Now let's look at power protection schemes wedded with the ability to keep working during a power crisis of some kind. There are redundant power supplies. These provide two or more fully independent power supplies within the same unit. If one fails, the other kicks in to keep you operational.

There are also two types of backup power supplies: a standard power supply (SPS) and an uninterruptible power supply (UPS). Before I explain their functions, let's review why these "backup" power supplies can be vital. Most of these protection/reserve schemes will not buy you a large block of time when electricity fails. What they will buy is a few moments to properly shut down a PC when sudden power losses, particularly those coupled with the severe rebound of a surge, would otherwise risk unsaved data or the hardware itself. Some models will keep you working for 15 minutes or more, buying you time to save and possibly complete a time-critical project. Since the majority of serious local power crises are resolved within 30 minutes, the use of one of these could eliminate any real down-time whatsoever.

Note, however, that if you choose not to implement any of the protection schemes discussed here, be prepared to power-down during known power disrupters, like a serious electrical storm. Once the PC is off, disconnect it and any peripherals connected to it from the wall outlet, remove the phone line from the modem, and expect to sit out the storm or other disruption. Of course, if you have a laptop with a charged battery, you can simply move your base of operations temporarily to it.

A standard power supply charges its battery while simultaneously monitoring the electrical current load for problems. The moment the SPS senses a power change, the battery is triggered into activation to provide backup current until normal power is restored or the SPS battery fails, whichever comes first. If you consider a unit such as this, be sure to check into the time that it takes to implement the switch of power from current to battery. If it is more than 5 milliseconds, it may be of far less help to you.

An uninterruptible power supply is the most expensive and the most reliable short-term solution overall. This is because it incorporates various levels of defense by combining a battery with both a power supply and a reverse power supply. They usually offer some surge suppression technology as well, putting the UPS battery between your PC and the source of power damage. In addition, unlike the SPS, there is not even a slight pause waiting for the battery to kick in. The battery is always charging and always ready to take over the load to provide a stable flow of power.

Some UPS units start as low as $66, offering up to 15 minutes of battery life for a standard PC without a lot of extras attached. While this is not an extravagant period of time, it does provide an adequate grace period. The amount of time you will have depends not only on the capacity of the battery itself but also on the PC's load. You don't hook up nonessential equipment to the UPS, since doing so will drain the battery much faster (another reason will be covered shortly). So plan to leave peripherals like a printer or scanner off the UPS connection.

However, UPS systems have their limitations as well. One is that they consume more power because you are adding an entire mechanism that needs constant power to be ready whenever power fails. More power also means more heat is generated.

A second and more significant issue is that some UPSs, particularly cheap ones, produce square-shaped wave currents. To your PC, which is designed for the rhythmic, alternating up-and-down curve of the sine wave, the square waves produced by a DC battery are rougher on sensitive electronics. It's very much the equivalent of rapidly turning electronic equipment on and off because of the aggressiveness of the power flow. This can damage components quickly or at least contribute to faster wear and tear. And this is another reason you don't want unessential peripherals like a PC printer, which tends to be especially sensitive to square wave flux, running off the UPS for best results and the least problems.

At a higher end of the spectrum, there are pseudowave UPSs that try to reduce the harsher effects of square wave currents, and then more advanced and far pricier sine wave UPSs, which attempt to eliminate the square wave form altogether.

Sadly, none of these protection schemes is perfect. You need to balance needs against cost while also figuring in the investment you have in your PC, whether for work, pleasure, or (like most of us) both, to determine which method to use. In addition, if you have multiple PCs, you may want to prioritize them for protection. High-end PII workhorses might warrant an uninterruptible power supply, while a 486 or older Pentium backup machine only need to be plugged into a decent surge protector.

In summary, I strongly recommend you do not overlook proper cooling and power protection techniques to safeguard your computing investment. Keeping your hardware protected and maintained reduces both risk and downtime. It also helps ensure your time is not squandered attempting to troubleshoot hardware failures triggered by physical conditions you may be unable to see with the naked eye.

Glossary

access time Time required for information demanded by a device from where it resides (in disk or memory) to arrive at its destination.

AUTOEXEC.BAT Automatically executed batch file run (when present) each time the computer is booted, in association with CONFIG.SYS. This file is optional in Windows 95 and 98 to load certain software and load a few drivers not included in CONFIG.SYS. If present, however, it must reside in the root, or C:\, directory.

benchmarks Tests designed to gauge the speed, accuracy, or reliability of a piece of hardware.

bus One of several different electronic avenues that move a signal from one part of the PC to another. Examples of a bus include ISA, EISA, PCI, and VESA local bus.

bus mastering Sophisticated hardware technology by which a specific device works with memory to transfer information, without the direct and constant supervision usually required by the CPU.

CD-ROM (Compact Disc Read-Only Memory) A high-capacity storage medium, the speed of which is usually represented by 16x or 32x.

clock speed Also known as clock rate; refers to the internal speed of either the PC itself or the central processing unit (CPU) specifically. The greater the clock speed, the faster a PC will perform a specific operation.

cluster Represents the smallest unit of space DOS can reference or acknowledge on a PC hard disk drive. Each cluster contains one or more contiguous sectors.

cold boot Refers to when you boot your PC by turning on the power (not hitting reset); typically reserved for severe freezes or hardware installs when you may have had reason to pull the power connection.

COM port   Serial communications port; usually available from a PC's motherboard but also provided by internal modems. Later versions of both DOS and Windows support up to four COM ports (but with only two IRQs covering all four, you are left practically to use just two at a time).

CONFIG.SYS   One of the DOS configuration files read during bootup, this is a text file that loads DOS-based memory management and DOS or real-mode drivers for operation of hardware while in DOS mode.

controller   Frequently a controller is a printed circuit board specifically designed to control the operation of a part of the PC; for example, the hard disk controller, the IDE controller, the keyboard controller, and the floppy drive controller.

CPU   (Central Processing Unit) The brain of the PC.

device driver   Specifically designed software interface between a piece of hardware and the operating system to allow the two to work together.

DIMMs   (Dual In-line Memory Module) Allows for a 128-bit data path by interleaving memory on alternating memory access modules (SIMMs are restricted to a 64-bit data path); often used on later PCs.

DMA   (Direct Memory Access) An alternate way for a PC to handle the transfer of information between a specific hardware device and memory without requiring the constant supervision of the CPU.

DRAM   (Dynamic Random Access Memory) One form of PC memory.

DVD   (Digital Video Disc) An optimal storage medium often used for movies or special interactive games that require a greater capacity than a CD-ROM.

EDO   (Extended Data Out Random Access Memory) An older form of PC memory now largely replaced by faster technology.

EISA   (Extended Industry Standard Architecture) A type of PC bus that expanded along ISA's narrow resources and data path (32-bit).

Fast Page   An older form of PC memory, not commonly in use today.

FAT   (File Allocation Table) Serves as the organizational table from which the contents of a hard disk drive are indexed.

FDISK   DOS-based utility for preparing a drive for use with DOS as well as for creating partitions (or segments) on a hard drive.

FireWire   Also known as IEEE 1394, a type of high-performance serial bus interconnect technology with transfer speeds of 100, 200, or 400 Mbps that accepts up to 63 peripherals or devices (high speed; slower-speed devices go to USB—see *USB*) and permits peer-to-peer device communication.

flashing BIOS   The act of upgrading your PC motherboard's BIOS to a later version; often used in conjunction with specific hardware upgrades, such as installing a much larger hard disk to an older PC.

FORMAT   DOS command by which a drive's DOS boot record, file allocation table (FAT), and root, or C:\, directory are created.

FPU   (Floating Point Unit) Also known as floating point accelerator.

grounding   Process by which you ground yourself, preventing you from carrying electrostatic shocks into a PC's inner components when you work beneath the case; such shocks could seriously damage the sensitive electronics within.

hard disk   Type of storage device that writes data to platters rotating within the unit itself.

heat sink   Simply a piece of thermally conductive metal, attached either to the central processing unit or other electronics within the case (such as a hot-running hard disk or a fast 3D video adapter), which works by drawing heat away from the heat production source (like a hot CPU) and radiating it out into the air of the PC, where it can be drawn out through a fan usually located at the back of a PC.

I/O   (Input/Output) The transfer of data/information between a peripheral device and the PC itself.

IRQ   (Interrupt Request) Hardware signals carried along hard-wired lines in a PC bus carrying signals from a peripheral to the PC itself.

ISA   (Industry Standard Architecture) Original PC bus design; still in use in a modified, enhanced format.

jumpers   A pair of wires covered (or not) by a plastic shunt; used to turn on or off specific features or attributes of a piece of hardware much like you might throw a switch.

LBA   (Logical Block Addressing) Used to increase the size limit for a single hard disk drive to over 8 GB.

LED   (Light Emitting Diode) Typically used to indicate power on an external hardware peripheral, such as a printer or scanner, or to show hard disk activity on the front display panel of a PC.

master/slave   When two drives share a single IDE controller connection to a PC motherboard, the first drive cabled directly to the IDE controller is called the master drive (and jumpered accordingly), and the second drive cabled directly to the first drive is called the slave drive (and jumpered accordingly).

modem (modulator/demodulator) A type of hardware that converts the analog signals from a phone line into digital data readable by the PC and vice versa, for telecommunications.

motherboard Also known as the main or system board, this is a printed circuit board that contains the bus(es) and the CPU, as well as chips and memory used for handling additional hardware additions.

overclocking The act of manipulating the clock speed on your system to achieve a faster CPU than the speed at which the CPU is rated to run.

parallel port Parallel input/output connection (and one of the slowest); typically used for printers; also called the printer port.

partition The act of dividing or partitioning one large single physical drive into one or more logical drive partitions, usually with its own file system; often used for better drive organization, to reduce the time to optimize a hard disk, and to better enable a multiple-boot situation, where more than one operating system resides on a PC simultaneously.

PCxx specifications Annual minimum (and recommended) standards published by a cooperation between Microsoft and Intel with input from key hardware manufacturers on the recommended standard components for a PC for the coming year.

PCB Printed circuit board, such as a motherboard.

PCI (Peripheral Component Interconnect) A faster standard of PC bus that provided improved performance in transferring of signals between an I/O device, such as a piece of hardware attached to the bus, and the CPU.

PCMCIA (Personal Computer Memory Card International Association) A type of easily changeable hardware add-on typically seen in portable computers. This name has been largely abandoned for the newer standard term, PC card.

Pentium (classic) 64-bit microprocessor introduced by Intel. Rated to run between 90 and 233 MHz, this was the successor to the 80486 architecture.

Pentium MMX Basically, a Pentium classic with multimedia extensions provided for better graphics and rendering for games and other multimedia applications.

Pentium Pro "Professional" level Pentium featuring internal RISC architecture; designed specifically with Windows NT in mind and for use with systems where dual CPUs are employed for better processing capacity.

Pentium II Current enhancement to the Pentium line, combining increased processing speed and capacity with the multimedia extensions; rated to run between 233 and 450 MHz.

Plug and Play (PNP) Hardware standard where the device contains information about itself that can be read by the PC during the hardware detection process, enabling the device to theoretically be plugged in, instantly recognized by a PnP-capable operating system and ready for use.

pointing device Any device (mouse, trackball, and pen are the most common types) that allows you to point to a specific area on your desktop and "click" to indicate an action.

POST (Power On Self Test) A series of hardware-specific tests run by your system as soon as it is turned on, before any configuration files or the operating system are loaded or devices are recognized for use.

power supply Electrical power source specifically designed to deliver reliable current to the electronics composing your PC.

refresh rate Speed at which your PC screen is redrawn during use.

removable drives As named, these are storage medium that can be moved literally from PC to PC as needed, sort of like high-capacity floppies. Iomega's Zip and Jaz drives, Imation's SuperDisks, and SyQuest's series of drives fall within this category, permitting between 100 MB and 1 to 2 GB of data to be stored on this removable medium.

resolution The maximum number of pixels that can possibly be displayed on a PC monitor (examples: 640x480 or 1024x768).

SCSI (Small Computer System Interface) Representing a higher-speed device interface, such as used in large-capacity hard disks and backup devices. Traditional SCSI is still somewhat more expensive than Enhanced IDE (EIDE) devices while offering roughly comparable speed. Fast SCSI, on the other hand, is more expensive but offers a speed and reliability-of-transfer boost over EIDE.

SDRAM (Synchronous Dynamic Random Access Memory) A faster type of RAM still in use in many PCs today (SGRAM is a variant of this found on some video cards).

serial port I/O serial device, also known as COM port.

UPS (Uninterruptible Power Supply) A power supply that permits you time to finish your work and properly shut down a PC even when power has failed to the main PC itself.

USB (Universal Serial Bus) An interconnect specification that is part of the Plug and Play ease-of-use technology; allows devices to be shared easily between PCs on a plug in/use/unplug basis and is somewhat faster than traditional serial.

virtual memory Hard disk space allocated and reserved for use as a short-term staging area, which uses the hard disk space much as one might use extra memory to page applications in and out from desktop use.

VRAM (Video Random Access Memory) A faster memory specification used to store an image that can then be displayed on a PC monitor.

WRAM Windows RAM, or a faster form of VRAM, first introduced by Matrox.

Online Sources for Hardware Help

GENERAL HARDWARE

AnandTech *http://www.anandtech.com*

CMPnet's TechWeb *http://www.techweb.com*

Robert Proffitt's DoubleDigit *http://www.doubledigit.com*

Hardware Forum, Microsoft/MSN ComputingCentral
http://www.computingcentral.com/topics/hardware (click on
Newsgroups to see the newsgroups available from beginners to
advanced video and drive controller issues)

Hardware One *http://hardware.s-one.net.sg/*

HPC Hardware Guide *http://hardware.pairnet.com/*

Microsoft Knowledge Base *http://support.microsoft.com/support*

PC Guide *http://www.pcguide.com*

Planet Hardware *http://www.planethardware.com*

SupportSource *http://www.supportsource.com*

Tom's Hardware Guide *http://www.tomshardware.com*

CHIPSETS AND PROCESSORS

Advanced Micro Devices (AMD) *http://www.amd.com*

The Brotherhood of the CPU *http://www.processor.org*

CPU Central *http://www.cpucentral.com*

CPU Review *http://www.cpureview.com*

Cyrix *http://www.cyrix.com*

IBM *http://www.ibm.com*

Intel at *http://www.intel.com* or Intel Support at
http://support.intel.com

MOTHERBOARDS AND BIOS

Abit *http://www.abit.com.tw/*

Aopen *http://www.aopen.com*

Asus *http://www.asus.com*

MrBIOS *http://www.mrbios.com*

SuperMicro *http://www.supermicro.com*

System Optimization home page *http://www.sysopt.com/bios.html*

Tyan *http://www.tyan.com*

Wim's BIOS page *http://www.ping.be/bios/faq.html#q1*

VIDEO

3Dfx *http://www.3dfx.com*

3D Labs *http://www.3dlabs.com*

ATI Technologies *http://www.atitech.com*

Bill's Workshop *http://www.billsworkshop.com*

Canopus *http://www.pure3d.com*

Cirrus Logic *http://www.cirrus.com*

Diamond Multimedia *http://www.diamondmm.com*

Matrox *http://www.matrox.com*

NVidia http://nvidia.com

Rendition *http://www.rendition.com*

Trident Microsystems *http://www.tridentmicro.com*

Voodoo Extreme *http://www.voodooextreme.com*

DRIVES/CONTROLLERS

Adaptec *http://www.adaptech.com*

Fujitsu *http://www.fcpa.com*

IBM *http://www.ibm.com*

Iomega *http://www.iomega.com*

Maxtor *http://www.maxtor.com*

Mitsumi *http://www.mitsumi.com*

Partition FAQ *http://www.webdev.net/orca/*

Plextor *http://www.plextor.com*

Seagate *http://www.seagate.com*

Western Digital *http://www.westerndigital.com*

SOUND CARDS

Aztech *http://www.aztech.com.sg/*

Creative Labs *http://www.creativelabs.com*

Ensoniq *http://www.ensoniq.com*

Diamond Multimedia *http://www.diamondmm.com*

Turtle Beach *http://www.tbeach.com*

MODEMS

3Com (US Robotics) *http://www.3com.com*

Diamond Multimedia *http://www.diamondmm.com*

Hayes *http://www.hayes.com*

SYSTEM DESIGN

Device Bay *http://www.devicebay.org*

FireWire/IEEE 1394 *http://www.firewire.org*

Universal serial bus (USB) *http://www.usb.org* (also check out *http://www.usbstuff.org* and *http://www.allusb.com*)

DRIVERS AND UTILITIES

Drivers Guide *http://www.driversguide.com*

Drivers HQ *http://www.drivershq.com*

WinFiles *http://www.winfiles.com*

TuCows *http://www.tucows.com*

Configuration Checklist

This table is provided as a checklist of information related to your PC and its configuration. You can keep this as a spreadsheet or table on your PC itself or print it out as a hard copy checklist. Filling it out and remembering to use it when you're planning for a new hardware installation, however, are two different things. So keep this list handy to consult before you pull the cover off your machine.

PC Make:	Operating System Version:	Model #:
Qualantex	Windows 98	XX450
Total RAM:	**Purchased:**	
64 MB PC 100	9/1/98	
OS Updates Applied:		
None		
Hardware Driver Updates Applied:		

Device Type/Make	System Resources Used (IRQ, DMA, I/O)	Notes
Monitor		
CPU		
Hard disk		
CD-ROM		
Floppy drive		
Video adapter-		
Regular		
3D		
Sound card		

COM ports:
1
2
3
4
Parallel ports:
1
2
Mouse

Keyboard
Modem
Printer
Network card
Additional storage:

SCSI

Universal serial bus
Other

Special Notes:

Serious Hardware Issues/Resolution:

Don't Try List (things you want to remember never to try again):

Hexadecimal Math Primer

A bit (binary digit) is the smallest unit of information that can be represented. A bit has two states, variously described as on/off, 1/0, true/false, and so on. The 1's and 0's lend themselves to the binary representation and arithmetic that is native to computers. Inside the central processing unit (CPU), registers are able to process strings of bits simultaneously. The size of the string of bits is the word size of the CPU.

Early microprocessors, such as the Intel 8080, had a word size of just 1 byte (8 bits). This meant that the 8080 could add two 8-bit binary numbers together in a single machine instruction. Intel's 8088, which was at the heart of the original IBM PC, was a limited 16-bit CPU; limited because it only accessed an 8-bit external data bus. Intel's 80286, used in the IBM PC/AT, expanded the data bus to 16 bits. Today's CPU's are full 32-bit implementations, giving them much greater power in processing and addressability.

One bit can represent two possible numbers, 0 or 1. Two bits can potentially name up to four binary numbers. With the addition of each bit, the range of numbers that can be represented is doubled. In fact, each bit position, reading from right to left, represents an increasing power of two. The rightmost position is the ones place ($2 \wedge 0$), the middle position is the twos place ($2 \wedge 1$), and the leftmost position is the fours place ($2 \wedge 2$). This continues for every bit position that is added to a machine word.

number	binary	hex	number	binary	hex
zero	0000	0	nine	1001	9
one	0001	1	ten	1010	A
two	0010	2	eleven	1011	B
three	0011	3	twelve	1100	C
four	0100	4	thirteen	1101	D
five	0101	5	fourteen	1110	E
six	0110	6	fifteen	1101	F
seven	0111	7	sixteen	1 0000	10
eight	1000	8			

Notice that in hexadecimal, which is base 16, the number sixteen is represented as "10". The capital letters A through F are used to represent the numbers ten through fifteen. Each group of four bits can be expressed conveniently as a hex digit. When you see a byte represented as a hexadecimal number like C4, it's just shorthand for binary 1100 0004 (refer to the above table).

Each successive bit position added to the left of a binary number adds a power of 2 to the address range. There are $2 \wedge 4$, or 16, possible values, from zero to 15, that can be assigned to a 4-bit number, as the above table shows. An 8-bit byte can have $2 \wedge 8$, or 256, possible values, from zero to 255. This is also the number of memory locations that can be directly addressed by an 8-bit processor. The first IBM PCs could directly address $2 \wedge 16$, or 65,536 (64 KB) of RAM with their 16-bit processors, and today's 32-bit processors can directly address $2 \wedge 32$, or 4 GB (slightly over 4 billion).

Each position from right to left in a hexadecimal number represents an increasing power of 16. The rightmost position represents 16 to the zero power, which is 1. The next hex digit is multiplied by 16 to the first power, or 16. So a four-digit hex number like B7A2h is really (in base 10) 2 times 1, plus 10 times 16, plus 7 times 256 plus 11 times 4096, which adds up to 47,010.

Adding and subtracting in hex is done the same way as in decimal, allowing for the six extra digits and the numbers 10 through 16 that they represent. In decimal, 8 + 4 = 12. In hex, 8 + 4 = C (which is still 12). Hex F + 1 = 10 (i.e., 16). Hex C + E = 1A (26). Hex A - 1 = 9. Hex E - B = 3.

When adding two hex numbers, digits are summed in each column from right to left, just like in decimal. If an overflow occurs, it is carried and added to the next column to the left.

```
  31A4h      40B0h      FF9Ch
+ 1234h    + 1EF4h    + 003Fh
```
_____

```
  43D8h      5FA4h      FFDBh
```

Subtraction is similar. If the digit being subtracted is too large, a borrow occurs from the next column right.

```
  31A4h      40B0h      FF9Ch
- 1234h    - 1EF4h    - 003Fh
```
_____

```
  1F70h      21BCh      FF5Dh
```

Four-digit hex numbers like these are common in the PC world, since they conveniently held the 16-bit operands and addresses contained in the original PC's 16-bit registers. The 64 KB address space made available to a single 16-bit address word was obviously not enough, so one of the registers was used to reference the PC's memory in chunks called *segments*. How this is done is a little bit arcane and has to do with limitations on the address bus of the old 8086 CPU that have grandfathered themselves into current designs. Memory locations are referenced as offset addresses "within the current segment," whose location is stored in one of several segment registers. Memory locations within the first megabyte of the PC's RAM are frequently specified as a segment address followed by an offset, separated by a colon. To obtain the linear address, multiply the segment address by 16 (10h), and add the offset. For example, FF00:001A is FF000h + 001A, or FF01Ah.

Understanding Error Codes Generated by Device Manager

Remember, where Device Manager is requesting that you update a driver, all that may be necessary is removing the current driver, shutting down then rebooting the machine, and letting Windows "find" the device and its driver anew. You may still need to obtain an updated driver from your manufacturer (these are usually available on their Web sites or via FTP (file transfer protocol) on the Internet.

NOTE This explanation is drawn almost exclusively from the Microsoft Knowledge Base, Article Q125174.

Error Code #	Error Message with Action Required
Code 1	This device is not configured correctly. (Code 1) To update the drivers for this device, click Update Driver. If that doesn't work, see your hardware documentation for more information. *Action required:* Update the driver, as indicated.
Code 2	Windows could not load the driver for this device because the computer is reporting two <type> bus types. (Code 2) *Action required:* If the type specified is ISAPNP, PCI, BIOS, EISA, or ACPI, no action is required; if the type is a DevLoader and indicates FLOP, ESDI, SCSI, etc., then you need to update the driver.
Code 3	The driver for this device may be bad, or your system may be running low on memory or other resources. (Code 3) *Action required:* Update the driver for the device identified.

Code 4	This device is not working properly because one of its drivers may be bad, or your Registry may be bad. (Code 4) *Action required:* Update the driver (it's more likely to be a corrupted or damaged driver than a problem Registry).
Code 5	The driver for this device requested a resource that Windows does not know how to handle. (Code 5) *Action required:* Update the driver.
Code 6	Another device is using the resources this device needs. (Code 6) *Action required:* Since this indicates a hardware conflict of some kind—more than one device trying to use the same IRQ at the same time, for example—troubleshoot this using techniques learned in this book.
Code 7	The drivers for this device need to be reinstalled. (Code 7) *Action required:* Reinstall this driver.
Code 8	The device is not working properly because Windows cannot load the file <name> that loads the drivers for the device. (Code 8) To fix this problem, run Windows Setup again using your CD-ROM. *Action required:* None. *or* The device is not working properly because Windows cannot find the file <name> that loads the drivers for the device. (Code 8) To fix this problem, click Reinstall Device to reinstall this device. *Action required:* Reinstall the driver in question. *or* The device is not working properly because the file <name> that loads the drivers for this device is bad. (Code 8) To fix this problem, click Update Driver to update the drivers. *Action required:* Update the driver as indicated. *or* Device failure: Try changing the driver for this device. If that doesn't work, see your hardware documentation. (Code 8) *Action required:* Update the driver.
Code 9	This device is not working properly because the BIOS in your computer is reporting the resources for the device incorrectly. (Code 9) *Action required:* None. *or* This device is not working properly because the BIOS in the device is reporting the resources for the device incorrectly. (Code 9) Contact the device manufacturer to get an updated BIOS for your device. *Action required:* None. Note, however: In both cases, you can try removing the driver to see if Windows can refind and reload properly, or you can check with the manufacturer for specifics on any modifications necessary to the Windows Registry or for an updated driver or BIOS.

Code 10	This device is either not present, not working properly, or does not have all the drivers installed. (Code 10) *Action required:* Update the driver; also check to make certain the device is plugged in properly, well-seated, and power lights, if any, are showing on and ready.
Code 11	Windows stopped responding while attempting to start this device, and therefore will never attempt to start this device again. (Code 11) *Action required:* Upgrade the driver. Also, run the Automatic Skip Driver utility from the System Information tool (discussed in Chapter 3).
Code 12	This device cannot find any free <type> resources to use. (Code 12) If you want to use this device, you must disable another device that is using the resources this device needs. To do this, click Hardware Troubleshooter and follow the instructions in the wizard. *Action required:* Use the Hardware Troubleshooter to try to resolve this conflict when the type listed is a resource type (IRQ, DMA, memory, or I/O).
Code 13	This device is either not present, not working properly, or does not have all the drivers installed. (Code 13) *Action required:* Select Detect Hardware.
Code 14	This device cannot work properly until you restart your computer. (Code 14) *Action required:* Restart the computer, as indicated.
Code 15	This device is causing a resource conflict. (Code 15) *Action required:* Since this is another typical resource conflict, click on Hardware Troubleshooter to try to resolve.
Code 16	Windows could not identify all the resources this device uses. (Code 16) *Action required:* You may need to click on the Resources tab in Device Manager and add any missing settings, if you know them or can get them from the manufacturer's Web site.
Code 17	The driver information file <name> is telling this child device to use a resource that the parent device does not have or recognize. (Code 17) *Action required:* Update the driver; remove the current driver and choose the Add New Hardware option in Control Panel.
Code 18	The drivers for this device need to be reinstalled. (Code 18) *Action required:* Reinstall the driver; if this fails, try removing the driver and using the Add New Hardware option in Control Panel to re-add it.
Code 19	Your Registry may be bad. (Code 19) *Action required:* Check the Registry (see Chapter 4). You may also need to run Scanreg.exe or scanreg /restore.
Code 20	Windows could not load one of the drivers for this device. (Code 20) *Action required:* Update the driver.

Code 21	Windows is removing this device. (Code 21) *Action required:* As prompted—since Device Manager is already removing this problem driver for you—restart your PC and see if it redetects the hardware and reloads a working driver.
Code 22	This device is disabled. (Code 21) *Action required:* Enable device, or remove the driver altogether and restart your PC to try redetecting.
Code 23	This display adapter is functioning correctly. (Code 23) *Action required:* None normally; if a secondary display adapter, check its Properties.
Code 24	This device is either not present, not working properly, or does not have all the drivers installed. (Code 24) *Action required:* Select Detect Hardware, or (with Plug and Play devices) update the driver.
Code 25	Windows is in the process of setting up this device. (Code 25) *Action required:* Restart your PC to see if this resolves. If not, a complete reinstall of Windows may be required to clear the error.
Code 26	Windows is in the process of setting up this device. (Code 26) *Action required:* Restart your PC to see if Windows loads the correct drivers the next time around. You also may need to re-add the hardware after removing the driver, or obtain a driver update.
Code 27	Windows can't specify the resources for this device. (Code 27) *Action required:* Remove the device driver and then run the Add New Hardware option in Control Panel. An updated driver may also be required.
Code 28	The drivers for this device are not installed. (Code 28) *Action required:* Reinstall the driver; this likely points to an incompletely installed hardware driver.
Code 29	This device is disabled because the BIOS for the device did not give it any resources. (Code 29) *Action required:* Check to make certain the device has not been specifically disabled in CMOS. If you cannot enable it, contact your hardware manufacturer.
Code 30	This device is using an interrupt request (IRQ) resource that is in use by another device and cannot be shared. You must change the conflicting setting or remove the real-mode driver causing the conflict. (Code 30) *Action required:* As indicated.
Code 31*	This device is not working properly because <device> is not working properly. (Code 31) *Action required:* Check the properties; this error occurs when one device is dependent on another device to be functioning.

Code 32*　Windows cannot install the drivers for this device because it cannot access the drive or network location that has the setup files on it. (Code 32)
Action required: Restart your PC first; if required, copy all the setup files onto your local hard drive and perform the setup from its new location.

Code 33*　This device isn't responding to its driver. (Code 33)
Action required: Check the physical hardware, since this is almost entirely seen with a full hardware failure.

Index

About the Author

Kate Chase is a writer, journalist, and online manager with more than 10 years of experience providing support for operating systems, applications, and PC hardware. She specializes in troubleshooting PCs Net primers, and Net law and the impact of technology. Her publishing credits include work for Que books, IDG computing magazines, and *The New York Times,* among other newspapers.